THE GOLDEN APPLE

THE GOLDEN APPLE
Changing the Structure of Civilization

Edgar J. Ridley

Africa World Press, Inc.

P.O. Box 1892
Trenton, NJ 08607

P.O. Box 48
Asmara, ERITREA

Africa World Press, Inc.

P.O. Box 1892
Trenton, NJ 08607

P.O. Box 48
Asmara, ERITREA

Front Cover—Pictorial of the presentation of an apple in Greek history. Mark Rosenstein: *In Praise of Apples,* Lark Books. Used with Permission of Lark Books.

Book design: Aliya Books
Cover design: Ashraful Haq

Library of Congress Cataloging-in-Publication Data

Ridley, Edgar J.
  The golden apple : changing the structure of civilization / Edgar J. Ridley.
      p. cm.
  Includes bibliographical references and index.
  ISBN 1-59221-588-2 (hardcover) -- ISBN 1-59221-589-0 (pbk.)
  1. Civilization, Modern--21st century. 2. Religion and civilization. 3. Symbolic interactionism. 4. Symbolism. I. Title.

CB430.R495 2007
909.83--dc22
                                          2007041791

Dedication

This book is dedicated to
Dato' Nik Zainiah Nik Abdul Rahman,
and
The National Productivity Corporation
and
To my wife, Linda, whose love and support is never ending

Contents

Illustrations

Figure 9:
Stimuli Funneling into the Human Brain 99

Figure 10:
Passage of Symbol Systems into Symbolic Behavior 118

Figure 11:
Passage of the Symptomatic Thought Process 118

Figure 12:
Cartoon Illustrating Accounting Errors 125

Figure 13:
Valley of Oaxaca - National Academy of Sciences 156

Figure 14:
Apple Wassailing 169

Figure 15:
Incense burner from Tomb L24 - known as a Censer 174

Table 1:
Word Table Illustrating Symbols vs. Symptoms 180

Table 2:
Business Interruption Events 196

Table 3:
Living Symptomatically vs. Symbolically 200

Figure 16:
Decapitated Enemies 222

Figure 17:
Clay sculpture of Narmer, first Pharoah of Egypt 223

Figure 18:
Atlas Bringing Apples to Heracles 235

Figure 19:
Cartoon of white hunters 239

Figure 20:
Ronald Reagan voodoo visit 240

Figure 21:
Laura Bush at UNESCO Headquarters in Paris 241

Preface

The Golden Apple: Changing the Structure of Civilization has been a journey that has taken several detours. It was originally intended to conclude a trinity that began with *An African Answer: The Key to Global Productivity,* and was followed by *Symbolism Revisited: Notes on the Symptomatic Thought Process.* However, the journey of writing about symbolism and its alternative, the *Symptomatic Thought Process®,*[1] has been an exciting and exhilarating experience, to say the least. As I spent countless hours in research that turned into months and years, it became apparent to me that this task would encompass several volumes if justice were to be done to this project. *The Golden Apple,* instead of being the conclusion, is but a continuation of my life's work: the examination of how symbols, with their resulting mythology and superstition, have affected man and civilization; how the *Symptomatic Thought Process*

must be used as an alternative to symbolic thought; and what symptomatic thinking can mean to civilization.

What is exciting about this present work is the realization that all the problems that have occurred in civilization are the result of a neurological misadventure that happened to primitive man as he tried to make sense out of his universe. I began this inquiry by asking myself, What happened to *Homo sapiens* to compel them to act the way they act? Why do we have the global conflicts and global enmity that have continued throughout history? My research has determined that the two primary causes of civilization's near destruction are the religious and racial wars that have taken place in practically every corner of the globe. These racial and religious conflicts are the core of the economic and territorial wars that have engulfed civilization from its genesis.

Because symbolic thought has been accepted as a natural occurrence of the human mind, writing about symbolism has been a challenge. Almost every academic discipline has been working under the assumption that symbols are a natural neurological process of the human brain. I maintain that by discarding symbols and ridding ourselves of superstition we can usher in a *Symptomatic Thought Process* that enables us to behave in a qualitatively different way from symbolic-thinking humans. Only time will tell whether this is the answer to civilization's global problems.

It would be impossible to name all of the people that have influenced my work and made it possible for me to continue. My research in Dakar, Senegal at the Radiocarbon Laboratory of Cheikh Anta Diop University enabled me to delve deeper into the disciplines of Egyptology, and of cultural, physical and social anthropology. The guidance and generosity of Dr. Cheikh Anta Diop, director of the Radiocarbon Laboratory, was invaluable. Dr. Diop, who has rewritten the entire history of the world, was pivotal to my understanding of how Africa played the leading role in the formation of civilization and the disciplines that are now a part of the global educational system.

Acknowledgement

This project would not have been brought to fruition without the encouragement and support of Dato' Nik Zainiah Nik Abdul Rahman, director general of Malaysia's National Productivity Corporation; Kassahun Checole, my publisher; and my wife, Linda. I would also like to thank Professors Domenic Sica and Ronald Sims for their valuable suggestions and encouragement. they are not only top-rate scholars, but caring people as well. Additionally, the feedback I received from Saira Ihsan Khwaja of the Pakistan Institute of Management was most helpful to me. Finally, I would like to thank the many individuals from all over the world with whom I have had conversations and debates about my ideas. These exchanges were extremely helpful as I formulated my concepts on the dynamics that shape civilization. All have helped me greatly to continue my life's work.

The conclusions drawn in this volume are solely mine.

Foreword

Domenic A. Sica, M.D.

It is with great interest that I read "The Golden Apple: Changing the Structure of Civilization" by Edgar Ridley. This is an extraordinarily insightful book, which delves into the symbolic workings of the mind, and more importantly the behavioral elements that have become the norm for what oftentimes is maladaptive societal behavior. Having spent the better part of the past four decades in the medical profession, I found the messaging in this book to be powerful and broadly applicable to not only the practice of medicine but also the myriad of other professions that comprise society.

To quote Edgar Ridley, "As we view the importance of symbolism, it becomes abundantly clear that the natural way to go is to live symptomatically rather than symbolically." Symptomatic illness knows no boundaries of race, age, or gender and, as such, encourages rational and non-prejudicial treatment practices. Symptoms are widely used in the medical profession to describe illnesses both mental and physical. It is not possible to think symptomatically and symbolically at the same time and behave soundly. The disconnect when both symptomatic and symbolic behavior coexist ultimately distorts reality. Moreover, symbolic illness is steeped in misperception, cultural bias, and relies heavily on the mythologic traditions of various cultures.

The visionary nature of this book can be captured from another quote by Edgar Ridley "Race has become metaphorical—a way of referring to and disguising forces, events, classes, and expressions of social decay and economic division far more threatening to the body politic than biological "race" ever was. Expensively kept, economically unsound, a spurious and useless political asset in election campaigns, racism is as healthy today as it was during the Enlightenment." Race has a profound "creep effect" in our society. One has to look no further than the recent approval of a heart failure medication based on race, which seemingly has ushered in an era of race-based therapeutics when in point-of-fact race is a very crude marker for genetic variation.

I encourage the readers of this book to carefully take the thoughts proposed herein and apply them broadly to their life practices. Dissemination of the themes so beautifully articulated in this book is important. This is not only for what they tell us in their current form but also for how the messages expressed in these writings might help shape the next iteration of these themes. Thematic evolution is a potent force. It gains momentum one small step at a time. If we have learned anything throughout the history of civilization it is that we are no more or less a product of our past – recent and distant. Yet, to change the past requires that we realign the thinking in the future.

Domenic A. Sica, M.D.
Professor of Medicine and Pharmacology
Virginia Commonwealth University
Richmond, Virginia

Introduction:

Getting the Most from This Book

Ronald R. Sims, Ph.D.

The *Golden Apple: Changing the Structure of Civilization* began life as an idea that Edgar Ridley, the author, had from his many years of passionate work devoted to trying to find the answers to the following questions: What accounts for the historically destructive nature of mankind and civilization? What is the relationship between symbols, mythology and superstition? How has this relationship affected man and civilization? Are symbols and their accompanying superstitions the seed of religious and racial wars? Can The Symptomatic Thought Process serve as a vehicle for minimizing and possibly eliminating global conflict and global enmity? Over time, Ridley has rigorously worked to find answers to these and similar questions. In his first two groundbreaking books, *An African Answer: The Key to Global Productivity* and *Symbolism Revisited: Notes on the Symptomatic Thought Process*, Ridley, now an internationally recognized scholar, speaker and consultant for his work on symbolic thought and The Symptomatic Thought Process, offers readers an extended look at the need for mankind to abandon its historical dependence on destructive symbols and the shackles of symbolic thinking once and for all in favor of the liberating Symptomatic Thought Process. Thus, the focus of his new book, *The Golden Apple: Changing the Structure of Civilization* which is a contribution and celebration of the passion he feels for the positive benefits of the Symptomatic Process as perhaps the last hope for mankind of reversing the destructive historical trends of a civilization with symbolic thinking as its DNA.

CONTENTS OF THE BOOK

The *Golden Apple: Changing the Structure of Civilization* is organized with three primary parts:

Part One: *The End of Symbolism: The Demise of Mythology, Superstition and Cultism* is an introduction to the concepts of symbolism and mythology and the two destructive outgrowths: cultism and superstition.

Part Two: *Symptomatic Thought Process* is a comprehensive overview and discussion with definitions, context, and a perspective on symptoms and the Symptomatic Thought Process as it relates to global leadership, change initiatives, technology and productivity, and medicine.

Part Three: *Changing the Structure of Civilization* explores the forces relevant to bringing about change in civilization, the role of The Symptomatic Thought Process in breaking the symbol, mythology, superstition cycle in the future and ultimately a civilization infused by symptomatic behaviors and thought processes.

2

CHAPTER OVERVIEWS

Part One begins with Chapter 1, "Ending Symbolism." Chapter 1 defines cultism and superstition, two of the harmful outgrowths of symbolism and mythology argues that superstition and religions are synonymous, while offering a more in depth look at the origin of symbolic thinking and calling for an end to symbolism if civilization is to bring to an end its history of destructive behavior.

In Chapter 2, "The Superstition and Myth of Fish and Apples" suggests that the fatal flaw of myths (mythology) and superstition is that they are too dependent on the individual who perpetuates the myth via a never ending manipulation of facts and entities. Unlike those who espouse the benefits of religious or mythical transitions as an advance of civilization over time, this chapter lays the foundation for much of the rest of the book as it argues instead that such accepted views are nothing more than the misread of the neurological misadventure that created the beginning of symbolic behavior in humans and/or the beginning of barbarism and the ongoing global conflicts and global enmity.

Chapter 3, "Ending Mythology," posits that despite the alternative scholarly views of mythology, only one mythology evolved over the years and took on different meanings in its diffusion from culture to culture. The chapter argues that racism and other superstitions result from mythological thought and become standard ritual which continues to threaten the survival of civilization.

Part Two begins with Chapter Four, "Definition and Use of Signs and Symptoms" provides several definitions of symptoms and highlights the various ways the concept has become ingrained in our society and been used to make sense of the history of civilization and our world. The latter part of the chapter challenges the position that symbolism is a natural occurrence in the human brain and human behavior along with attempting to answer the following questions: How mankind began to think symbolically? If symbolic thought arose out of a failure to deal with reality or arose spontaneously? The chapter concludes with a discussion of language as a symptom and how language becomes symbolic when it is mythologized.

Chapter 5, "Doing Business with a Symptomatic Attitude," argues that symptomatic thinking affects business performance or productivity through the behaviors of its leaders and the critical role that leadership can play in eliminating behavior globally. The chapter also offers examples of global leaders-in-action who have demonstrated a commitment to decisions that are not based on a mythological foundation but instead defer to The Symptomatic Thought Process.

Chapter 6, "Reconciling the Dynamics of Symbols and Symptoms in Bringing About International Change," begins with a discussion of the need for consultants involved in global change to recognize the role they play in hindering the true productivity improvements and change by creating new metaphors that become superstitious rituals. The chapter also offers further discussion of the relationship between mythology and change and the need for consultants to change their in practice mindset through The Symptomatic Thought Process.

Chapter 7, "How Thought Processes Impact Technology for Productivity," considers the relationship between research and development and problem solving, and suggests that productivity and growth, which should evolve from technology, are stagnated instead because they are isolated from cultural problems which emanate from real-world experiences. The chapter also stresses the role of research and development to the success of organizations and civilization especially if it is based upon a factual and symptomatic approach.

Chapter 8, "Symptoms and Medicine" discusses the relationship between symbolic thinking and medical procedures and methodologies and behavior patterns that perpetuate unhealthy lifestyles. The chapter also makes the argument that a relationship exists between symbolic thinking and racism which is a disease in need of treatment like any other disease and can best be treated or eradicated through symptomatic thinking and related initiatives.

Part III consists of three chapters. Chapter 9, "The Dynamics of Changing Civilization," first offers a look at how the concepts of symptoms and symbols have been used by some scholars to help trace, define and view civilization. The relationship of religion and mythology and symbolic thinking is also discussed along with the importance of recognizing the distinction between symptoms and symbols and their role and use by scholars in trying to understand human behavior and civilization. The chapter concludes with a discussion of how religious thought and mankind has historically been dictated by symptoms and symbols which clearly has contributed to the destructive nature of civilization.

Chapter 10, "The Symptomatic Thought Process and the Future," argues that symptomatic thinking is a viable method for countering symbols, superstition and myths. The chapter suggests that living symptomatically as opposed to symbolically results in a willingness to face reality head on as opposed to mythologizing and relying on neurological misadventure which is nothing more than the avoidance of the true facts.

The final chapter, Chapter 11, "The Golden Apple" provides a look at the impact of mythology and views of scholars on the African continent, its people, race and religion. The chapter concludes by revisiting the dynamics of signs and symptoms and extols again the virtues of The Symptomatic Thought Process as the one best opportunity for mankind and civilization to once and for all bring an end to or decrease the never ending global conflicts and global enmity which is so pervasive in our world today.

Ronald R. Sims, Ph.D.
Floyd Dewey Gottwald Senior Professor
Mason School of Business
College of William and Mary
September 2007

PART ONE

THE END OF SYMBOLISM

The Demise of Mythology, Superstition and Cultism

CHAPTER ONE

Ending Symbolism

To anyone who has read my previous two books, it should be apparent that I have made the case that symbolism must be eliminated. Once we end symbolism, we are also participating in the demise of cultism and superstition. Webster's Dictionary defines the word *cult* as a system of religious worship and its adherents. *Superstition* is defined as a belief founded, despite evidence to the contrary, that is irrational, a belief resulting in faith in magic or chance. Cultism and superstition go hand in hand with symbolism and mythology. Cultism and superstition are byproducts of mythology. Once we understand how superstition has affected the behavior of human beings as they mythologized one another, it becomes easy to see why the end of symbolism must be greeted with joy and celebration.

Superstition and religion are synonymous. This statement may be a cause of great controversy among people of different faiths. Nevertheless, once we understand that religion is mythology evolving via symbol systems, and that mythology has produced both superstition and cultism, it should be readily clear that religion stems from a foundation known as symbolic thinking. Superstition has led humans to a myriad of unreasonable deeds that are supported by irrational decision-making.

The Greek historian, Herodotus (ca. 484 B.C.), in *Book II of The Histories*, writes that, "The Egyptians were the most religious of all humans."[1] This statement was so provocative that the translator was compelled to add a footnote: that "The extreme religious views of the Egyptians became at length a gross superstition and were naturally a subject for ridicule and contempt."[2] We have maintained and continue to maintain that superstitious behavior led to Egypt's downfall. That same type of behavior has caused all the problems and conflicts that we see in the world today. A few words about Herodotus: It is my belief that if it were not for *Book II of the Histories*, Herodotus would be as celebrated as an Einstein in academia. However, because he insisted on the blackness and the Africanness of the ancient Egyptians, white academia has not only dismissed *Book II of the Histories*, it has accused Herodotus of being a great liar of history. This accusation is solely based on how he saw the ancient Egyptians; that they were a black, African people. Herodotus may have made some historical errors, as all historians have done, but we must at least give him credit, as the late Professor John Henrik Clarke would say, for having good eyesight.

One of the main functions of superstition is to keep human beings religious. Since all religion is inherently superstition, being superstitious is being religious in its most depraved and fundamentalist form. Religion is the most unifying and dividing force in civilization. Much of the wars that the world has seen have religion at their core. It is incredible that in the twenty-first century we are still fighting battles over ancient religions. However, when examined closely, it becomes clear that the battle is over symbol systems that produce the very religious conflicts that have been prevalent since the beginning of mankind. Religious clashes are necessarily ancient due to the antiquity of symbol systems. What is really incredible is that in all of the scholarly work that has been written about religion, religious wars, and religious conflicts, the symbol systems that have produced these conflicts have not been studied or adequately dealt with as an incipient cause of human misery in the world. If left unchecked, the damage that symbol systems cause to the neurological process of the human brain and its resulting symbolic behavior will ultimately cause the demise of civilization as we know it. The conflicts we see in the Middle East, Europe, Africa, and Asia will surely escalate unless we eliminate symbolic behavior and rid the world of a superstitious-behaving humanity.

Terrorism is one of the unfortunate symptoms of people immersed in cultism and superstition. The United States government will never be able to effectively deal with terrorism until it stops terrorizing its own nonwhite population. Terrorism can never be eliminated by counterattacking it with terrorism. That, unfortunately, has been the mode of behavior of the United States and its allies. The leadership in the United States needs to heed the sentiments of Malaysia's former prime minister, Dr. Mahathir Mohamad, who stated that the attitude of the West is symptomatic of a new racism reminiscent of that practiced by the British in colonial times. He added that, "The feeling is that a Western life is much more valuable than anybody else's. It is alright for others to die, but don't you dare touch Westerners."[3] It should be fully understood that in the United States, in particular, a white life is considered much more valuable than a black one. Racism abounds in the United States, and the American mythology justifies that racism.

While religion is definitely a powder keg in many areas of the world, religion and racism easily rank among the leading causes of all conflicts around the globe. Religion and racism, which are fostered by symbolic-behaving people and the main reasons that people continue to kill each other, easily outdistances the desire for power and all economic disputes as the leading causes for upheaval in the world. It must be understood that behavior patterns are at the root of much of all power struggles, racial differences, religious differences, and economic disputes.

WHEN HUMANS BECAME HUMAN

Most scientists, if not all, would agree that early man became human when he began to walk permanently on two legs and actually became a tool-making human. But the big question that remains is *when* these anatomical humans begin to think symbolically. No one knows exactly when modern man began to think symbolically.

Another big question widely debated concerns the origin of modern human behavior. Archaeologists had long believed that modern human behavior originated 40,000 years ago in Europe. But new findings are pushing the origins tens of thousands of years earlier and thousands of miles southward.

New discoveries at Blombos Cave, 200 miles east of Capetown, South Africa, are turning long-held beliefs upside down. It has been traditionally held that modern human behavior was assumed to have been a very late and abrupt development that seemed to originate in a kind of creative explosion in Europe. The leading proponent for this explosion phenomenon is Dr. Richard G. Klein, a Stanford University archaeologist. Dr. Klein has a neurological hypothesis: He suggests that about 50,000 years ago, a genetic mutation took effect that rewired the brain. According to Klein, these rewired modern humans, called Cro-Magnons, were at the forefront of creativity. This type of Eurocentric thinking is beginning to collapse with the findings in Capetown, in the last half of the twentieth century, of African stone etchings that are said to be about 77,000 years old. Christopher Henshilwood, an archaeologist and researcher at the State University of New York – Stony Brook, said that these findings show that modern human behavior developed in Africa, even earlier than in Europe. This obliterates the hypothesis of Dr. Klein, who favors a European origin of modern human behavior and creativity. What has to be understood, and made clarified, is that since we know that man's origins, including symbol systems, started in Africa, any reasoning of a European starting point for human behavior is an outgrowth of the traditional and ongoing racist beliefs of the inferiority of Africans and the superiority of Europeans. Charles Murray further documents this in his book *Human Accomplishment: The Pursuit of Excellence in the Arts and Sciences*. Murray, the American who coauthored *The Bell Curve*, which emphasizes the supposed intellectual inferiority of black people worldwide, states unequivocally, in his book *Human Accomplishment*, that all excellence and creativity in the arts and sciences were achieved by whites, and that Africans and all other peoples of color contributed practically nothing in the areas of the arts and sciences.

As stated above, no one knows the exact time or date of the origin of symbolic thinking. However, it is understood by anthropologists and archaeologists that thinking symbolically is the foundation of all creativity, including art, music, language, mathematics, science, and the written word. This has been the traditional understanding of symbols for almost as long as man has been articulating and defining symbolic thought. One of the most puzzling questions that have confounded the experts in a multitude of disciplines is the event(s) that took place that caused man to initiate a symbolic thought process that would lead to mythology. It is extremely important to understand that humans began to think symbolically in response to a certain set of circumstances that eventually developed into the origins of mythology. It has been traditionally accepted that this was a normal and natural process of *Homo sapiens*. However, in reading the literature, it is becoming increasingly clear that humans were in a special state of mind when they created symbols. That special state of mind is what I call a neurological misadventure, a disease state. The German scholar, Friedrich Max Müller, stated that:

> the Mythopœic Age... is a period in the history of the human mind, perhaps the most difficult to understand, and the most likely to shake our faith in the regular process of the human intellect....Was there a period of temporary insanity, through which the human mind had to pass, and was it a madness, identically the same to the South of India and the North of Iceland?[4]

Similarly, the scholar, Cheikh Anta Diop, stated:

> The attitude that consists of resorting to an insane misinterpretation of text instead of accepting the evidence is typical of modern scholarship. It reflects the special state of mind that prompts one to seek secondary meaning for words rather than give them their usual significance.[5]

This is an extremely important point: for Diop is describing that special state of mind that man was in as he developed symbolic mythological thought. It is indeed a state of insanity. Müller goes on to express the sickness of mythological thinking:

> How does it render intelligible that phase of the human mind which gave birth to the extraordinary stories of gods and heroes – of gorgons and chimae-

ras – of things that no human eye had ever seen, and that no human mind in a healthy state could ever have conceived?[6]

Müller caps off his thesis with his famous phrase, "Mythology is...a disease of language."[7] Of course, Müller was criticized by academia for suggesting that the state of mind that produced mythological thought was a diseased one. However, as I have stated in my books, *An African Answer* and *Symbolism Revisited,* the neurological process that produced symbolic thought and subsequent mythological behavior was indeed a neurological misadventure of primordial man.[8] Indeed, that misadventure caused a period of insanity from which modern *Homo sapiens* has not recovered. The same type of symbolism that caused symbolic behavior in antiquity is present in our own behavior in every area of people activity.

There have been countless instances in early history describing the activity of symbolic thought. Diop describes one particular trait in Egypt and in the rest of Black Africa:

> Certainly there can be found, as a particular trait in Egypt and in Black Africa, this unrestrained worship of animals, this zoolatry, which the Greeks jeered at so much, and of which André Aymard remarks that no traces were to be found in Semitic Asia. These beliefs – whether they are given the name of totemism or zoolatry – which make possible the identification of a human being and an animal, taken and analysed from the outside, misled, for a certain time, Western thinkers such as Levy-Bruhl. It was following a generalized study of these that the latter affirmed that the principle of identity ought not to operate among peoples whose members were capable of considering themselves as one and the same time as animals and authentic human beings; they would be ruled by a primitive pre-logical mentality, the difference between which and that of the civilized adult

white male could not be made up by intellectual progress accomplished in a human lifetime. There were two distinct levels. The author before his death retracted this and considered that the word "symbolism" would be more exact to characterize this type of mentality.[9]

It should be understood that mythology is synonymous with symbols, symbol systems, metaphor, superstition, and folklore. Since all these entities are a result of symbolic thinking, a description of any one of these phenomena includes the symbol systems that produced them. This is extremely important. As John Fiske states in *Myths and Mythmakers*:

> The religious myths of antiquity and the fireside legends of ancient and modern times have their common root in the mental habits of primeval humanity. They are the earliest recorded utterances of men concerning the visible phenomenon of the world into which they were born.[10]

Therefore, a discussion of religious history includes symbolic and mythological history, which, of course, leads to cultism and superstition. Whenever mythology is present, there will be an accompanying superstition; in fact, superstition will be present long after the myth has degenerated or disappeared altogether. Fiske states further:

> The medieval belief in werewolves is especially adaptive to illustrate the complicated matter in which diverse mythological conceptions and misunderstood natural occurrences will combine to generate a long enduring superstition.[11]

It is important to point out that there is one symbol system, which means there is only one mythological system. That mythological system started in Africa and migrated throughout the entire world. Remember, the origins of symbol systems and myth occurred when man had no explanation for the phenomena experienced in his environment. When early man did not comprehend something, he created a myth to explain it. John Fiske continues:

> Primitive men had no profound science to perpetuate by means of allegory, nor were they such sorry pedants as to talk in riddles where plain language would serve their purpose. Their minds, we may be sure, worked like our own, and when they spoke of the far-darting sun-god, they meant just what they said, save that where we propound a scientific theorem, they constructed a myth.[12]

> Here, on the other hand, we see what a heterogeneous multitude of mythical elements may combine to build up in course of time a single enormous superstition, and we see how curiously fact and fancy have cooperated in keeping the superstition from falling.[13]

As we know, racism has its origins in symbol systems and mythology. As long as those symbol systems remain, racism will remain. Note: African-American psychiatrists are pressuring the American Psychiatric Association to declare racism a mental illness. It goes without saying that racism is, indeed, a mental illness, due to the fact that it was created by a mental state of mind that produced a neurological misadventure.

It is becoming increasingly clear that an event occurred in the neurological process of humans that caused a disruption in the mind, where humans began to create delusions, which an increasing number of scholars are saying is insane. Müller described it as "breaking the regularity of the early strata of thought and that convulsed the human mind like volcanoes and earthquakes arising from some unknown cause."[14]

As I stated earlier, Müller thought there was a period of temporary insanity through which the human mind had to pass. That special state of mind is what I call a neurological misadventure. That neurological misadventure produced a mythology that has been described as absurd, irrational, and, even in its best cases, not worthy of man. Scottish anthropologist David Mac Ritchie posed the question:

> The future student of mythology will ask, "is there any contemporary stage of thought and of society in which the wildest marvels of mythology are looked on as the ordinary facts of experience, and as laws regulative of phenomenon?" And they will find that condition of thought surviving among contemporary, and historically recorded of departed races of savages.[15]

Mac Ritchie's question is extremely important, for it underscores the fact that race, which was created by mythology, and the absurdity of racism based on color, is looked upon as a natural mental process and state of mind. When you consider that people are judged in this contemporary world on the basis of the color of their skin, it is absurd and insane. The mythology that perpetuates such judgment has to be eradicated, or it will become a permanent superstition. In fact, it is considered a permanent state of mind that is ingrained so deeply in culture that it has been called a lasting and permanent fixture of civilization.

Another phenomenon that is also considered a permanent part of civilization is religion. Like racism, religion was created by mythological thinking via symbolic thought. The murder and suffering that humans have endured in the name of religion is incalculable. Religion is as old as the symbol systems that produced it and is considered a gross superstition that has the power to manipulate humans more than any other phenomenon. The great nineteenth century French scholar, Charles François Dupuis, stated:

> Is it not a superstition, which makes millions of people believe, that the Deity passes into a wafer,

after pronouncing over it some mysterious words? That which a philosopher calls superstition, the priest calls a religious act, and makes the basis of his worship. Is it not the priest, who keeps up all the most absurd superstitions, because they are lucrative and keep the people under his dependence, by making his agency almost a necessary one in almost all the instances of our life?[16]

Religion preys on the emotional vulnerability of people and manipulates them in such a way that it dictates their behavior and their pattern of thought - all this in the name of superstition. Dupuis realized the superstitious nature of all religions in a way that has been unparalleled. Only the nineteenth century British anthropologist Gerald Massey rivals Dupuis in his understanding of the mythological element that made religion such a dangerous phenomenon in civilization. Both scholars understood the superstitious nature of religion. Massey was never considered a "proper" scholar by Western academia. The reasons are obvious – his insistence on the African origins of civilization and on the fact that ancient Egypt was a black civilization. Dupuis also recognized the blackness of the ancient Egyptians. Not only did Dupuis recognize the blackness of the Egyptians, he believed that the first inhabitants of Greece and the founders of Athens were also black. Dupuis' *Memoirs* mentioned:

> Dupuis has also published the following works: 1) Memoirs on the Pelasgi, inserted in the collection of the Institute, class of ancient literature. The object of the author was to prove by all the authorities, which he could collect from monuments and from history, that the Pelasgi came originally from Ethiopia, and were a powerful nation, spread over all parts of the ancient World, and to which Greece, Italy and Spain owed their civilization.[17]

Because the vast use of symbols by *Homo sapiens* is so apparent, the neuroscientist and evolutionary anthropologist Terrence Deacon has designated that *Homo sapiens* be called *Homo symbolicus*. This new species designation would apply to all hominid symbol users. That designation is very appropriate because of the devastating effect symbols and symbol systems have had on civilization via humankind. It is further appropriate due to the fact that humans have been labeled mythmakers by various scholars in practically all disciplines. The challenge for *Homo symbolicus* is to become *homo symptomaticus*. Psychiatrists Sigmund Freud and Carl Jung, and their followers, emphasized the turning of symptoms into a symbolic process. That is the core of the neurological misadventure and the period of temporary insanity that Friedrich Max Müller talks about. Unfortunately, this is not a period of temporary insanity but a continuum that borders on permanent insanity. The continual use of symbol systems has unequivocally caused all of the problems that civilization has experienced.

The call for an end to symbolism is a bold and provocative act, but it is an end that must be achieved, or we risk the future of civilization. The symbol systems that have been embedded in our minds have caused harm so devastating that it is considered mere folly to seek any other alternative. We all must do whatever we can to understand the function of symbols, how they originated and flourished, and the damage they have done not only in the past but what they are doing in our present and what they will do in our future. I am sure that some will insist that the eradication of symbols is neither possible nor desirable. However, that is not an option. Any thorough reading of history will show the predominance that symbolic thought has had on the behavior of humans since the beginning of time. How we determine our behavior patterns determines the future of the world.

Chapter Two

The Superstition and Myth
of Fish and Apples

No foodstuff has been more symbolized and mythologized than apples and fish. No foodstuff
has created more superstitions that have
evolved into cults than fish and apples. Benjamin O.
Foster details the myths and superstitions that have
surrounded the apple in so-called classical antiquity. "For
instance, in modern Greece, throwing an apple is a sign
to express love or to make an offer of marriage."[1] James
Frazer tells of a custom amongst the Kara-Kirgiz, in
which barren women roll upon the ground under a soli-

tary apple tree in order to obtain offspring.[2] Frank Browning states:

> Many of these folkloric customs crossed the Atlantic with the immigrants who settled America, and because apple trees have covered farmland in nearly all the eastern half of the country, the myths have flourished as local superstition — nowhere more than in the hills neighboring our farm in Kentucky.[3]

The form and shape of the apple contain further mysteries still more appealing to the richly superstitious medieval mind and its emerging Manichaean view of the world. In an era of alchemy, numerology, and witchcraft, nothing about the physical fruit could be taken for granted.[4]

A newly married Montenegrin woman will throw an apple against her husband's house to encourage the birth of many children. In provincial towns of northern France, a young woman will twirl an apple peel three times around her head and throw it into the air, and when it falls it will form the first letter of her true love's name. In the Walloon county of Belgium, a young woman tests her fate with apple seeds: she places the seeds on the lid of a hot pan and asks, "Will I like him?" If the answer is yes, the seeds will explode. The game continues through a succession of questions –"Will he marry me?" "Will my first child be a boy?" — And each time the answer is yes if the seeds pop open. Finally, she asks how many children she will have, and the answer is the number of seeds that have burst.[5]

Still the apple presents a mystery that has long puzzled anthropologists, folklorists, students of ancient myth, and even contemporary genetic sleuths. How is it that Norse Odinists, Greek and Roman pagans, Judeo-Christian monotheists, and Indian Vedantics bear such remarkable inter-reflections about the sacred tree and its fruit? The gods and the myths persist even as they change their names and the trees with which they are linked. Oaks become laurels. Oranges become apples and apples become pomegranates. But as we peel apart the gods and their sacred fruits, we find shadows and antecedents that sweep across the continents and the millennia. Did the Greeks steal from the Norse or the Norse from the Romans? Was the sacred fruit of the Roman Apollo the same as the sacred fruit of the Greek Apollo, whose name, after all, is neither Greek nor Roman? Were the evil, mortal giants of Crete kinsmen to the evil giants of Germania, and did their evil schemes to steal forbidden fruit shape the much later Christian story of the stolen fruit?[6]

Mark Rosenstein further supports this thread: "Apples are more than something to eat. For centuries, they've been intertwined in the myths, economics, culture, and developing technologies of countries throughout the world."[7] What is important to understand is that whenever mythology is involved, changes can occur at any time and place according to the whimsy of the mythmaker. For instance, Edith Hall states:

> Ethnicity could be proved or challenged by inventing genealogies and mythical precedents....In myth the ethnicity of heroic figures is remarkably mutable. Heroes can change their ethnicity altogether according to the ideological requirements of the imagination interpreting their stories.[8]

This is one of the core problems with mythology: Myths are totally driven by the mythmaker and his desire to manipulate, which means the endless manipulation of facts and entities. Rendel Harris states:

> Similar results to our own have been reached by Mr. A.B. Cook, who has studied the legends in the Celtic literature with such astonishing industry and effect. He finds out in fact, from these legends, that the apple-tree was almost as sacred as the oak, that it had nearly as good a claim as the oak to the title

King of the Wood, that on the one hand it represented the Sky-God, and on the other the life of a king or hero with whom it was associated. Mr. Cook suggests that the "religious or mythological transition from oak-tree to apple-tree corresponds to an actual advance in pre-historic civilization."[9]

The suggestion that religious or mythical transition is an actual advance in prehistoric civilization is part and parcel of the misread of the neurological misadventure that created the beginning of symbolic behavior in humans. That statement shows the assumption held by scholars today that the advance of civilization occurred because of the advancement of the human mind to produce symbols and symbolic-behaving humans. The main argument given by scholars for the necessity of symbolic thought is that civilization would not advance at all were it not for the ability of mythmaking humans. On the contrary, the neurological misadventure of primordial man that occurred in prehistoric civilization is most assuredly the beginning of barbarism, and we have borne the brunt of its effect throughout all of civilization and history. Rendel Harris is profound when he states: "We see through it, down a long vista across which many shadows are passed, the reasons which made man a religious animal and not merely the superstitions that keep him so."[10] That statement undoubtedly reinforces the fact that it is superstition that keeps man religious, and these same superstitions, which have symbolism as their origin, have caused the most harmful events in the history of mankind. As the late scholar Friedrich Max Müller affirmed frequently, these superstitions have created racism, greed, and indeed insanity. Müller stated:

> Never do I remember to have seen science more degraded than on the title page of an American publication in which among the profiles of the different races of man, the profile of the ape was made to look more human than that of the Negro.[11]

That degradation of science that Müller points to is caused by the mythologizing of the facts so that an insane portrayal of African Americans is made to stand. Müller understood quite clearly the damage that mythology has caused the human race. He may not have been able to articulate the origins of mythology correctly, but he understood quite clearly that mythology was indeed a disease of language. That disease of language has its origins in a neurological misadventure of primordial man that was created by symbolic thinking. Müller was also correct in insisting that mythological thinking was a mental aberration, which is entirely consistent with the understanding that early man indeed suffered a neurological misadventure. As he stated, "The mythological age is a period in the history of the human mind, perhaps the most difficult to understand, and the most likely to shake our faith in the regular process of the human intellect."[12]

THE IMPORTANCE OF FISH IN EGYPTIAN MYTHOLOGY

In *Natural Genesis*, Egyptologist Gerald Massey writes "Fish were considered an abomination by the ancient Egyptians who did not use them as an article of diet."[13] Fish were very important symbols for the ancient Egyptians and were prominent in their religious literature. Massey gives fish a prominent role in the Egyptian mythological system, whereas the scholar, Martin Bernal, contends that "Fish were not prominent in the Egyptian religious tradition."[14] In his book, *Black Athena*, Bernal further states:

> In Egypt, certain fish were associated with certain gods, and in some Egyptian "nomes" or districts particular species of fish were worshipped and considered taboo. Furthermore, in late times, legends arose that fish had eaten Osiris' phallus and the word *bwt* (fish), written as such, could mean "abomination". Nevertheless, fish cannot be considered in any way central to Egyptian religion.[15]

25

Massey, an Egyptologist, displayed a thoroughgoing understanding of the role fish played in ancient Egyptian mythology. In his book, *Ancient Egypt*, Massey stated: "When the sun sets at night or in the autumn season, it sank down into the waters of the abyss below the horizon, which Horus Sebek swam as a fish...."[16] Massey goes on to say:

> The fish, a figure of plenty brought by the Inundation, was continued as a symbol of Atum-Horus. The type might be changed from the crocodile of Sebek to the silurus or electric eel of Atum, but the fish remained as an emblem of Ichthus, or of Ichthon, that saviour of the world who came to it first in Africa by water as the fish. We have already seen that the mystical emblem called the "Vesica Pisces," as a frame and aureole for the virgin and her child, is a living witness to the birth of Jesus from the fish's mouth, as it was in the beginning for Iusa or Horus of the Inundation. This will also explain why Ichthus, the fish, is a title of Jesus in Rome; why the Christian religion was founded on the fish; why the primitive Christians were called Pisciculi, and why the fish is still eaten as the sacrificial food on Friday and at Easter.
>
> Horus, or Jesus, the fulfiller of time and law, the saviour who came by water, by blood and in the spirit, Horus the fish and the bread of life, was due according to precession in the sign of the fishes about the year 255 B.C. A new point of departure for the religion of Ichthus in Rome is indicated astronomically when Jesus or Horus was portrayed with the sign of the fish upon his head, and the crocodile beneath his feet.[17]

Bernal emphasizes the importance of fish in Christian iconography, yet contends that fish were not important in Egyptian mythology. Bernal fails to understand the role Egyptian mythology played in creating Christianity. Therefore, he underestimates the central role fish plays in Egyptian mythology. In *Black Athena*, Bernal stresses the dynamics of fish in both Old and New Testament, but because of his lack of expertise in Egyptology, he, like Massey, fails to understand the importance of fish as it diffused from an Egyptian mythology to Christianity and other religions. The following *New York Times* excerpt shows how fish is used in the mythology of other countries:

> This African country [Eritrea] may take its name from the Greek word for the Red Sea, which laps around its long shoreline, but for several centuries the idea of eating anything that came out of these waters was Greek to most people who live here.
>
> Even when drought ruined crops and decimated livestock, a complicated brew of religious taboos, cultural traditionalism, lack of refrigeration and poor cooking kept Eritreans convinced that seafood was inedible. The resulting famines took lives that the sea could have saved.
>
> Religion also played a part. The Islamic half of the population worried about sea creatures that were too insect-like such as shrimp and gravefish, and also fish apparently without scales, such as tuna, which some readings of the Koran deemed off the menu for Muslims. For the Christians, meanwhile, fish eating is an extricable link with Lenten traditions or fasting and self-denial. Eating it becomes a penitence — especially since hardly anyone knows how to cook it properly. Highlanders would boil it for hours, like camel meat, and be repelled by the bony, tough and tasteless result.
>
> During the Italian colonial period, from around the turn of the century to the 1940s, a few Eritreans learned to fillet and deep fry. But while fish is cheap in Eritrea, running around a third a cost of meat per pound, cooking oil is such an expensive luxury that it wiped out any savings. So deep-frying fish made about as much sense as cooking baked beans in vin-

tage Bordeaux. In addition, filleting, which wastes 60% of a fish's nutritional value, was a poor use of food in a country where many people are malnourished.

But [things are changing] if Eritrea's newly independent government has its way. With the tenacity and sense of purpose that helped win a 30-year war of independence against Ethiopia, the former fighters now have declared war on Eritrea's eating habits. To promote fish eating, they have assembled a front that includes international big guns such as the United Nations' World Food Program, and enlisted local talent, such as an Eritrean comedian who has developed a routine making fun of meat-eaters. Eritrea's answer to Julia Child is cooking fish on the airwaves, and fish is most definitely on the menu at state dinners and school lunches.

In fact, school children have become guinea pigs in a piece of social engineering. As a captive audience, they're being fed seafood that Eritreans find especially unpalatable, such as deep-fried fish and sardines. "If you start with school children, maybe in ten years they get used to it," Mr. Etoh explains.

There's a new modern fish market in the capital city, Asmara, and a refrigerated fish van that patrols the back streets, trawling for impulse buyers by playing songs extolling the delectability of fish. Fish-promoting slogans appeal to both the palate and the patriot: "Eat Fish — It's Good for Us and Good for Our Country."[18]

Fish appear in the dynamics of race and the mythological behavior patterns of man, as shown in the following two incidents. The legend of the first 14½-pound brook trout caught provides an interesting panorama of storytelling, and, hardly unique to this story, it seems that the involvement of African contributions is always minimized, if not wholly dismissed, as stories are repeated. In Nick Karas' book, *Brook Trout*, he describes

Figure 1: Catching of the Big Trout by Webster and Lige
Reprinted by permission of Globe Pequot Press/
Lyons Press – Public Domain

how a 14½-pound brook trout was allegedly caught by Daniel Webster and pulled in by his slave, a man called Lige. A Currier & Ives print capturing Webster "catching" the trout also shows the slave, Lige, landing the trout. Karas relates a second version of the catching of the big trout: Writer Edna Trappell authored a story suggesting that not only Webster, but several men present, including future president Martin van Buren, all attempted to land the trout. The contribution of the slave, Lige, was dismissed in Trappell's account; in fact, she credited the landing of the fish to Sam Carman, the local gristmill owner. Unfortunately, when Black people participate in any significant event, their role and contribution are always in question.[19]

Another fish story involves Comoran fisherman Ahmed Hussein. Hussein caught the historic fish known as the coelecanth, which has been touted as the missing link between sea and land mammals. By catching the rare fish in 1952, Hussein put the island of Comoros on the scientific map. Notwithstanding his contribution, Hussein received a small reward for his labors, as other fishermen took the credit. In fact, it was not until 2005 that Hussein was even recognized. When the old fisherman was asked whether he had been acknowledged by historians, he stated, "It was as if they never wanted to see me again."[20]

CHAPTER THREE

Ending Mythology

Gerald Massey and Friedrich Max Müller were the two scholars who established new ways of thinking about mythology. It is very interesting to note how Western scholars view the works of Massey, a nineteenth century British Egyptologist. Massey emphasized the black, African origins of humanity and Egyptian civilization and was virtually ignored by white Western scholars. He and his colleagues, notably the surgeon, Albert Churchward, were not considered proper scholars by the Western academic establishment. Even the African American scholar St. Clair Drake in volume one of his book, *Black Folks Here and There*, states: "Only devotees of mystical literature will be able to assimilate the contents of Gerald Massey's six-volume work, *A Book of the Beginnings.... Natural Genesis...*and *Ancient Egypt."* [1] When comparing Massey's work along with other scholars who attempt to correct the falsification of African and world history, it becomes very clear that Massey was denigrated because of his emphasis on Africa as the origin of civilization and/or the contribution of black Africans to world history. In neither of the two volumes of Martin Bernal's *Black Athena* does he mention Massey even once. Yet Bernal talks a great deal about Charles François Dupuis. Both Dupuis and Massey underscore the black African origins of Egypt and civilization and the African mythological origins of all religions.

The reason why white academia refuses to give Gerald Massey his due is completely understandable. They want to minimize the influence of his writings as much as possible. So it is equally understandable why a black scholar like St. Clair Drake, who was educated in a Eurocentric model of thought, can render Massey academically irrelevant.

Meanwhile, black scholars like Charles Finch and the late John G. Jackson have done much to expose blacks the world over to the importance of Gerald Massey's scholarship.

Massey challenges the concepts of the Oxford Orientalist Max Müller. Müller and Massey had a basic disagreement, Massey taking exception to Müller's pronouncement that "Mythology is a disease of language." I think confusion arises where Massey takes that to mean mythology has its origins in language rather than in behavior. Mythology is indeed a disease of language. But that does not mean that humans became mythmakers because their language abounded in mythology. Conversely, the human language became myth because the humans who spoke it were mythmakers. In other words, mythology has its origins in symbolic thought, and that symbolic thought produced language that was mythological and metaphorical.

African people tend to put a great deal of importance and emphasis on mythology. Mythology, which is a conglomeration of symbols told in story form, can also be defined as a metaphor for human experience, a way to communicate that experience and to ascertain its meaning. It has been stated that one of the reasons African people talk and act mythologically is that like all people, the pain of reality and experiencing that reality is too much for the human psyche to receive and experience. Therefore, mythologizing becomes a mode of thought to ease the pain of reality. However, to think mythologically is to compound and extend the pain and frustration that one experiences in the world today. The more one mythologizes, the more one strays further into the abyss of unreality and mental illness. Not only does one experience the damage of mythology in real life situations, but one can see the damages of mythology in literature, whether in fiction or nonfiction. In black writing, myth is emphasized repeatedly. The African American writer, Toni Morrison, is well known for her ability to weave mythology and metaphor throughout her novels to describe the experiences and dilemmas of black people.

> In *The Bluest Eye*, a tale of paternal rape and incest, Morrison uses the first person narrator to tell the story of a childhood playmate, Pecola. The story is then filtered through the playmate's intelligence. In this way, the reader is twice removed from the pain of the tale. Two narrative voices move the story...like a Greek chorus, giving the story a mythic quality....Later, three little Black girls all strongly respond to media images (e.g., Shirley Temple and Mary Jane). Pecola eats Mary Jane candy trying to become the European aesthetic of Mary Jane.[2]

Seen from this perspective, the elimination of mythology is a foregone conclusion if people, wherever they reside, are to live harmoniously and peacefully in the space that they occupy. Mythmaking is a neurological misadventure that expressed itself as a disease of language as humans communicated with each other. Morrison herself states:

> Race has become metaphorical - a way of referring to and disguising forces, events, classes, and expressions of social decay and economic division far more threatening to the body politic than biological "race" ever was. Expensively kept, economically unsound, a spurious and useless political asset in election campaigns, racism is as healthy today as it was during the Enlightenment. It seems that it has a utility far beyond economy, beyond the sequestering of classes from one another, and has assumed a metaphorical life so completely embedded in daily discourse that it is perhaps more necessary and more on display than ever before.[3]

It must be clearly understood that mythology, since its emergence in Africa, has created all superstitions that humans have believed and/or practiced. As *Homo sapiens* spread throughout the entire universe, they have also spread their mythology. Yet, that mythology is basically one mythology: There are not two or many mythologies; there is but one, and that one mythology takes on different meanings in its diffusion from culture to culture.

The late American scholar and mythologist Joseph Campbell has written extensively on mythology and its effect on different cultures throughout the world. He was an expert on storytelling and mythology's participation in those stories. In Campbell's many books, he ably describes the dynamic of symbols as they interact with universal forces. His insistence on the importance and necessity of mythology and its relationship to symbols and metaphor is brilliant. However, because Campbell does not have a clear understanding of the dynamics of the symbol systems that appeared in Africa and the mythology created by those symbol systems, he lacks the ability to analyze mythology in a way that breaks with the European tradition.

Notwithstanding, Campbell's work is extremely important for its emphasis on the role myth has played in civilization. It is important to understand that people who decry mythology as falsehood fail to realize that mythology is, in fact, a metaphor that permeates our daily existence. Those who proudly proclaim that their mind is clear of mythological thought yet continue to practice racism and other superstitions in their daily existence fail to understand that the very racism and all other superstitions that they practice are, in fact, mythology. Because of the frequent occurrence of that mythology, it has become a ritual of daily existence in our universe. Because that very mythology is a superstition, it has become standard ritual. Civilization itself becomes ever more barbaric. For that reason alone, the end of mythology must take place. Indeed, it is a necessity if civilization is to survive in any form.

It must be clearly understood that the quagmire into which the U.S. has fallen in the Middle East, and our precarious relationships with Asia and Africa, are a product of how mythological thought in the U.S. is practiced and implemented, which makes for a very perilous situation that will lead to destruction.

Part Two

THE SYMPTOMATIC
THOUGHT PROCESS

CHAPTER FOUR

Definition and Use of Signs and Symptoms

As noted in my previous two volumes, Susanne Langer defines a symptom as a natural sign that is part of a greater event or a complex condition in which it is a notable feature.[1] Elsewhere, Cirlot[2] and Garber[3] define symptoms as signs. To sum it up, there is a distinct difference between a sign and a symbol. A sign is a symptom, and a symptom is always a part and has the original stuff to which it points. However, a symbol can never possess the original stuff to which it points, because it is a substitute and has no originality.[4] Symptoms are widely used in the medical profession to describe illnesses both mental and physical. But in reality, symptoms were first used as cultural indicators in antiquity. In fact, symptoms are older than symbols. As Deacon points out, the very first symbols ever thought or acted out grew out of the symptoms of an ancient socioecological dilemma.[5] When we think and experience things symptomatically, we are literally rewriting the history of the world. When archaeologists and anthropologists make discoveries that reshape world history, these discoveries are always made by symptomatic means. These scientists make these discoveries by finding natural signs that provide evidence of what happened in the past.

It is important to understand that symptoms are cultural indicators. They are signs that culminate into history. Symptoms are ways to read history — in fact, symptoms are a reading practice. Symptoms are languages without metaphor. The following examples of symptoms, below, give us an authentic reading of history.

As Marjorie Garber states, "...Symptoms are cultural practices and cultural signs. They are something to be read..."[6]

We continue with the late anthropologist Louis B. Leakey, whose fossil finds in Africa indicated that all of humanity originated in Africa rather than in Asia. That was followed by other numerous fossil discoveries that showed unequivocally that all of humanity has its roots in Africa. Fossils are important because they are a perfect example of natural signs and/or symptoms.

Paleontologists developed a new appreciation for the diets of prehumans when they uncovered signs. It had previously been thought that *Australopithecus africanus* – an upright, walking hominid that lived in Southern Africa – ate little more than fruits and leaves. By analyzing carbon atoms locked up in tooth enamel, researchers determined that these prehumans ate not only fruits and leaves but also grasses. The signs and symptoms present were the shape of *A. Africanus'* teeth

— the microscopic scratches and pits on the molars, and the chemical composition of the tooth enamel. By examining these signs, scientists were able to offer new suggestions of a hominid diet.[7]

Another member of the Leakey family used signs to establish the possibility that a species other than *Australopithecus afarensis* (known as "Lucy") could have been an early ancestor of human beings. Meave Leakey examined the signs and symptoms surrounding *Kenyanthropus platyops*, found in Kenya. Those signs were an unusual combination, having a large, flat face and small teeth, compared with Lucy's generally big teeth and different facial structure. These signs led Leakey to conclude that the odds were the same that either Lucy or *K. Platyops* could have preceded us.[8]

Symptoms are so powerful that they can present themselves in living fossils. One such living fossil is the coelacanth, a fish that dates back to antiquity, from 360 million to 80 million years ago. When that fish was discovered on December 22, 1938, off the coast of South Africa, debate began on the evolutionary link of fish to the human race. Many biologists believe that lung fish, which absorb oxygen through primitive air-breathing lungs as well as ordinary gills, were the true aquatic ancestors of the land-dwelling tetrapodes, the line that gave rise to the human race. Therefore, the debate persists between the coelacanth and the lung fish as being the evolutionary link to the human race. In terms of the analysis of blood proteins and the amino acids chain sequences, the dynamics over this phenomenon are all symptomatic. These signs will ultimately settle the debate. "Both the lung fish and the coelacanth were originally known only from fossil remains dating from the Devonian period, 370 million years ago. Both fish were believed to be extinct."[9]

Paleoanthropologists used signs to buttress the argument for the single-origin theory of modern human evolution. By analyzing over 1000 skulls, scientists found evidence that Neanderthals differ substantially enough from humans to be a separate species. That analysis, done in 3-D, focused on the same fifteen "landmarks" on the cranium and face to determine even the finest variations in shapes. With these signs, the researchers were able to provide tangible proof that Neanderthals were indeed a separate species.[10]

The presence of signs can provide tantalizing evidence to science, even when exploration has been hindered. Recently, paleontologists came across a prehistoric human site in the Tenere Desert of Niger, home of a little-known population of some 5,000 years ago called the Tenerian culture. Using symptomatic evidence easily accessible, scientists came across 130 skeletons and innumerable stone and bone tools, fish and animal bones, including domesticated cattle. The signs inherent in this find suggest a culture of people with a comprehensive economy networking from the Sudanese Nile all the way across the Sahara. This find is significant since it draws attention to the central African interior, the culture of which has not been as widely studied as Egyptian civilization. Although the team is seeking financing and other archaeologists to continue the expedition, the symptoms thus far uncovered provide great insight into the Tenerian culture.[11]

Unfortunately, notwithstanding the value of signs, some scientists are unable to resist mythologizing symptomatic results. After unearthing two fossils near the Sterkfontein caves north of Johannesburg, South Africa, scientists determined that the fossil pair was, rather than direct ancestors of modern humans, "kissing cousins" of our ancestors. This determination led to christening the fossils Orpheus and Eurydice after the lovers in Greek mythology. The fossils are 1.5 to 2 million years old and have been categorized as *Paranthropus robustus*. This hominid line became extinct one million years ago. It is ironic that although signs and symptoms can point unequivocally to a distant African origin, scientists are still enticed to overlay Greek mythology in naming the signs.[12]

In the ongoing search to solve the puzzle of human evolution, signs and symptoms play an integral part. Scientists uncovered the most credible contender for a direct ancestor of modern man with the finding of a skull near a lake in Ethiopia's Afar Desert. Fossilized tidbits provide signs that a humanlike creature, named *Australopithecus garhi,* survived in that region during an era when apelike creatures evolved into our human predecessors.[13]

To come to an understanding of human physiology, scientists are using the signs presented by fossils to compare primordial man with modern man. Anthropologists can support the finding that humans are a different lineage from Neanderthals by examining not only hominid fossils from 1.6 million years ago, but present-day chimpanzees and humans. The shortening of one bone at the brain base, the sphenoid, had rippling effects through the remainder of the skull, resulting in the shrinking of the brain case, making the head smaller. This dynamic also shortened the space between the mouth and the top of the windpipe, impacting the vocal tract and speech. These signs and symptoms of evolution are further confirmation of the hypothesis that modern humans evolved in Africa and migrated worldwide 100,000 years ago.[14]

There are still those scientists who continue to debate the identity of man's immediate ancestors. Paleoanthropologists are examining signs from a partial hominid skull, known as "Madeleine," that actually has features of both *Homo sapiens* and *Homo erectus* (an earlier species). By examining these signs, scientists concluded that this fossil possibly had an aptitude for verbal communication similar to that of modern humans. Signs indicating the same were the thick cranial bone and heavy brow ridges typical of *H. erectus.* Conversely, the fossil's forehead rose vertically in a dome shape more like *H. sapiens*, along with an asymmetric brain. Madeleine's contradictory signs only enrich the discussion regarding the evolutionary distance between *H. erectus* and *H. sapiens*.[15]

Paying attention to signs provides scientists with valuable clues. By geologically dating volcanic ash surrounding fossil bones found in Kenya, scientists confirmed that a leg bone came from a hominid species known as *Australopithecus anamensis* that walked on two feet 4.07 million years ago. This caused scientists to wonder whether there was a relationship to the female hominid known as Lucy (*Australopithecus afarensis*) believed to have walked upright as early as 3.9 million years ago. Continued examination of these signs allowed anthropologists to conclude that *A. anamensis* was a mixture – with limbs similar to humans, jaws and teeth like apes, and a small brain.[16]

Even symptoms such as sea mud allow anthropologists to explore whether a relationship exists between climatic and evolutionary events. An abundant deposit of hominid fossils accompanied by ashes was located in the Gulf of Aden off the coast of East Africa. Geologists analyzed the sediments from the sea floor to obtain accurate links between fossil records and climatic fluctuations. Examination of these signs allows scientists to ascertain what biological reasons caused the human family tree to separate.[17]

Another fascinating methodology for examining the origin of humans and Neanderthals is the analysis of mitochondrial DNA from Neanderthal remains. This analysis enabled a scientific team to conclude that the Neanderthal ancestry is four times older than that of humans. These signs point to a conclusion that Neanderthals were a genus distinct from modern humans.[18]

Signs can provide valuable evidence for the rewriting of history. The remains of eighteenth century Africans found in Lower Manhattan (New York City) were uncovered during preparation for the construction of a federal office building. The location of the skeletons enabled the building site to be designated a historic site. Additionally, the analysis of the human remains led to the conclusion that Africans were significant and valuable contributors to the economic health of colonial New York. This was contrary to the previously-held view that Africans did not play a part in the building and sustenance of New York City during colonial times.[19]

An article in the *New York Times* describes how a fossil shows signs that the earliest known bird could fly. This article is important, for it shows how natural signs become symptoms that allow an accurate reading of historic events. It is very important to realize and understand that a symptom is a state of affairs. With that in mind, it is important to understand that everything is symptomatic. There is no such thing as anything being symptom free, for life itself is a symptom. We must remember Susanne Langer's statement in her book, *Philosophy in a New Key*,

> A sign indicates the existence, past, present and future, of a thing, event or condition. Wet streets are a sign that it has rained; a smell of smoke signifies the presence of fire. All examples here produced are natural signs. A natural sign is a part of a greater event or a complex condition and to an expert observer, it signifies the rest of that situation, of which it is a notable feature. It is a symptom of a state of affairs.[20]

With the understanding that symptoms are a state of affairs — as opposed to the popular understanding, as in medicine, that some diseases present themselves as symptomless – the symptoms appear as cultural signposts long before their use in medical journals. So it must be clearly understood that symptoms present themselves as a state of affairs in all life endeavors. There is no such thing as a symptom free existence. A *New York Times* article (August 5, 2004)was pertinent in its description of how symptoms present themselves in fossils as signs. A research team led by Dr. Angela Milner, a paleontologist at the British Museum, showed how fossil signs were the leading ingredient in showing how an ancient bird had a brain conducive to flight. This study shows how symptoms rather than symbols are the necessary ingredient for analyzing how important events are recorded in history. We must remember — the analysis of symptoms is a reading practice. It is the missing link between what is real and unreal.

> Scientists have determined that Archaeopteryx, the earliest known bird, was definitely bird brained, meaning no disrespect. Indeed, they consider the fossil's brain size decisive evidence that Archaeopteryx had what it took to fly.

> The new research suggests, moreover, that birds probably started flying millions of years earlier than scientists previously thought. It is just that fossils of those first flying birds — predecessors of Archaeopteryx — have never been found.

> The researchers, at the Natural History Museum in London, based their findings on the first X-ray examination and reconstruction of the braincase and inner ear of a 147-million-year-old Archaeopteryx specimen. They found that in size, shape and volume, its brain was similar to that of the modern eagle or sparrow.

> The research team, led by Dr. Angela Milner, a paleontologist at the British museum, wrote that until their investigation of Archaeopteryx, "Little was understood about the extent to which its brain and special senses were adapted for flight."

> Dr. Milner said the new study not only established that Archaeopteryx was capable of "controlling the complex business of flying," but also showed "how much there is still to discover about when and how bird flight began."

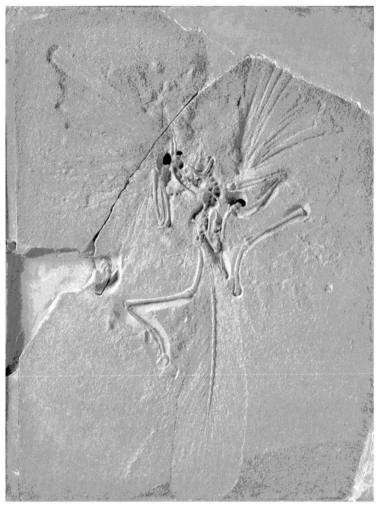

Figure 2: Archaeopteryx
Reprinted by permission of the Natural History Museum,
London

In a statement issued by the museum, Dr. Milner said, "If flight was this advanced by the time Archaeopteryx was around, then were birds actually flying millions of years earlier than we'd previously thought?"[21]

Symptomatic signs had the neurological and structural adaptations necessary for flight for the ancient bird, Archaeopteryx. This is extremely important, for it shows how symptomatic signs were a natural, neurological process; to introduce a symbolic presentation is truly a neurological misadventure. It brings to mind the statement by Max Müller, that mythology, which was the bane of the ancient world, is in truth a disease of language. The symbolism that produces the mythology is in fact a disease that infected all areas of human activity. That disease must be eradicated. This also follows the Dupuis' assault as he attacks the superstition that symbols bring as "diseases of which the germ is transmitted by the fathers to the progeny for a series of ages and against which art has no remedy to offer." DuPuis goes further to suggest that "it is an evil the more incurable, as it makes even fear the remedy which might cure it."[22]

My book, *An African Answer*, delineates symbols as a neurological misadventure of the human mind. That process has proven to be correct by the symptomatic findings of all the disciplines of science. It is impossible to get an adequate picture of the dynamics of history without a symptomatic reading of those events. So, symptoms are not only ways of speaking, they are a language. That language is disease free, as opposed to symbolic language that is riddled with disease. This completely turns upside down not only the way we see history but how we view behavior. If our behavior is symbolic, then it must become symptomatic.

A perfect example of how to turn symbols into symptoms is the work done by the late physicist and anthropologist, Cheikh Anta Diop, as he examined the myth of Atlantis through radiocarbon analysis. Diop examined a natural catastrophic event, a volcanic explosion on an island located in the Mediterranean Sea between Egypt, on the African continent, and Greece, on the Eurasia land mass. The explosion, which occurred during the eighteenth Egyptian dynasty, was a symptom of a complex situation.

> The volcanic eruption of the island of Santorini has been dated at 3050+150 B.P. or 3370+100 B.P. These two dates have been calculated from a piece of wood under the thirty-meter-thick layer of ashes that had covered the whole group of the Cyclades Islands after the explosion. This wood is therefore contemporaneous with the volcanic explosion that was to give birth to the myth of Atlantis. The second date; 3370+100 B.P., was obtained after the extraction of the humic acid that had accumulated in the ligneous material with time, and which constitutes an organic impurity likely to engender false analysis results. Thus 3370+100 can be considered the most probable date of the eruption of Santorini.[23]

An inability to comprehend the depth of the explosion led historians to mythologize the event; hence, the story of Atlantis.

> The eruption of Santorini had an impact on Greek mythology and legends. The long-term meteorological changes that accompanied it, affecting the aspect of the sun and the moon, must have given it a supernatural character in the eyes of witnesses, who would never have understood the exact nature of the event, which thus remained enshrouded in mythology.[24]

The piece of wood found under the layer of ashes that Diop talks about is what we call a natural sign, and it was analyzed using radiocarbon dating, a technology used to date natural signs or symptoms. Radiocarbon analysis is a very important tool in validating events and in putting these events in their proper perspective. It is not error free, for nothing in this life is, but when correctly used, it is a very reliable instrument that allows symptoms to reveal our early history in a way that is void of myth. The humic acid mentioned by Diop is also a natural sign that validates and removes any possibility of symbolic or mythological importance. Clearly, Diop placed little importance on symbols and myth. As noted by the scholar St. Clair Drake, "Diop makes very sparing use of mythology and folklore."[25]

Martin Bernal states, "In much of *Black Athena*, I have been trying to use myth and legend to help understand events and processes. Here I shall be attempting to do the reverse. That is, to use known and datable events — the Thera eruption, the expulsion of the Hyksos and the invasions of the people of the sea – to interpret myths and legends."[26]

Indeed, Martin Bernal uses mythology to understand the historical dynamics of the past. He leans on the myths and superstition of antiquity to such an extent that some of his conclusions are based on the same mythological evidence of modern scholarship that he attacks. If he relied more on the symptomatic evidence that is at his disposal, his conclusions would be more concrete.

One very interesting and telling procedure of turning symbol systems and myths into symptoms is used by folklorist Adrienne Mayor. Mayor, by connecting myths of ancient peoples with the bones buried on their land, is turning the symbol systems into symptomatic results.

HUMAN BEHAVIOR

In the nineteenth century, Gerald Massey stated, "The simple realities of the earliest times were expressed by signs and symbols."[27]

In the twentieth century, artist David Hammons prepared for his work by practicing the fine art of observing pedestrians, which he called "reading the signs and symbols of the street."[28] It is interesting to note that Massey made his observation pertaining to the antiquity of man in ancient times when the realities of life were expressed by signs and symbols. As expressed by David Hammons, it was as true then as it is now.

Human behavior is dictated by how one reads and reacts to signs and symbols. As stated earlier, it has been traditionally assumed that all stimuli experienced in life are ultimately given symbolic expression. That symbolic expression is a mythological thought process that translates into symbolic behavior of a highly superstitious nature. This causes man to act in a confused and barbaric manner, which is entirely inappropriate and incompatible in a civilized world. This mode of behavior has caused all of the problems that we face in today's world. This basic assumption of symbolic-behaving humans perpetuates a behavior pattern that causes world wars, intertribal conflicts, and a thoroughgoing corruption of human life. The alternative to that behavior is to react to life's stimuli in a symptomatic way. This will produce a symptomatic behavior that is void of all mythological thought processes. By seeing things symptomatically, behavior is void of racist, superstitious assumptions, and there is no need to distort the truth. It is impossible to think both symbolically and symptomatically simultaneously or interchangeably. This creates a schizophrenic individual who is unable to make sound decisions or to think rationally.

It must be thoroughly understood that out of the symbolic experience came religion and racism. It must be understood very clearly that without symbolism, we would not have religion or racism. Symbol systems are at the origin of all religions and mythological thought, and have produced all forms of mental illness. Mental illness is a product of symbolic-behaving *Homo sapiens.* An inability to face reality initiates a mythological process in the human mind, which results in a thoroughgoing inability to behave productively.

This inability to deal with reality creates an atmosphere that is highly charged with falsehoods. This is an environment where conflict and war are viewed as not only natural but sound. Not unlike the cultural conflicts and wars continuously wreaking havoc around us, today's global terrorism is a reaction to the absurdities that we are experiencing with disconnected people who are reacting to the stimuli of a world gone mad. However misplaced that terrorism is, it is their reaction to the myth. Indeed, in the larger society, myth is manipulated to achieve far-flung goals, such as domination, racism, and a strange mentality that only comes from a multitude of mythological assumptions. Gerald Massey stated:

> Misinterpreted mythology has so profoundly infected religion, poetry, art, and criticism, that it has created a cult of the unreal. Unreality is glorified, called the ideal, and considered to be poetry, a mocking image of beauty that blinds its followers, until they cannot recognize the natural reality.[29]

Symbolic-behaving people, indeed, produce a civilization in which what is normal and natural is perpetuated as the unreal. Conversely, what is abnormal is perpetuated as real. In his book, *Decolonising the Mind*, the Kenyan writer, Ngugi wa Thiongo, spoke of the consternation among some Europeans that Thiongo was writing in his native language, Gikuyu. Thiongo stated:

> It was almost as if, in choosing to write in Gikuyu, I was doing something abnormal. The very fact that what common sense dictates in the literary practice of other cultures is questioned in an African writer is a measure of how far imperialism has distorted the view of African realities. It has turned reality upside down: the abnormal is viewed as normal and the normal is viewed as abnormal."[30]

Later he would add:

> "Africa actually enriches Europe: but Africa is made to believe that it needs Europe to rescue it from poverty. Africa's natural and human resources continue

to develop Europe and America: but Africa is made to feel grateful for aid from the same quarters that still sit on the back of the continent. Africa even produces intellectuals who now rationalize this upside-down way of looking at Africa.[31]

Living in a civilization where mythmaking is the norm produces an individual that is literally upside down. Living in a civilization where facing reality is considered abnormal produces a permanent state of mental confusion.

The idea that symbolism is a natural occurrence of the human brain is a falsehood that must be eliminated from our assumptions about human life. It has been a long-standing assumption that in order to be creative, symbolic thought must be prevalent. That alone is the reason why we truly live in a barbaric civilization that has no end in sight. Whitmont was wrong when he suggested that we live symbolically and symptomatically at the same time. It is very clear that we cannot live effectively if we continue a behavior that is both symbolic and symptomatic. Throughout history, human behavior has been based on a symbolic process that has laid the foundation for all the conflict and suffering that we experience in this world today. In order that civilization be just, the symbol system that produces a superstition that is transported by rituals from culture to culture must be totally eliminated.

Scholars have studied the behavior of ancient Africans. A recent stone that was etched with intricate patterns and dated 77,000 years old suggested that Africans were capable of complex behavior patterns and sophisticated thought earlier than once believed. Scholars have studied the human behavior of humans using symbol systems as a yardstick for creativity. They have surmised that the etchings found on the stone indicated symbolic thought and the creativity that comes from symbolic thought. These scholars state that abstract

53

symbols are the foundation of all creativity, art and music, language, and more recently, mathematics. These scholars insist that the environment out of which such symbolic thought came was, indeed, the nursery of all advancement that man is likely to see.

It is interesting to note that because the stone was dated using radiocarbon analysis, the very material that was found had to be interpreted symptomatically. Said another way, the approach to extract data and information about this event was totally symptomatic. Out of that situation, the scholars emphasized the suspicion that early man began to think symbolically; that symbolic thought process is the key to creativity and an effective way of life.

All scientists that are interested in the field of human beginnings and qualitative behavior change have raised the question, When and how did man begin to think symbolically? It must be clearly understood that there can be no qualitative behavior change by way of symbol systems. These same symbol systems create a thoroughgoing mythological world where confusion is the rule of the day, and decisions are made entirely in a mythological, superstitious way. This, in turn, has caused virtually and literally all the turmoil that we see in the world today.

One's attitude is an important ingredient in relationships. It is important to understand that if we approach life with a symbolizing attitude, we will have chaotic and difficult relations among not only people, but also between whole countries. A symbolizing attitude is one that presents metaphors in not only our mode of speech but in our daily life. When we encounter people from different cultures, we mythologize that person and his existence; and we make up a description of him according to our own prejudices and idiosyncrasies based on superstition.

The idea — that symbolic thinking is not only essential to our thought pattern but is embedded into our self-conscious that no act or will can eliminate — is false. We are in control of our own thought processes. If there is a subconscious, it is totally irrelevant. The idea that symbols operate in the subconscious independent of our will is open for debate. For a symptomatic-behaving individual, the subconscious is non-operable. If symbols do come into play, they quickly dissolve into symptoms. There is a true desire for *Homo sapiens* to remain sane, without a superstitious nature. As Max Müller stated, man underwent temporary insanity as he became a mythmaker. That is why symbol systems can never be a natural neurological process.

As stated before, it must be emphasized that symbolism is a neurological misadventure. It is a disease, and this disease causes mythology and superstition, which in turn creates racism and other prejudices that are unhealthy and detrimental to all humans that partake in them. When we see each other as we really are without adding distorted images, we are, in effect, thinking symptomatically. Then and only then are we open to the energy and forces, or whatever we want to call the stimuli that make the world what it is. When we react to the stimuli, we are reacting to the symptoms that emanate from that stimuli. During that phenomenon, there is no symbolic activity taking place at all. We become healthy individuals who are able to love and appreciate people for who they are. All neurosis is eliminated, if it is present at all, and then we are able to make the kind of business and personal decisions that are not only sound but liberating.

The response to stimuli is a key event in people behavior. Traditionally, all responses to stimuli have been symbolic since the neurological misadventure took place. What is critical here is that any response to outside stimuli needs to be symptomatic. The stimuli can either be internal or external, but the response must be symptomatic. As stated earlier, any suggestion that the response be both symptomatic and symbolic creates a schizophrenic individual unable to make healthy decisions that would benefit the individual, or the people with whom he/she comes in contact. Man's choice is whether to respond symptomatically or symbolically to stimuli.

What is at stake is civilization itself. All human behavior studies that have been based on a symbol system without considering the symptomatic approach are wrong. All assumptions that a symbolic attitude is natural and essential are incorrect. The symbolizing attitude has affected every area of people behavior and academic discipline. It has been stated repeatedly that it is impossible to stop symbolic thought; that stopping symbolic thought is synonymous with stopping thinking. That particular attitude is taken because of the failure to understand that humans began to think symptomatically before they invented symbolic thought.

Symbolic thought arose out of a failure to deal with reality. If mythology is a disease of language, then symbolic thought is a disease of the neurological system. The assumption that symbols are never consciously devised but arise spontaneously is erroneous. Dr. Randall White, an archaeologist at New York University, states: "People had a capacity for symbolic thinking. That's important. Then they invented it in response to a certain set of circumstances."[32] If in fact symbolic thoughts do rise spontaneously, they are easily eradicated by our natural will to think and behave symptomatically. We must always remember that when one mythologizes, it is out of a failure to confront and deal with reality. That, by the way, is the definition of mental illness: the inability to deal with reality. It is easy to see the impact of the phenomenon of symbols and systems on human behavior.

Edward Whitmont stated, "The world of myth has its own laws and its own reality."[33] Whitmont's statement was compatible with the following statement by Ki-Zerbo: "Myth governed history and was at the same time responsible for justifying it."[34] The idea above is that civilization is governed by myth. The fact that civilization based on myth has its own laws and its own reality shows that we are presently in a barbaric civilization. Whitmont states further: "The myth's truth is accessible only to the symbolic view...The whole of life can be seen as a symbolic quest."[35]

These statements are extremely important for they show the role symbolic thought plays in civilization, and that the world of myth has its own laws and its own reality.

> The mythical approach in fact is common to all peoples. Every history starts off as religious history, but sometimes the mythical current overwhelms a nation's attitudes, opinions or ideology. Under the Nazi regime, for instance, the myth of race, substantiated in ritual that went back into the remote past, led mankind into one of the most terrible periods in all its history.[36]

What the evidence points out is extremely disturbing. It shows that we are living in a society that is not civilized at all. Even those nations that consider themselves the most powerful and wealthy are in fact the most hypocritical, i.e., the United States and the European countries. Indeed, it comes as a cultural shock when one realizes the kind of civilization that we live in — one borne out in conflicts experienced around the world in Africa, Europe, the Middle East, and other parts of the globe. The conflicts that are presently affecting the world are created by symbolic-behaving people.

Thinking symptomatically is seeing people as they really are without mythologizing their existence. How does one mythologize? For instance, when someone encounters another person who does not look like him or her.

In Fig. 3, the white individual mythologizes a person who is black. The sociologist St. Clair Drake states:

White person   **Black person**

Figure 3: White Person/Black Person

Social scientists, historians, and men and women of
letters sometimes present evidence to show that the
word for *black* in a specific language has numerous
derogatory synonyms and referents. Some then add
a comparative dimension by studying the meaning
associated with *black* in a variety of contexts cross-
culturally, contrasting these associations with those
made with the word *white*. A few scholars have ex-
plored the extent to which black people themselves
make negative appraisals of blackness. Some are con-
vinced that not only is there a universal dislike of
"darkness" in abstract symbol systems but also that
invidious distinctions are made everywhere between
light and dark people.[37]

The so-called black-white symbolic metaphor is used continuously to denigrate people of color. Frantz Fanon
wrote: "In Europe, the black man is a symbol of evil....In
Europe, the Negro has one function: that of symbolizing the lower emotions, the baser inclinations, the dark

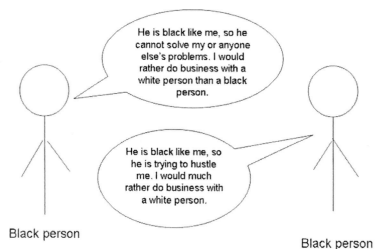

Figure 4: Black Person/Black Person

side of the soul...the color black - symbolizes evil, sin, wretchedness, death, war, and famine."[38] Fanon was quite explicit about the black-white polar contrast.

Fig. 4 illustrates how colonization and the educational system, with its penchant for mythologizing the existence of black people, has caused severe damage to the neurological process and self-esteem of black people.

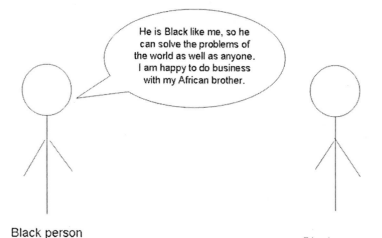

Figure 5: Black Person/Black Person with Symptomatic Thinking

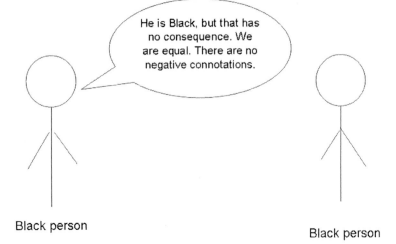

Figure 6: Black Person/Black Person with Confidence and Trust

They lack confidence in themselves and do not trust each other in a way that would be productive for themselves and black people globally. This is the syndrome that black people are in when they are initiators and victims of a global symbol system. However, when one thinks symptomatically, a correct and natural neurological process takes place.

Fig. 5 shows how nonsymbolic people relate to each other without using metaphoric language.

Fig. 6 shows two African brothers who are proud of their Africanness and are confident in each other. They feel that they can solve any problem that is put before them, or, at the very least, they can be as effective in problem-solving as anyone else. They are not mythologizing each other's existence — they are thinking and behaving symptomatically.

Symptoms force one to deal with reality. Zizek states that symptoms enable one to "deal with the truth about his desire, the truth that he was not able to confront, that he betrayed."[39] When a symptom is symbolized, it disintegrates. Thereafter, people once again become mythmakers, and they return to the bad habits brought on by superstition. To show how symbols affect color culminating in behavior change, St. Clair Drake states:

> Color words such as *Black* or *Yellow* or *White* or *Red* are used as shorthand symbols for configurations of physical traits, not for skin color alone; but they may also apply to the assumed heredity of a person not immediately manifest visually. For instance, the culture of the United States is frequently cited as one in which the color terms have become detached from the actual appearance of individuals when they are used to provide cues for discriminatory behavior. The state of Virginia carried a law on the books for many years that defined a "Negro" as anyone with "an ascertainable trace of Negro blood." *Thus many ostensibly "white" people are "Black," showing that people react to the presumed ancestry - -to a concept - - not to the actual phenotype.* Jokes and apocryphal tales are legion as well as a few documented cases of how behavior changes when a white person has been treating another as white and, then, becomes aware that the person has some Negro ancestry.[40]

It is imperative to understand that all human behavior is dictated by our use of symbols, or the use of mythology and signs, always recognizing that symptoms and signs are synonymous, as symbols are synonymous with myth. As stated earlier, the origin of human behavior goes back to Africa, and all research involving ancient behavior patterns of *Homo sapiens* are dictated by the use of symbols. Our main emphasis here is to show how color symbolism affects human behavior and our relationships with people globally. Drake is especially eloquent as he addresses this very problem when he states:

> A large amount of research has been carried out by psychologists on color symbolism and color preferences in the abstract....*Our primary concern is not with color symbolism per se, but with how it affects social interaction, social structure, and psychological states, that*

is how the designation of some people as Black and their relegation to an inferior position in socioeconomic hierarchies has affected individuals and groups. [Emphasis Drake's] The approaches of both comparative anthropologists and of social psychologists interested in cross-cultural research are vitally necessary. Controlled research on race and color in the Muslim East and Latin America are especially needed.[41]

Traditionally, the engine that runs human behavior has been understood and recognized by behavioral scientists and scholars from other disciplines to be symbol systems. However, we have found it to be incorrect that symbol systems are an effective engine that culminates in healthy human behavior. Only by incorporating a *Symptomatic Thought Process* can we initiate healthy human behavior in order to make this a truly sane and just civilization.

LANGUAGE AS A SYMPTOM

It has been understood by most scholars that language is a symbol system that evolved out of the human brain. It has been understood that language, the ability to speak, is what separates humans from other animal life. Deacon suggests that language should reflect a new mode of thinking symbolically. However, our research has found that language is not naturally a symbolic system. Language is a symptom, as Garber states: "Symptoms.... are ways of speaking. And the analysis of symptoms is a reading practice."[42] The Orientalist scholar, Max Müller, who was renowned for his theory on language, stated emphatically that mythology is a disease of language. When language is symbolized, it becomes distorted and highly metaphoric. It is important to understand that the brain has a language organ that is unique to humans. Stated another way, the neurological processes that produce language are symptomatic due to the uniqueness of the human brain. It is incorrect to say that language is symbolic in its natural and healthy state. Carl Jung, who was famous for symbolizing everything, stated that "language, in its origin and essence, is simply a system of signs or symbols."[43] Jung is correct in suggesting that language could either be a system of signs (symptoms) or a system of symbols (metaphors and myth). Language only becomes symbolic when it is mythologized. That is, indeed, a disease of language and it is prevalent in a neurological misadventure.

This understanding of language turns previous assumptions upside down. It has vast implications on how we speak and interact with each other. We are reminded of the words of Max Müller when he stated:

> Even if we take only that part of mythology which refers to religion, in our sense of the word, or the myths which bear on the highest problems of philosophy — such as the creation, the relationship of man to God, life and death, virtue and vice — myths generally the most modern in origin, we find that even this small portion, which might be supposed to contain some sober ideas, or some pure and sublime conceptions, is unworthy of the ancestors of the Homeric poets, or the Ionic philosophers.[44]

So Müller was correct when he suggested that humanity went through a period of insanity when it began to create mythology. Unfortunately, that insanity became permanent.

CHAPTER FIVE

Doing Business
with a Symptomatic Attitude

This section shows how symptomatic thinking affects the decisions that lead to productivity in every area of economic life. As we have repeatedly stated, the global business community has assumed that a symbolizing attitude is the correct approach to usher in profit, quality, and productivity. Consulting firms have used the technology emanating from various business gurus whether for reengineering, process engineering, or best practices. These concepts have made millions for their creators but have done little to facilitate business efficacy. All of the concepts taught in business schools, seminars, and workshops are based on a symbolizing attitude. Symbolism generates circular concepts that are faddish and hence disappear quickly. One need only pick up the *Harvard Business Review* to see what management concept has been declared royalty. That concept will be used in major corporations in the Western business world. Then, no matter how ineffective these concepts are, they eventually work their way into Asia, Africa, and Latin America.

The business schools do not produce students who are prepared to be effective in a highly technological and complex world that is basically nonwhite. Because of a huge falsification of history and an educational system that is ruptured to its core, pedagogical influences are based on the thought processes and habits of the status quo, which makes education a mockery. With globalization, a premise is ushered in that could have positive effects on the global economy. But because globalization is built on a foundation of myth and superstition, it has become totally impotent and exacerbates further the disparity that is so rampant in today's civilization. There have been some bright spots in the global economy: Daring leaders such as South Africa's Nelson Mandela and Malaysia's Mahathir Mohamad have provided the kind of leadership that is courageous, sage, and productive. Mahathir Mohamad, the former prime minister of Malaysia, rejected the advice of the World Bank and International Monetary Fund (IMF). Instead, he enacted his own policies to usher in a new productivity level for Malaysia as it rebounded from the economic crisis that engulfed the Pacific Rim. The following sections show how and why the behavioral sciences are imperative in all the agendas and concepts that are put forth to improve productivity and quality control.

UNDERSTANDING THE DYNAMICS OF GLOBAL LEADERSHIP

Effective leadership takes on two forms: The first teaches people to eventually lead themselves; the second simply realizes its motivations and goals. The quality of leadership is a product of the times in which one lives. Unfortunately, too often, today's global leadership is severely lacking due to the narrow-mindedness and the inability of those in positions of power to understand the dynamics that shape the modern world. Today's global leadership requires one to push the agenda and mandates that have shaped the present environment, with its ills and complexities.

This section focuses on what needs to happen to make leadership effective not only in Western countries, but in Africa and Asia as well. In doing so, we hope to lay bare the dynamics that shape the decision-making of the leaders of these countries as they push their agenda in a world that is truly confused. What do I mean by confused? As long as there is an environment that perpetuates destructive forces, it is all the more critical to have effective leadership that allows openness in which creativity can take place.

WHAT IS LEADERSHIP?

Leadership is as good as the behavior patterns of those who would consider themselves leaders. Most global leadership as practiced today is a vehicle that perpetuates the results of a highly symbolic civilization that glorifies the unreal as reality. The danger of today's leadership is that it perpetuates and globalizes the most destructive forces that have become prevalent worldwide. These destructive forces are, by unanimous decision, racism and religion. In a suggestion to the European community that they should use their influence to convince the United States to reverse its uncompromising stand against the regime of Iraq's Saddam Hussein, Malaysia's former prime minister Mahathir Mohamad offered several suggestions. While classifying the US approach as "symptomatic of a new racism," he stated:

> If the attack on Saddam Hussein is mounted there will be more willing recruits to the terrorist ranks. The perception is that Muslim countries seem to be the target everywhere – Libya, Sudan, Somalia, Chechnya, Iran, Iraq. It is a question of injustice. It seems that it is all right for Palestinians to die and Afghans to die. Thousands of Bosnians died, 200,000 died, and the world watched on TV and did nothing. But if you kill anybody else that is wrong. The feeling is that a western life is much more valuable than anybody else's. It is all right for others to die but don't you dare touch Westerners.[1]

Racism and religion have been the cause of most if not all of the conflicts that we now experience globally. After religion and race, the two other forces that are understood to be destructive are the quest for power and economic superiority. Each country and each group selects leadership that they believe will best promote and propagate their agenda. The key to that leadership is the ability to create an environment where the people can eventually lead themselves to perpetuate the agenda mandated to their particular leadership. To be sure, one can have effective leadership without that leadership being a force that would enhance civilization as a whole. In other words, an effective leader can perpetuate destruction, if that is the agenda; just as effective leadership can perpetuate good. Said another way, effective leadership can promote justice and enhance civilization; or effective leadership can promote evils such as racism, religious discord, and confusion around the world. So be clear: Effective leadership can promote issues and agendas good and bad. A case can be made that both Adolf Hitler and Nelson Mandela provided good leadership for their constituencies. As a matter of fact, Hitler, it has been said, created such "magic" for the people he persecuted, that they often saluted and cheered him as fervently as did his followers. Conversely, Nelson Mandela's leadership and personality were so effective that even his most ardent opponents were impressed by his charisma – they saluted him and showed him respect, even while he was imprisoned. Leadership is simply providing and taking on the agenda of the people who appointed it.

HOW SYMBOL SYSTEMS DICTATE THE EFFECTIVENESS OF LEADERSHIP

One cannot discuss the dynamics of leadership without understanding the effect that symbol systems have on human behavior. Because we live in a universe that is governed by symbol systems and their resulting mythologies, rituals, and superstitions, leadership is really at the mercy of the usage and interpretation of these symbol systems in their individual scenarios and environment. Symbols have an extraordinary effect on human behavior. If one understands that myths and symbols are synonymous, then you understand that mythology has governed history and justified it at the same time.

Man's attitude is basically a symbolizing attitude. Unfortunately, this symbolizing attitude has led to a penchant for never-ending mythmaking. All symbols were created out of a symptomatic existence. When *Homo sapiens* began to symbolize their symptomatic existence, a neurological misadventure took place in which man began to act out, or to initiate, symbolic behavior patterns. Accompanying the birth of symbolic behavior was the tendency for humans to make decisions based on mythological assumptions. Some scholars have even called the human species symbolical savants because of our propensity to see everything in symbolic terms.

> Most scholars of symbolism have stated that symbolism is as natural as breathing; and the ensuing mythology is not only natural, but it is what keeps hu-

mans civilized. Psychoanalyst Rollo May states that mythmaking is essential in gaining and maintaining mental health. "History is determined by its mythology."[2]

Modern-day scholars are emphasizing the importance of symbols and myths that vindicate the earlier concepts of Gerald Massey and Albert Churchward. My basic assumption is that all religions stem from symbolism, which means all religions are mythological.

Unfortunately, most people do not understand how symbolism is used to mythologize history, manipulate behavior, and set in motion a way of thinking that creates the phenomena of racism, greed, neurosis and other forms of mental illness. Although Jung and May both postulate the belief that mythological symbolism is essential for mental health and well-being, symbolism, through its mythological content, has caused the distortion of scientific facts and created a barbaric civilization. Instead of being a panacea for humanity's thrust into fulfillment, it is a plunge into despair, derangement, and frustration for the whole of civilization.[3]

This symbolizing attitude has doomed humankind to creating leadership that perpetuates a ritualistic way of life that has made mythological existence the norm. This dynamic has caused today's leadership to perpetuate a mythological existence, by way of symbolic thought, that has caused destruction, and made destruction a permanent way of life in today's civilization. Accordingly, the leadership we experience in today's world is a guidance that spreads the results of a symbolizing attitude that affects every area of human existence. This leadership has made possible the distribution of ideologies and concepts that are the engine for the conflict and discord that we see operating in all areas of human activity. This explains today's prominent global conflicts. As mentioned earlier, effective leadership takes on two forms: the first gives people the ability to eventually lead themselves; the second realizes the leadership's motivations and goals. The description of good leadership does not necessarily mean that that leadership is working towards the common good of everyone. Effective leadership can have destructive goals and still be good leadership. Because we live in a mythological universe, the goals that are perpetuated and realized are often destructive and harmful to the universe as a whole. This is easily verified by the conflicts that we are experiencing throughout the world, which are motivated by symbol systems that emerge as superstition. These superstitions are utilized and perpetuated by symbolic-behaving people.

Malaysia's Mahathir Mohamad, former prime minister of Malaysia, was the leader of a country that was pivotal in the economic surge of Southeast Asia. Malaysia, which had one of the fastest growing economies in the world, has been a source of concern to the Western world. This concern was prompted by Mahathir's audacity and decision-making. Dr. Mahathir has never been afraid to challenge the racist attitudes of the United States and the West and their conspiracy to control the global economy. When commenting on America's attempts to remove Saddam Hussein from power, Dr. Mahathir said:

> ...[that the U.S.] attitude was symptomatic of a new "racism" reminiscent of that practiced by the British in colonial times. "The feeling is that a Western life is much more valuable than anybody else's. It is all right for others to die but don't you dare touch Westerners."[4]

Dr. Mahathir had a unique situation as he tried to control Malaysia's ethnic and religious conflict and at the same time keep the country on track as a leading economic force in the region. His joint ventures with African countries were a source of irritation to the European Union. The Western world has always had problems with countries that are populated by a nonwhite majority. Mahathir Mohamad had the wisdom and the courage to stand up to the International Monetary Fund (IMF) and the World Bank as they tried to lay out their agenda for the developing world.

> [Malaysia] had experienced ethnic riots in the past. Malaysia had done a lot to prevent their recurrence, including putting in a program to promote employment for ethnic Malaysia. Mahathir knew that all the gains in building a multiracial society could be lost, had he let the IMF dictate its policies to him and his country and then riots had broken out. For him, preventing a severe recession was not just a matter of economics, it was a matter of the survival of the nation."[5]

Though Prime Minister Mahathir's policies trying to keep interest rates low and trying to put brakes on the rapid flow of speculative money out of the country were attacked from all quarters, Malaysia's downturn was shorter and shallower than that of any of the other countries.[6]

What made Mahathir exceptional was his refusal to be fooled by the mythological manipulations that the West tried to impose on Malaysia.

> Early on in the 1997 economic crisis, IMF chief Michael Camdessus announced that Malaysia's banks were in a weak position. An IMF/World Bank team was quickly dispatched to look at the country's banking system. The standard way to assess the strength of a banking system is to subject it...to stress tests and evaluate its response under different economic circumstances. The Malaysian banking system fared quite well...and was remarkably strong. [IMF staffers had difficulty] writing the report: how to formulate it without contradicting the managing director's assertions and yet remain consistent with the evidence.[7]

Prime Minister Mahathir's dealings with Zimbabwe's President Robert Mugabe were of special consternation to Europe. One of the Western world's worst nightmares is that Asia and Africa engage in joint ventures and other business dealings. Of course, that is solely because of the racist attitude of whites in the Western world. When leadership is established and mandated on the liberation of a country's people, the agenda of that leadership is simplified. Prime Minister Mahathir Mohamad provided the kind of leadership that made Malaysia economically strong, and that positioned the country to be basically sound in multiple areas that he was able to touch.

LEADERSHIP EXHIBITED IN THE AFTERMATH OF SEPTEMBER 11, 2001

Rudy Giuliani, former mayor of New York City, was lauded for his leadership of New York City after the bombing of the World Trade Center. Prior to September 11, 2001, the majority of New York's populace experienced the racially divisive leadership of Giuliani. Many maintained that Giuliani fostered an atmosphere of racial tension throughout the city. He was seen as an uncaring mayor who perpetuated an attitude of vindictive behavior and unfairness throughout his administration. In countless instances, nonwhites experienced the inequitable treatment of Giuliani during his so-called leadership.

> [In his attempt] to enforce "one standard" for all New Yorkers, Giuliani rarely reached out to any minority leaders. The city's black and Latino leaders did not like it. They complained that his aggressive cops were practicing racial profiling, stopping and frisking people because of their race. [As a result] three awful brutality cases came to define the Giuliani years.[8]

73

Abner Louima was a Haitian immigrant who was sodomized with a plunger handle by members of the police department. This was one of the most barbaric acts known to so-called civilization. Giuliani showed not only a lack of concern for the victim, but downplayed the significance of the act, and once again showed unwavering support for the New York Police Department. Amadou Diallo, an unarmed African immigrant, was shot forty-one times by New York police officers while standing in his doorway. Giuliani unequivocally supported the Police Department and showed no sympathy for Diallo's family. Finally, Patrick Dorismond, an unarmed African-American security guard trying to hail a taxi, was a victim of a case of mistaken identity, when New York police working under cover shot him to death. Not only did Giuliani unshakably support the offending policemen, the mayor then proceeded to condemn the dead man, suggesting he was a criminal.

> After Dorismond was killed, Giuliani's instinct to defend the police led him to attack the unarmed victim; the mayor authorized release of Dorismond's juvenile records to "prove" his propensity for violence. The dead, Giuliani argued, waive their right to privacy. Even old friends and supporters were appalled. The man who had saved New York City saw his job approval rating drop to 32%".[9]

Rudolph Giuliani created an atmosphere of fear, distrust, and disdain for people of color in New York City. It was evident to those in the black community that a black person's life meant nothing. However, the vast majority of whites showed support for Giuliani mainly because of his racist leanings and his dictatorial style of running the city government.

> The public, shocked and delighted that the streets were actually safer and cleaner – didn't care how it happened. If Giuliani picked fights big and small, if

74

he purged government of those he deemed insuffi-
ciently loyal, so be it.[10]

Giuliani cared very little about the prospect of unity
between blacks and whites; but after September 11, he
perpetuated an atmosphere that hypocritically reached
out to the city's nonwhite population to support his self-
contrived attempts at leadership. Giuliani's objective
was to uphold the mythic image of the white warrior
being in control. As long as the white warrior was in
control, everything would be all right. The very blacks
that he denigrated throughout his term in office were
supposed to rally around him as a hero. Because America
is fundamentally racist, Giuliani's actions during and
after September 11 were considered heroic, and he was
reborn in the public's mind as the hero of the country's
worse internal disaster in modern times. Consequently,
he made the cover of *TIME* magazine as its Man of the
Year. September 11 actually saved Giuliani's reputation
and reinvented him as the mythic savior of New York
City. Giuliani's leadership was opportunistic at a time
when an unfortunate occurrence took an enormous
number of human lives. The fact that he was so readily
accepted as a hero by the white community only illustrates how determined they were to deify him because
they agreed with his racist attitudes.

THE CASE OF THE UNITED STATES OF AMERICA

Giuliani's leadership of New York City was symptomatic of the leadership of the United States as a whole.
We currently have a president, George W. Bush, who
has no respect for the United Nations or for the value
of any multilateral action that embraces attitudes and
concepts from non-Western groups. Realizing that his
ascent to leadership was one that grew out of a corrupt
political system, George W. Bush is simply mimicking
the attitudes of white American citizens. Bush did not
win the 2000 presidential election by vote of the people,

but was put into office by the U.S. Supreme Court. The vast majority of black Americans did not vote for George Bush to be President of the United States. In the state of Florida, for example, Black voters were intimidated at the polls, and in many precincts their vote was not counted. What makes these actions so glaring is the disconcerting fact that the United States prides itself on having fair and free elections, an integral part of the democratic process, and that it has criticized other countries for their corrupt voting practices. Nowhere in the world has leadership been as hypocritical as that displayed in the United States of America.

The U.S. does deserve special credit and emphasis for its sophistication and its ability to manipulate symbols to a degree that far surpasses that of other countries in the world today.

> There are many people in the US...who are unsettled by public professions of faith from the White House. "We have a president who is about to plunge the world into chaos by starting an unjustifiable war and he does that in part by wrapping himself in the mantle of religion," says George Hunsinger, a Presbyterian minister who teaches at Princeton Theological Seminary.[11]

The U.S. government's ability to oppress people of color, especially African Americans and immigrants of color, is unprecedented in world history. The United States is able to manipulate symbol systems in such a way that causes the oppressed to believe in their own oppression. That is especially the case with African Americans. It is appalling to see the contentment and apparent resignation of blacks in the United States when it comes to confronting their status as second-class citizens. The United States leadership understands the dynamics of symbols and how they influence people of color. A very effective way to keep people of color in a state of satisfaction is to create a mythological existence under the guise of success and status. This is done for a small elitist segment of the black community who believe that they have attained the status that would make them, at least subliminally, honorary whites. That same elitist black group perpetuates a symbol system of success that they encourage the black majority to follow, as if to reach the end of a rainbow. This behavior exists in every area of human endeavor. Those blacks who resist are usually destroyed and/or exhibited as examples of what happens to blacks who dare step out of the box to promote real equality, justice, and fairness in one of the most racist systems in the world. One prime example was the 2000 "election" of George W. Bush, who, after failing to gain the majority of the vote, manipulated himself to a position that left the decision of the presidency to the conservative Supreme Court. Nowhere is it more visible to the pattern of leadership in the United States than in the case of Clarence Thomas, where the conservative Republican leadership placed a black judge on the Supreme Court who, for all practical reasons, is a totally dysfunctional individual who undoubtedly has issues that do not allow him to be an effective advocate for the African American community. However, Clarence Thomas certainly provides effective leadership for the white, racist leadership of the United States of America. That leadership readily understands that African Americans, like their African ancestors, are a symbolic people, for: "...Africans are the most symbolic behaving people on earth. Such behavior is inadequate for doing world-class business."[12] Because of symbolism, Africans are easily manipulated to living out a mythological existence disguised as the American dream of success, which entails attending the "proper" schools from elementary to the graduate level; attending the "right" church; living in the "acceptable" neighborhood; buying the "right" home; and behaving in a way that whites see as non-threatening and, indeed, subservient — even if that subservience is masked in a way that appears not to be dehumanizing.

The question must be asked and answered: Why do blacks tolerate the insults and dehumanization from the U.S. leadership that forces them to die at a younger age than anyone else not only in America but at an age comparable to those in the worst-case scenarios in the developing world?

> Poor urban blacks have the worst health of any ethnic group in America, with the possible exception of Native Americans. It makes you wonder whether there is something deadly in the American experience of urban poverty itself. ...Since the time of slavery, physicians have noted that the health of impoverished blacks is, in general, worse than that of whites....The experience of racism and discrimination in everyday life is also still very real, and very stressful....Arline Geronimus, University of Michigan professor of public health says that blacks are faced with a society that institutionalizes the idea "that you are a menace – and that demeans you." Nancy Krieger, a Harvard researcher, found that working-class African Americans who said they accepted unfair treatment as a fact of life had higher blood pressure than those who challenged it.[13]

As the United States population becomes increasingly nonwhite, its leadership is projecting symbol systems that indeed cause identity confusion among people of color. Nowhere is that more apparent than in the attempts to categorize people of color by the U.S. Census Bureau. The option is given for people to mythologize their racial identity. This simply means inventing new identities that categorize as neither black nor white. The nation's Hispanic population is now mythologizing racial categories that they feel will erase the stigma that is usually associated with people of color.

An advertising sales director is uncomfortable picking one race because the words white and black carry political baggage...."White means mostly privilege and black means overcoming obstacles...." In 2000, 48% of Hispanic respondents [to the U.S. Census] identified themselves as white; 2% chose black...[however] the way Hispanics see themselves may ultimately be irrelevant if they are still subject to other people's biases.[14]

Because of the racist (symbolic) attitude of whites, and their treatment of people of color, blacks who have some degree of physical characteristics that are not associated with African Americans prefer to identify themselves other than black. The United States puts such great emphasis on the degradation of black Americans and the continual mythologizing of their existence that it is undesirable to be identified as an African American. Those people who feel as though they can get away with identifying themselves as anything other than black will do so. While this is indeed a tragic and unfortunate scenario, what needs to be emphasized here is that whites and their leadership see this strategy as a way of maintaining power and domination over the nonwhite majority. And make no mistake about it; they do that by manipulating a symbol system that is ingrained in every area of people activity. It is especially prevalent within the U.S. educational system, with its penchant for initiating standardized testing as a method of excluding people deemed undesirable. Invariably, those who are deemed as such are people who pose a threat, perceived or real, to the white leadership structure of the United States. As long as blacks fail to understand these symbolic dynamics, they will continue to be a people that are intellectually and physically enslaved by a white leadership that continues to see them as inferior. This is why it is paramount to comprehend the role of symbols and their ability to produce a superstitious mode of existence that keeps people docile and subhuman. That is one of the reasons why America is becoming a South Africa in its racial identity and in its way of enslaving a majority people who are indeed, in reality, an African people.

America prides itself on being the leader of the world. But America can be proud of perpetuating a leadership that is able to set an example of racism and hypocrisy. America is a perfect leadership paradigm for its mastery of the use and manipulation of a symbol system that produces a mythology that is able to confuse and disorient its population.

> Until recently, blacks in America had the numerical strength to cause grave concerns on the political scene. But all this was to change with the introduction of the class, "Hispanic" into the American census vocabulary. The change started some 20 years ago when the US government came up with the term "Hispanic" to describe that part of its citizenry whose origins were from Spanish-speaking countries. Note that censuses are not conducted for frivolous reasons. Census statistics have political and economic impact.....The surprising issue is why the black leadership of America never challenged this classification.[15]

The U.S. government created the term *Hispanic* to confuse the racial identity of its nonwhite citizens and at the same time dilute the African American power base. The U.S. Census Bureau and its racist mythological agenda stripped what power black Americans had by creating a mythological new minority that would rob African Americans of the so-called privileges they have obtained by being the so-called largest minority group in the country. African Americans continuously fail to see the damage that the government causes by its manipulation of symbol systems and the creation of a system built entirely on myth. Given this system, it is impossible for creativity or any kind of effectiveness to prevail due to a mythological foundation.

The new categories on race that have been added to the census forms only make matters worse; these categories are akin to the racial groupings used in South Africa. My book, *Symbolism Revisited* details why Dr. Mustapha Hefny filed a lawsuit against the U.S. government for declaring him legally white.

> Caramel-hued, wooly-haired Hefny filed his lawsuit after a citizenship interviewer told him that he would become legally white after becoming a U.S. naturalized citizen. The interviewer used guidelines established by the U.S. Office of Management and Budget, which stated that persons having origins in the peoples of Europe, North Africa and the Middle East are considered white. In his suit, Hefny requested that he and other Nubians, who are in fact Egyptians, be legally declared Black. Hefny has darker skin than Colin Powell, his hair is kinkier, and he was born in Africa. Yet in the United States he is declared white, and Colin Powell is declared Black. Hefny maintained that the present U.S. system is a racist system. By denying the Black African origins of the Egyptians, Hefny stated that for the last 400 years many white scholars have tried to resolve the logical dilemma of the ideology of white superiority and Black inferiority by separating Egypt from Africa and by claiming that ancient Egyptians were not indigenous Africans but a branch of the white race."[16]

When whites are in a minority, they mythologize the facts of race to cause confusion among people of color. This is a perfect paradigm that shows the need for whites in leadership to turn symptoms into symbols so that history can be mythologized. This must cease in order for us to understand correctly the dynamics of civilization.

GLOBALIZATION

Globalization is another perfect example of how a phenomenon that was meant to signify integration and unity has failed the world's poor, polarizing instead of unifying. Because of leadership that bases economic decisions on myth, globalization never had a chance to succeed. The Western world's advocacy of globalization as a force to enhance the developing world's economic situation proved to be nothing less than a symbolic venture that was not meant to aid the poor nations of the world. The leadership of the Western world did not intend for globalization to work for everyone. That leadership will always want the have-nots to continue to have not and the haves to continue to have.

> The World Trade Organization was designed as a meeting place where willing nations could sit in equality and negotiate rules of trade for their mutual advantage, in the service of sustainable international development. Instead, it has become an unbalanced institution largely controlled by the United States and the nations of Europe and especially the agribusiness, pharmaceutical and financial services industries in these countries. At WTO meetings, important deals are hammered out in negotiations attended by the trade ministers of a couple dozen powerful nations, while those of poor countries wait in the bar outside for news.[17]

This is the logic of a leadership of destruction that is built on racism, power, and greed. Leadership should promote justice in all levels of human activity to eliminate racism, religious discord, and confusion. A just leadership is one that is built on a nonmythological framework and legitimizes its existence by eliminating systems that are perpetuated by symbolic manipulation. That leadership eliminates behavior built on superstition that keeps people intellectually confused and mentally disoriented. The majority population can never function productively while in a state of confusion and discord. That confusion and discord, again, is based on a population behaving symbolically.

JUST LEADERSHIP

Effective leadership that would qualitatively enhance the world in such a way as to be truly just is one leadership that would eliminate symbolic behavior globally. This leadership is not based on myth but on the realities of any given situation. This leadership would be committed to eliminating all decisions based on a mythological foundation. There have been world leaders that have indeed accomplished such a mode of leadership; although criticized extensively, they were endowed with courage and resolve as they endeavored to create a truly civilized environment.

One such leader was the Senegalese scholar Cheikh Ante Diop (1923 – 1986). Dr. Diop was director of the Radiocarbon Laboratory at what is now renamed Cheikh Anta Diop University, formerly the University of Dakar, Senegal. Diop's last book before his death, *Civilization or Barbarism* (Lawrence Hill Books), was the culmination of a series of writings that rewrote world history. More than anyone else, Diop changed the falsification of history that had been written by racist white scholars, and he subsequently changed how we view world history. Consequently, he was vilified by European scholars, who refused to accept the revisiting of history for fear of unveiling the true history of the universe and the leading role that Africans played in it. Diop had the courage of his convictions. Self-aggrandizement and mythology were never factors in his decision-making. His only commitment was to making the world a better place for everyone by increasing our understanding of history and civilization. Cheikh Anta Diop and W. E. B. DuBois (1868 – 1963) were honored as two who exerted the greatest influence on African people in the twentieth century at the World Black Festival of Arts and Culture held in Dakar, Senegal, in 1966. However, the ferocity with which Dr. Diop was attacked by European scholars shows the commitment of white and European scholars to maintain a status quo that has racism as an integral part of the global culture. This status quo keeps blacks in a permanent state of worldwide servitude.

Cheikh Anta Diop exhibited the kind of leadership that should be prevalent the world over. However, because he was a black African who had the courage to reject the falsification of history that is a permanent conceit of Western academia, he became the principal target of those who wanted to perpetuate a continual state of imperialism and racism. Leaders such as Cheikh Anta Diop and Mahathir Mohamad, along with Nelson Mandela, exhibit the courage required to initiate the type of leadership that will benefit all people. The fact that these men were and are nonwhite should not be lost, and that fact perpetuates the most severe criticism and attacks against them. However, their unswerving bravery enabled them to carry on.

Amadou-Mahtar M'Bow, a Senegalese leader and former secretary general of UNESCO, the United Nations body responsible for education, culture, and science, had the courage to exhibit the leadership that would liberate the pedagogical circumstances that the world found itself in. Under M'Bow's leadership, UNESCO forged programs to reeducate the world away from the distorted historical perspective perpetuated by the West. Secretary M'Bow proposed that UNESCO establish a Third World news agency that would offer an alternative to the dominant Anglo-Saxon news agencies; however, the United States and England objected. M'Bow's pedagogy was responsible for the initiation of the eight-volume series of books called *The General History of Africa*, which set out to expose the distortions perpetuated by the Western world about the history of the world generally and the history of Africa specifically.

> For a long time, all kinds of myths and prejudices concealed the true history of Africa from the world at large....there was a refusal to see Africans as the creators of original cultures which flowered and survived over the centuries in patterns of their own making and which historians are unable to grasp unless they forego their prejudices and rethink their approach....[A] phenomenon that did great disservice to the objective study of the African past was the appearance, with the slave trade and colonization, of racial stereotypes that bred contempt and lack of understanding and became so deep-rooted that they distorted even the basic concepts of historiography. By demonstrating the inadequacy of the methodological approaches which have long been used in research on Africa, this *History* calls for a new and careful study of the twofold problem areas of historiography and cultural identity, which are united by links of reciprocity.[18]

The United States believed M'Bow was challenging so-called American cultural imperialism and racism and pulled out of UNESCO. These views were shared by the Thatcher government in Britain, which pulled the United Kingdom out of UNESCO a year later. By removing their countries from participation in UNESCO and discontinuing their funding, the United States and the United Kingdom demonstrated the lengths to which the Western world would go to preserve their own version of history, one based on overt racism. M'Bow's position is symptomatic of a leader challenging the racist structure that Europe and America perpetuate globally on people they classify as nonwhite. Conversely, the return of the United States to UNESCO in 2003 came as a result of UNESCO's change in focus. This is significant, because it led to the untenable situation at the United Nations with its former secretary general, Kofi

Annan. During his tenure, Annan exhibited courageous and wise leadership. Notwithstanding, the U.S. has been the UN's strongest critic. In fact, the U.S. has accused the UN and, indeed, Annan himself, of being anti-American. Needless to say, Kofi Annan had to walk a tightrope as he carried out his duties as secretary general, for no matter what decision he made, there would be at least one country that would be critical. It didn't help that Annan is a black African from Ghana, which made him a special target for people who did not wish to see an African in such a position of power. Yet, while President Bush is called the president of the United States, Kofi Annan has been called the president of the world. The U.S. leadership did whatever it could to belittle the UN and Annan's tenure as secretary general. In his opposition to the U.S. lack of leadership in the Iraq war, South African leader Nelson Mandela stated:

> Why does the United States behave so arrogantly? Their friend Israel has got weapons of mass destruction, but because it's their ally they won't ask the UN to get rid of it. They just want the oil. Is this because the secretary general of the United Nations is now a black man? They never did that when secretary generals were white.[19]

Kofi Annan showed extraordinary leadership in initiating decisions that were based on a balanced and fair assessment of global situations that arose continually affecting millions and millions of lives. However, Western leadership is focused on maintaining a permanent state of haves and have nots, assuring that those who classify themselves as white are always the haves.

Good and effective leadership based on establishing a system of justice requires a great deal of courage and wisdom. Living in a world that is based on myth and its prevailing symbol systems keeps the world in constant turmoil and crisis. Unfortunately, many of today's leaders base their decisions on the perpetuation of symbol systems which allows mythology to prevail in all areas of people activity. It is quite ironic that the United States chooses to consult with organizations like the American Enterprise Institute – a conservative think tank that perpetuates racism — for intellectual guidance to justify leadership decisions, over and against an organization like UNESCO, which seeks to correct the falsification that has caused severe harm to the educational system globally. The quality of leadership needed today is that which Amadou M'Bow and Kofi Annan exhibited in their very difficult situations, past and present.

THE CHALLENGE TO LEADERSHIP

The mythological environment in which we currently live makes it imperative that leadership take on a certain shape. Because we are symbolic human beings, we live in a mythological world with superstition being the base upon which people make decisions. Because we live a mythological existence perpetuated by symbolism, we live in a racist environment that perpetuates greed, dishonesty, and a continual type of barbarism that has not been experienced before due to the advanced stage of symbolic behavior in our population. This state of civilization makes it imperative that leadership take a proactive role in the elimination of symbols and symbolic behavior by the populace. Mythology, which has been created by symbols, has been allowed to spread. That symbol-created mythology has been allowed to remain unchecked, creating a most barbaric environment. Leadership must lay out a program that exposes the dangers of symbolic behavior and unveils the treacherous decision-making that superstition fosters.

There may be a realization that superstition is operating only because of a civilization driven by symbols. Sir James Frazer, in his book, *The Golden Bough*, revealed how modern society' attitude towards the natural environs of the world is similar to that of the ancients during antiquity, in that the same symbolic-driven superstitions that occupied the mind of the ancients are still present in modern-day decision-making and behavior.[20] Unlike the assumptions of the past on the role leadership takes, it is imperative that leadership becomes a savant for the elimination of symbols and symbolic behavior. Such a mandate has not been made before because of the assumption that symbolic thought is a natural neurological process. Symbolic thought is not a natural neurological process; it is indeed a neurological misadventure. The nineteenth century scholar Max Müller was determined to expose the absurdities of mythological thought to the extent that he called mythology "a disease of language."[21] For this reason, Müller was ridiculed as being naïve. Müller expressed outrage at the lunacy of mythological thought as it was expressed by the ancients. He noted that the same symbolic thought was prevalent throughout the entire universe. In his book, *Comparative Mythology,* Müller mused that humans must have passed through a period of insanity to come up with the various mythological stories that he deemed worthless and wasteful of human thought.

Because we live in a highly superstitious and ritualistic civilization, unpredictability has been the rule of the day. Because the very nature of mythology is change, i.e., apples become oranges, bananas become pears, the changes of names and situations are at the mercy of the mythmakers. When reality seeps in, myth takes over to the extent that it changes situations to suit the desires of the mythmaker regardless of reality. In other words, what hinders the smooth running of the symbolic circle is the traumatic presence of the real.[22] On the other hand, a symptom (which is indeed the real) dissolves after we have symbolized its presence. What is being said here is that the general populace of the world has not been taught to deal with reality. Indeed, when confronted with reality, man has been taught to mythologize because it is considered easier than facing the brutal facts of reality. However, what is truly needed is a civilization without myth. Such a civilization would have no mythmakers, and symbolic *Homo sapiens* would be nonexistent. There would be no symbolic thought, and the *Symptomatic Thought Process* would be the rule of *Homo sapiens*. Since such an existence would eliminate superstition and ritual, racism would be absent in all its forms, decisions would be just, and problems stemming from poverty like starvation and disease would be eliminated. This is not a utopia, but an understanding of how life in civilization would be ordered without the damaging effect of mythology. The leadership present in such a situation would allow people to lead themselves without the limitations that stem from racism, sexism, and classism. There can be no other mandate for any type of leadership that does not focus on the elimination of symbolic behavior and its damaging effects. Unfortunately, that type of leadership would be a marked leadership in terms of the standard backlash against people who wish to make qualitative change, for there is a sizeable segment of people in the world today that benefit from the injustices that man faces. These people would not easily give up the benefits that they enjoy from a barbaric civilization that is dominated by symbolic-behaving humans.

GLOBAL LEADERSHIP

What has just been described above is the role that global leadership must take. It is a daunting task but entirely feasible. We have seen the remnants of such leadership in people like Nelson Mandela, Mahathir Mohamad, and Amadou M'Bow. These leaders have been vilified by some and praised by others. The effective global leadership needed today will always run the risk of criticism. They will be labeled tyrants, dictators, and other kinds of misnomers geared to impede their effective leadership. Realizing that no man or situation is perfect, it is easily understood that the leadership that is most needed today is the leadership of courageous individuals who are able to withstand the utmost scrutiny and the cruelty that a barbaric civilization will heap upon them. What South Africa's Nelson Mandela had to endure under 25 years of unjust imprisonment is symptomatic of what can happen to effective leadership that is unwanted or denied. Former Malaysian Prime Minister Mahathir Mohamad stood up to the Western world's racism, with courage and confidence, rejecting the economic policies of the World Bank and the IMF. Indeed, this is symptomatic of the leadership needed if we are to usher in a true civilized world.

GLOBALIZATION AND THE DEVELOPING WORLD

It is no accident that Nobel laureate Joseph Stiglitz stated, "The faceless symbols of the world economic order are under attack everywhere."[23] Indeed, the mythmaking of the international bureaucrats has given rise to a foundation that has made globalization, as it is now practiced, impossible to succeed.

The intent of globalization is to enhance world trade relationships by the eradication of prior boundaries. True globalization would integrate the worldwide community with fairness so that economic stability would result for all. Unfortunately, globalization has failed terribly because of the fundamental mindset of its architects. This mindset is built on a mythological system that has racism, imperialism, and greed as its highest priority.

We can look to Asia to see how countries such as Malaysia and China rebuffed the strategies of global institutions like the World Bank, the International Monetary Fund, and the World Trade Organization. Malaysia, under the courageous leadership of Mahathir Mohamad, totally rejected the IMF's programs and implemented a very successful economic initiative. True to form, Prime Minister Mahathir has frequently criticized the West for its racist attitudes, which, he said, were symptomatic of its behavior toward the nonwhite world.

Globalization, in and of itself, is neither good nor bad. It can benefit everyone if it is managed properly. This would mean establishing behavior patterns that are void of decisions based on mythology and superstition. Such decisions result from thinking symbolically.

As it is presently practiced, globalization has not benefited Africa at all. It is no secret that Africa has always been a major object of scorn and criticism perpetuated by the West. In fact, African leaders can justifiably raise the same uncomfortable questions as former Prime Minister Mahathir. I suggest that African and Asian leaders go even farther. A strong and united Africa doing business with a strong and united Asia is the West's worst economic nightmare. This would dramatically shift the balance of economic power to those regions.

The attitude of superiority of the so-called developed nations is built on a racism so deep-seated and widespread that the French scholar Jacques Barzun called it a "superstition." This superstition must be eradicated if we are, indeed, to have a civilization, let alone globalization. Superstitious thinking is a direct result of symbolic thinking. In reality, those who would refuse to abandon the notion of white superiority never really intended that developing nations be equal with the developed world. That in itself makes globalization totally impotent and useless in its present form. The onus of productivity and economic equality is on the ability of undeveloped countries to forge economic unions and cartels that would enable competition that benefits them and the world.

Let me say here that I see no real difference between the developing world and the developed world.

The late consultant W.E. Deming stated that America could "well be the most underdeveloped country in the world"[24] due to its misuse and abuse of the skills and knowledge of the American workforce in all areas of industry. As I stated in my previous book, *Symbolism Revisited: Notes on the Symptomatic Thought Process,* the United States is no longer the economic powerhouse it once was. The United States has used methods to manipulate its image around the world to present a misleading view of its strengths and weaknesses.

A perfect example of the inequities of globalization, and the mindset of the developed countries involved, is the case before the World Trade Organization (WTO) against U.S. cotton subsidies. In 2007, four West African countries - Chad, Benin, Burkina Faso, and Mali - banded together, inspired by Brazil, to stand up against the debilitating policies of the U.S. cotton subsidy program, which subsidizes American cotton farmers in violation of U.S. — WTO commitments. These subsidies result in increased U.S. production, which ultimately depresses world prices. The African Cotton Growers' Association expressed dismay about the actions of the U.S. Not only is the very survival of the African cotton industry at risk, but, the Africans argue, the losses generated by the U.S. cotton subsidy policy far outweigh the benefits of American aid to those West African countries. In taking their cases before the WTO, Africa and Brazil show the kind of unity that must take place if the developing nations are to achieve parity with the developed world. [Incidentally, it is important to note that the aforementioned subsidy program only benefits white American farmers; African American farmers continue to suffer gross inequities and enjoy no benefit from any subsidies.]

Although the European Union has criticized the working relationship between Zimbabwe and Malaysia, African leaders must follow the economic example of countries like Malaysia and China. Africa is the richest continent in the world. As exemplified by President Bush's overtures to Africa's oil-producing countries and the worsening situation in the Middle East, the West finds itself uncomfortably relying on Africa for its resources. This is a golden opportunity for Africa to join forces with Asia and other developing countries to form unions and cartels that will enhance their economic might and upgrade their independence. It is imperative that countries in the developing world have an attitudinal change about their own self-worth. They must support each other in ways that have not taken place in the past. This can only come about if members of developing countries eradicate myths about each other's capabilities, intellectual prowess, and worthiness — those elements that the West has so aptly denigrated. This behavior change is essential if developing countries are to be successful in the global economic struggle for parity.

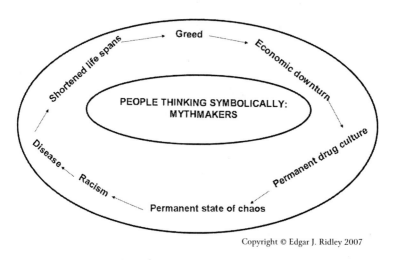

Copyright © Edgar J. Ridley 2007

Figure 7:
Leadership Using the Symbolic Thought Process

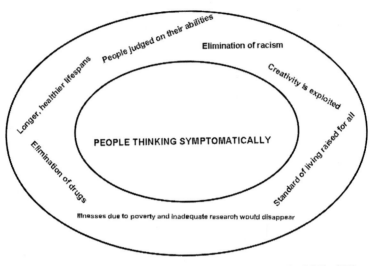

Figure 8:
Leadership Using the Symptomatic Thought Process

Reconciling the Dynamic of Symbols and Symptoms in Bringing about International Change

Change, as we all know, is easier said than done. Unfortunately, traditional change management methodologies have proven impotent in our present economy. A major impediment to change implementation involves risk that few are willing to take. Because so few people have the necessary courage to follow through on programs that would produce qualitative change, the situation leads to concepts that are circular – aka business as usual. Accordingly, it is a misnomer to suggest that we need new concepts for a "new economy." This so-called new economy still has the same ambitions, trends, and goals as the so-called old economy. It does not usher in a qualitatively new world or qualitatively new concepts. In short, the new economy is really the old economy given new names.

The engines currently in use for qualitative change are hoped to be quick fixes for our economy. One of those engines is the trend toward globalization. However, globalization is a sophisticated method for keeping developing countries in a mode of permanent underdevelopment with no possibility for competitive growth.

> The impact of globalization is extremely uneven. It implies rising inequalities within countries. It leads to greater polarisation across countries; and has resulted in greater vulnerability to macro-economic shocks that lower growth and employment rates resulting in widening the gap with developed countries.[1]

Today's change consultants must bring new tools to the table in order to challenge the status quo.

THE NEED FOR CONSULTANTS TO UNDERSTAND CHANGE

Management consultants are called upon to solve some of the most crucial problems facing the world today. Twenty-first-century consulting firms will have tremendous influence on not only the companies they serve but on the universe as a whole. With emerging economies and technological advancement, complex symbol systems have surfaced that have produced a myriad of myths and metaphors that regulate every phase of our daily life. To be sure, consulting firms use symbol systems to produce new metaphors. (In fact, consultants were coined "symbolic analysts" by Robert Reich, former U.S. labor secretary.[2]

Over the past several years, these new metaphors, also known as mythological symbols, have been presented as new business jargon such as *reengineering, pro-*

cess engineering, or even *best practices*. However, nothing ever really changes. As stated earlier, it is business as usual. This is why we agree with Professor Max Müller, who wrote many years ago, that "Mythology is a disease of language, and the ancient symbolism was a result of something like a primitive mental aberration."[3] We call this mental aberration the "neurological misadventure of primordial man."[4] That neurological misadventure caused brain activities that produced mythological thinking, which resulted in symbolic behavior. With that state of being in place, superstition and ritualistic behavior become the norm. We cannot make sound decisions and there is little or no chance for productivity or cultural harmony.

Productivity improvement has not taken place on a global scale consistent with our technological advancement. This is because business leaders continue to make decisions from a mythological framework that renders technological advances impotent. Until we realize the necessity of living in a world without myth, our global economy will never be stable. Symbol systems produce metaphors that are totally inadequate for addressing the changing trends in the global workforce. A new concept must be applied, and that new concept is the Symptomatic Thought Process.

It is important to understand what a symptom is. A symptom is a natural sign.

> A natural sign is immeasurably more valuable than a symbol. Where it has been held in the past that signs were inferior to symbols, that is totally incorrect. "A sign indicates the existence, past, present and future, of a thing, event or condition. Wet streets are a sign that it has rained; a smell of smoke signifies the presence of fire. All examples here produced are natural signs. A natural sign is a part of a greater event or a complex condition and to an expert observer, it signifies the rest of that situation, of which

it is a notable feature. It is a symptom of a state of affairs."[5]

Thinking symptomatically is seeing things as they really are, in their ultimate state. There is no going behind the actual entities to find anything more real. The sign, then, is the concrete form, the symptom, of an invisible and inner reality, and at the same time, the means by which the mind is reminded of that reality. "It has been traditionally held that when the brain crystallizes stimuli, it creates a symbol. That is a misadventure. When the brain crystallizes outside stimuli, the correct process is that it creates a natural sign."[6]

The Symptomatic Thought Process replaces the symbolic thought process, which has been a standard since time immemorial (see Fig. 7 and 8). The reader should understand that the symbolic thought process is one that produces mythology, ritual and superstition. This symbolic thought process can be called a neurological misadventure. The neurological misadventure can be described as an event in human history that occurred when symbols and symbol systems evolved in a symptomatic environment. In other words, when man began to symbolize and mythologize out of his symptomatic environment, a neurological misadventure took place at that moment. Out of that scenario, all the events that we know as history began to take place — through the industrial revolution all the way to the information revolution that produced the digital economic system and the Internet.

I maintain that as long as consultants insist on creating metaphors, they will continue to be bogged down in a global mythological abyss. The only way for consultants to serve their client base effectively is to cease creating new metaphors. These mythological metaphors that become superstitious rituals inhibit true productivity. To completely eliminate metaphors, the Symptomatic Thought Process should be implemented.

THE FRICTION BETWEEN SYMBOLS AND SYMPTOMS

What has to be understood is a step-by-step method in which the Symptomatic Thought Process is implemented. The Symptomatic Thought Process makes it possible for individuals to interact with each other in a way that is sincere without pretension. It opens up relationships as never before. The dynamic of a Symptomatic Thought Process on the brain is the most important experience one could ever have in one's lifetime.

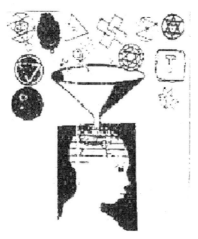

Figure 9: Stimuli Funneling into the Human Brain
Diagram courtesy of E. Curtis Alexander, Ed.D.

The above figure depicts matter, or stimuli, being funneled into the human brain. These matter are natural signs, not symbols. They have not yet been processed neurologically. Only the human brain can create a symbol. There is no such thing as symbols existing before they are processed within the human brain. All entities that exist before being processed within the human brain are natural signs. What does that mean for us as we go about our daily lives? This means that whenever we see anything, we look at it without the mythological symbols that produce connotations. We do not think in connotations. We see things as they really are in their ulti-

99

mate state as they are presented to us. This is extremely important for when we see things in their ultimate state as they are presented to us we do not mythologize about these entities.

The human brain processes energy and entities continually and that processing is the key to individual decision-making. As stated before, that process is what we have called the neurological misadventure of primordial man. The correct and effective behavior process is the Symptomatic Thought Process. The stimuli that the brain processes become symptoms of a state of affairs. These symptoms are always qualitatively ultimate not only in their character but in the matter that makes up the entities. The correct neurological adventure that takes place is that the brain crystallizes natural signs from our experiences. These natural signs, or symptoms, create reality, or bits of reality, from ultimate reality, which are those experiences that are originally part of our core truth.

We know that countries that are oriented towards symbol systems produce mythological cults that destroy productivity. What we maintain here is that the area of crisis is the dynamic that occurs between symbols and symptoms. As we look around the world, we see the results of those clashes between symbols and symptoms. That is why Marjorie Garber, in her book *Symptoms of Culture*, states that "One of the most striking symptoms of culture in our time has been the phenomenon of the so-called 'cultural wars', a conflict that might be located precisely in the clash between symbols and symptoms."[7] Garber goes on to state, "We should look for a theory of the symptom."[8] That theory is the Symptomatic Thought Process, which replaces the symbolic thought process.

Former United Nations Secretary General Kofi Annan has expressed bewilderment and puzzlement at the viciousness of acts around the globe. These acts are caused by mythological symbols played out as rituals, and the countries that participate in these acts on a large scale are usually the poorest countries, usually dependent on the World Bank and International Monetary Fund for handouts. These countries have not yet realized the potential of their own human resources to resolve their economic plight. One might ask, What does this have to do with the economy or economic growth or even productivity? The degree to which a country is able to resolve that friction between symbols and symptoms is the degree to which that country's economy will be stable and productive.

Symptomatic thinking — in other words, seeing things as they really are — can liberate developing countries from an overdependence on the West for problem-solving. For example, during his briefing at the 2001 World Economic Forum, South African President Thabo Mbeki noted that it is now time for Africans to step to the forefront to solve their own problems.[9] African leadership is slowly discarding the model of total disregard for African resources and sweat equity. African leadership is coming together to plan growth initiatives via partnerships that includes the best African minds in concert with world business leaders — this is symptomatic behavior at its best.

OPPORTUNITIES FOR QUALITATIVE CHANGE IN A NEW ECONOMY

The United States workforce has suffered negative labeling, not the least of which has been characterizations of sexism and racism among corporate managements. The reason is obvious: 95 percent of America's top corporate positions are populated by white males. Interestingly, the nation is about to undergo a demographic sea change. A recent U.S. Census report revealed that the states of California and New Jersey are now predominantly nonwhite. The report predicted a white minority throughout the United States by the year 2050. This changing workforce is the engine causing apprehension and paranoia among whites who have traditionally been thought of as the majority. There has been a rush to solidify white empowerment and entrenchment in the upper echelons of corporate and political life. This reaction is caused by an unreasonable fear that the workforce will become saturated with people of color from top management on down. Such fear is understandable in light of the manner in which blacks and other people of color have been treated by the white majority. The sheer number of lawsuits that corporate America has faced and/or is settling currently is an illustration of the roadblocks that have been placed to bar achievement by people of color. These roadblocks are erected by individuals who oppose change. Whether overt or subtle, that opposition is harmful. Of no small consequence is the collateral damage heaped upon the corporate landscape by the litigation experienced by such giants as Coca-Cola, R.R. Donnelly, Texaco, American Airlines, Eastman Kodak, and Denny's Restaurants. The lucrative settlements only serve to shrink corporate profits.

In 2000, Coca-Cola settled a racial bias lawsuit for $192.5 million, in which eight current and former African American employees accused Coca-Cola of discrimination against black employees in pay, promotions, performance evaluations, and terminations. If that weren't enough, the company also faced a $1.5 billion lawsuit filed by a separate group of four former workers, who allege that Coca-Cola maintained racially biased hiring practices and a hostile work environment for blacks.

Reaching even further back into the corporate landscape, we can't forget the infamous Texaco crisis, in which senior executives were audiotaped making cruel comments about black employees as well as discussing the destruction of documents that were linked to an ongoing discrimination lawsuit. Texaco settled this lawsuit for $115 million in cash plus salary adjustments for the 1400 employees involved.

Change consultants should recognize that the symbolic behavior that generates workplace bias can reach proportions that exceed the egregious. American Airlines received a $10.5 million racial harassment lawsuit in which a Black airline mechanic endured hanging rope nooses, having his photo placed on a dartboard, and racist scribbles in the men's room.[10] This worker, like many before and after him, lived within this environment with no assistance from his superiors, who were reluctant to handle the problem and allowed it to worsen.

A similar atmosphere existed at R. R. Donnelly & Sons Co. At this commercial printing firm, systematic bigotry existed:

> Black workers [were] prohibited from training for senior-level jobs and routinely denied promotions that went to less qualified whites; white co-workers dressed as Ku Klux Klansmen for laughs; and joke fliers were distributed that described "hunting season" on black people...however, the firm denies any wrongdoing.[11]

The previous examples scratch the surface of what black workers experienced at R.R. Donnelly. Needless to say, a change consultant entering this environment would be severely challenged, given the firm's denials. The irony is that R.R. Donnelly's corporate diversity program was highlighted in 1999 as a national best practices case study by Watson Wyatt Worldwide Consulting.[12] This is a perfect illustration of a business-as-usual stamp placed on a firm by consultants who are ignorant of the dynamics of symptoms and symbols.

Often, bias in the workplace is so subtle that it can easily be argued that it doesn't exist. Nonwhite executives are dismissed, disrespected, and embarrassed in a myriad of small ways. A 1999 court case shed light on the damage caused by "unthinking stereotypes or bias" in a lawsuit against Eastman Kodak.[13]

> Racial discrimination can occur '"whether the employer consciously intended to base the evaluations on race or did so because of unthinking stereotypes or bias...skewed perceptions may have come into play...discrimination may arise from stereotyping, which is unconscious."[14]

This so-called unconscious behavior is an excellent illustration of symbolic behavior; instead of viewing nonwhite executives symptomatically through a prism that only sees skills and performance, a mythology of inferiority is introduced. This happens repeatedly. True change is difficult if not impossible to implement in corporate environments such as those described above. Change management consultants must fully understand this dynamic if they wish to be effective in advising corporate management.

A symptomatic approach was the course of last resort for Denny's Restaurants. Denny's "became a national punchline and a symbol of the resilience of racism in America."[15] However, after a stinging lawsuit that resulted in a $54 million settlement, Denny's initiated a complete culture change within the corporation.

> As this country grows in the next 15 years the racial composition of the country will change dramatically...if you're not in touch with the tastes of minorities or in a position to reach them through ads, you're going to miss an incredible opportunity."[16]

Denny's recognition of the changing demographics is a symptomatic response. Denny's reaction to its crisis was to proceed symptomatically rather than symbolically. Denny's understands that it must cultivate its core client base (nonwhite customers) as opposed to allowing negative behavior by its employees against those customers. Prior to the lawsuit, Denny's employees nationwide were free to discriminate against nonwhite customers, by refusing or delaying service, as well as by providing substandard service in general. It was common for people of color to be asked to show identification when ordering food, to pay for their food in advance, to wait until all other diners were served, or not to be served at all. Denny's management, in typical symbolic behavior, maintained a posture of denial, until the lawsuit generated reams of negative publicity as well as lost sales. Cynics may infer that Denny's had no choice other than to change course. However, Denny's response can only be described as symptomatic, when, instead of remaining in denial about its racist practices, new management looked reality in the face and didn't flinch. Denny's management recognized that a cultural overhaul was necessary in order to win back its nonwhite customers since its very livelihood depended on them. Denny's new management launched a multimillion-dollar public relations campaign targeted toward people of color. They initiated a corporate diversity program that tied executive compensation to diversity goals. Managers were given diversity training, and waitstaff were given communications training. The company increased the diversity of its workforce, and also increased its partnerships with minority suppliers for all business from 0 percent to 18 percent. Additionally, prior to the lawsuit, less than 1 percent of Denny's franchisees were owned by people of color; new management expanded that ownership to 36 percent. This is clear evidence of management's willingness to disregard the mythologies surrounding people of color (i.e., thinking symbolically) instead of capitalizing on the contributions offered by such diversity. This is symptomatic behavior.

HOW MYTHOLOGY PREVENTS CHANGE

The corporate world perpetuates myths to enforce practices that are destructive to the overwhelming masses employed in the global workforce. Subliminally, such myths are documented and entrenched in the corporate lexicon by books such as *The Bell Curve*,[17] and *Not*

Out of Africa.[18] The change consultant must be clear: The philosophy espoused by a book such as *Not Out of Africa* attacks the revamping of African history to reflect an honest view of the African contribution to civilization. This philosophy supports a global philosophical viewpoint of whites that intellectually justifies their superiority and dominant position in the global arena.

Racism is easily the number one impediment to qualitative change and productivity in the corporate arena. In *The Bell Curve,* the authors emphasize that no matter what level of academic or professional achievement, blacks will always be subordinate due to their genetic inferiority. The authors allege that this inferiority is because of lower IQ scores than those of Asians or whites. Michael Dixon states, "What IQ tests actually gauge is the ability to reason with information presented through the medium of systems of symbols...The ability to reason is in terms of a symbol system, which is essentially the same as 'general intelligence....'"[19]

In other words, IQ tests are symbol systems that have no relevance in measuring either intelligence or performance. IQ tests perpetuate myths. The philosophies of *The Bell Curve* and *Not Out of Africa* simply reinforce the notion of racial superiority in the white population. This philosophy provides academic justification to those industrial psychologists consulting with corporate management — it allows whites to continue to think of blacks as inferior no matter what degree of success they attain. As David Olsen points out: "IQ has been used to exclude people from educational opportunities from which they would benefit and from jobs that they are entirely capable of handling."[20] It is imperative that change consultants understand this philosophy when servicing corporate clients. Indeed, a philosophical approach is critical. One only has to read George Soros' approach to the global economic picture to understand the importance of philosophical orientation.[21] Corporations are simply a microcosm of the larger society. The climate within an organization is fostered by the attitudes and beliefs of management, and it trickles down to the common employee. Americans, and American management, are in severe denial regarding the issue of race. However, because of systemic racism, blacks in the corporate world live in a totally different world than their white peers.

A familiar example is Joseph Jett, a top bond trader at the former Kidder Peabody & Co. Jett was charged with masterminding one of the largest securities scams in Wall Street history. He was eventually exonerated but only after going through the experience of "living while black." Jett's impeccable credentials from MIT and the Harvard Business School, as well as a golden resume that included General Electric, Morgan Stanley and First Boston, mattered little. The fact remained that Jett was a black man, and, according to the doctrine of *The Bell Curve*, he would always be genetically inferior to his white counterparts. Stated Jett: "If my white counterparts said one and one is two, it would be fine; if I said one and one is two, they'd say, I'll get back to you on that.... I was wrongly accused and made the scapegoat for a culture in which racism remains rampant."[22]

The specter of racism within corporations is an unpleasant subject at best. However, change consultants must focus on so-called diversity issues when advising corporate management. These consultants must be sophisticated and learned enough to recognize that typical corporate diversity programs rarely reach beneath the surface to thoroughly remove the symbolic behavior effectuating itself as institutional racism. Hammonds notes that "The corner office remains an exclusively white preserve....Explicit racial bias impedes progress....In most industries, blacks remain invisible. That's business' loss."[23] This is very important. The backlash behavior of whites within corporations does not emerge from a vacuum. Inappropriate stereotyping and unfortunate belief systems (also known as symbolic behavior) come to work with white employees. A 2001 article in the *Wall Street Journal* reports that "Whites 'feel more and more powerless. They have less and less control and influence. Whites feel like they're losing their grip. It's provoking a kind of racial angst."[24]

Of course, corporate managers are not going to broadcast their personal biases for public consumption. Instead, those biases are integrated within the corporate culture, in subtle, insidious ways. It is critical that change consultants put a name to this behavior, if they wish to provide advice to their corporate clients that is noncircular.

General Electric has been held up as the nation's leader when it comes to innovative management systems. American firms routinely imitate GE's management training initiatives. Yet this industry leader is stymied when it comes to locating talented executives that vary from the white male norm. This is consistent with the typical symbolic thinking — that white men are more skilled at running companies and manufacturing earnings for their shareholders. One G.E. executive stated, "If I managed my business the way I had managed diversity, I think I'd have gotten fired."[25] "General Electric," writes Mary Williams Walsh, "requires every business unit to be first or second in its market, or risk sale or closure. There is no such requirement for diversity."[26] The fear of a non-white majority workforce causes absurd and ridiculous concepts such as those found in *The Bell Curve*, which, as we know, states that no matter what the level of education and achievement of Black people, Blacks will always be inferior to whites due to a symbolic I.Q. score.

The theories of Herrnstein and Murray derive from a deeply-held mythological view in which racism and hysteria rule the thought patterns of the authors. It is important to understand that the origins of such unhealthy feelings are in the myths that serve as a vehicle for those feelings to be transported to all levels of human activity. The danger of these myths is that they serve to undermine and inhibit the productivity essential for qualitative change in the global workforce. Unfortunately, consultants and academia have acted in concert to not only reinforce these unhealthy concepts, but to use them as a justification to impose a sense of unworthiness and inferiority in the workforce. Again, it is important for the reader to understand clearly that behavior does not present itself in a vacuum; instead, it emanates from a culture that reinforces white superiority over the input and contribution of nonwhites.

We point to an academic example: Gunter Dreyer, head of the German Archaeological Institute, discovered clay tablets in southern Egypt from the tomb of King Scorpion, representing the earliest known writings by humankind. When Dreyer's find was published, academia noted that the discovery would rank among the greatest ever in the search for the origins of the written word, since carbon dating placed the tablets between 3300 B.C. and 3200 B.C. The problem with this announcement was the unchallenged suggestion and inference that no scholarship preceded Dreyer's.

"The idea that language originated in Egypt rather than Mesopotamia is not a new one, " [Dr. Molefi Asante as cited by Chad Glover]. Asante cited the works of Cheikh Anta Diop, a Senegalese professor, who wrote a book in the 60's that claimed that the Egyptian language is older than Sumer, which was an ancient country in the area known as Iraq. "African and African-American scholars made this argument many years ago," Asante said. It has only received press attention because it was a German scholar who was now saying it."[27]

In short, the archaeological discovery would have had no merit were it not endorsed by the German scholar, as opposed to volumes published by African scholars many years prior. Academic examples provide valuable fodder for the explanation of symbolic thinking, and change consultants must be educated and clear about this type of symbolic behavior. It is ingrained in American, indeed, in Western, corporate culture, that contributions of significance do not emanate from nonwhites. This allows the traditional mode of doing business to remain in place. There is no change in the way business is done or in who runs the businesses.

There is strong resistance to change especially when dealing with racial issues. The change agent must be courageous; he/she has a daunting task. Fear of repercussion, such as demotion or dismissal, is pervasive in the mind not only of the change agent but of anyone who would seek to break the myths that inhibit qualitative change. In corporate America, people have significant fear of retaliation if they were to step out of their box and change their behavior to one of advocacy for a just and nonracist workforce. We can, however, take certain steps to solve this problem when we understand how symbol systems produce the mythologies that produce an unhealthy workforce. These symbol systems that produce these mythologies call for superstitious, ritualistic behavior. This disrupts harmony and prohibits a just environment.

> The effect of unchecked workplace discrimination can be deep, and corporate culture is partly to blame....because the tone for tolerance is set at the top. A company's personality is a living and "enduring thing"....Employees who are sought and promoted often are compatible with the existing culture and therefore perpetuate it.[28]

Those of us who are charged with instituting change within corporations have to exhibit the courage required to break the circle.

Edgar J. Ridley & Associates was approached by a Southern African company for assistance on an infrastructure project. The emphasis of the consulting assignment was to secure funding; on-the-ground management of the project was of less concern. Unfortunately, many African projects deemphasize management and behavior procedures that will affect critical business decisions. Symbolic thinking has led Africans to feel that currency alone will solve their problems. This has often not been addressed in Africa, an oversight that has led to chaos and nonproductive behavior. A serious problem in Africa has been its dependence on symbol systems to provide relief. Africans don't realize, as noted by Aleksandr N. Solzhenitsyn, the Nobel Prize-winning Soviet writer, that "Symbols, for all their apparent power, do not bestow greatness. You cannot save a dying country with symbols."[29]

Conversely, an ASEAN country in the Pacific Rim expressed an interest in implementing the Symptomatic Thought Process in their management arena with an emphasis on management and productivity. That Asian country makes prolific use of its natural resources and management decision-making is nonsymbolic. Accordingly, management decisions enhance efficiency and create a scenario of independence and information sharing.

Additionally, Ridley & Associates was called to China to provide advice on management concepts for increased productivity. The unique methods of productivity improvement are part of the Symptomatic Thought Process. Because of its emphasis on proper behavior patterns and effective business decisions, China is growing at an extremely rapid rate, achieving an excellent measure of economic independence.

Consultations emphasized the need to evaluate the damage caused by symbols in the creation of mythology and superstition. By exploring the necessity of eradicating decisions based on myth, managers can go to the core of cultural beliefs. This core is often difficult to isolate. The change consultant must remember that assumptions are based on long-held beliefs. The objective in change management should be to convince managers to think symptomatically — i.e., to see things as they really are — and to encourage people to make decisions void of superstition or mythological assumptions. This would lead to smoother business transactions and to the elimination of damaging behavior.

There is no getting around it: behavior patterns and increased productivity are not just closely related but synonymous. An encouraging example of symptomatic thinking has to be the attempts by many countries in Africa to remove the obstacles to trade within African countries. It is well known that much of African productivity had been hindered by the lack of a common market among African nations. An attempt to overcome this has been the formation of COMESA (the Common Market for Eastern and Southern Africa). COMESA's mission is to remove trade barriers preventing intraregional trade. This initiative owes its success to the cooperation and symptomatic behavior of its twenty member states.

Many African economies suffer from numerous ills, not the least of which are considerable bureaucracy, inadequate infrastructure, skills in short supply, and the high cost of transporting goods from one region to another. These challenges need to be met by the African leadership, and the removal of trade barriers between countries is certainly a giant step in the right direction. It is well known that Africa has minimal to no manufacturing relative to the global economy. Intraregional trade between African countries would go a long way towards enhancing the view that Africans can solve their own problems rather than depend on entities outside their regions, such as the West. Although economists differ on whether intraregional trade would accelerate, rather than reverse, deindustrialization, an important component of this process is the degree to which African countries cease their symbolic decision making. It is symbolism that drives African managers to only consider business expertise if it is delivered from the mouths of Western policymakers. The belief that Africans cannot solve their own problems is driven by symbolism. The extent to which the various countries are liberating themselves from this mindset is the degree to which a Symptomatic Thought Process is taking place.

A paradigm for symbolism vs. a Symptomatic Thought Process is the dynamics surrounding events in Zimbabwe during a July 4, 1986 U.S. Embassy reception. This is one clear-cut case where Africans acted in a symptomatic way as opposed to symbolic overtures. Former President Jimmy Carter walked out of this July 4 reception because of criticism of the U.S. administration for rejecting severe economic sanctions against South Africa while imposing them on Nicaragua, because Carter felt that those statements were improper at a celebration. This is very interesting, since Jimmy Carter, during his presidency, was known as a President of symbolism because of his symbolic overtures while in office. This is a case where a Western leader wanted to remain in the realm of symbolic activity and criticize the African official for expressing concrete and true statements about the Ronald Reagan administration. In fact, the timing of those remarks by the Zimbabwean official was entirely appropriate. The July 4 celebration has severe connotations of freedom for all people. However, that freedom is a myth in terms of the U.S. commitment towards non-white people (in this case, South Africans). It is inarguable that the Reagan administration had no real rationale for not supporting sanctions against South Africa due to U.S. relations with other countries such as Nicaragua and Poland. President Carter was wrong by walking out and admonishing the Zimbabwean official.[30]

It is critical for change consultants to understand the ramifications of symbolism in neurological thought that affects judgment and decision making. Ultimately, that always translates and transfers to the business and corporate arena.

The following is another perfect illustration of a Symptomatic Thought Process being used in place of a symbolic one. A 1997 *Wall Street Journal* article described a black MIT graduate, Omar Green, and his relationship with his boss, the CEO of Xionics Document Technology, Inc. This symptomatic behavior ultimately raised the productivity of the company and made it possible for new ideas to form and take shape.

> Mr. Gilkes, who was hired as a change agent for Xionics, did not look at Omar Green symbolically, but symptomatically:

For Mr. Gilkes, Mr. Green represents technical and entrepreneurial thinking critical to his company's future, a chance to shake up resistant middle managers who have bucked many of his efforts to change Xionics. "'He can tell me things I am not seeing as a 58-year-old white man,' Mr. Gilkes says." (Jonathan Kaufman, *Wall Street Journal,* as cited by Edgar J. Ridley).

> All things did not go smoothly, as there was some discomfort: 'One day, he [Omar Green] startled a roomful of senior engineers by questioning the power capacity of a Xionics computer chip. 'Who the hell is this loudmouth, smart-aleck kid?' Mr. Morris, his fellow engineer, recalls thinking at the time. Mr. Green was later put in charge of testing the new chip, overseeing eight engineers, most of them at least ten years older.' "

What is key here is that Gilkes looked at Mr. Green and saw a Black man, but did not mythologize Mr. Green's existence as a Black man. Instead, by making him a member of an important team, Mr. Gilkes saw the contribution that Mr. Green could make to the company. The *Wall Street Journal* article goes on:

Mr. Gilkes says he sees Mr. Green as crucial in his drive to turn around Xionics. In his 2½ years as CEO,

Mr. Gilkes has taken Xionics public, doubled the number of employees to more than 200 and boosted sales to an estimated $40 million this year from $9 million in 1994. Mr. Gilkes has assigned Mr. Green to an elite team to develop an easy-to-use box that would give users access to their televisions, stereos, VCRs and computers, enabling customers to send and receive everything from music to computer files.[31]

This is a clear-cut example of productivity derived from using a Symptomatic Thought Process. There was no mythologizing, no connotations, but seeing things as they really are in their ultimate state. This is extremely important. Gilkes saw things as they really are — he saw reality — he did not add to it - he did not mythologize the facts. This importance cannot be overemphasized. If this situation were approached from a symbolizing point of view, things would have turned out much differently.[32]

The so-called new global economy can never prosper as long as symbols affect the neurological process of the human brain, which causes people to act out in totally irrational and unreasonable ways.

A CHARGE TO CONSULTANTS

Consultants must understand the dynamics between symbols and symptoms if they are to be effective in solving the immense diversity of problems they face in the world today. Remembering that symbols and myths are synonymous, it is easy to see the havoc caused by myths in civilization today. Again, we use academia to illustrate our point. David Mac Ritchie, in his book *Ancient and Modern Britons*, quotes Andrew Lang in his statement on mythology:

Max Müller observes that most of the ancient myths are absurd and irrational, savage and senseless. "Was there a period of temporary insanity through which the human mind had to pass? Indeed, wherever we look, in every part of the world, we find the same kinds of stories, the same traditions, the same myths.[33]

David Mac Ritchie goes on to state, "The future student of mythology will ask, is there any contemporary stage of thought and of society in which the wildest marvels of mythology are looked on as the ordinary facts of experience?"[34]

Despite all the literature, the one example that we try to avoid is racism. Racism must be weeded out if corporate productivity is to be realized. Racism is the "one absurd myth" that we experience in our corporate lives all over this world. Racism is the myth that answers the question posed by Mac Ritchie. As long as mythologies exist, racism will exist. In order to eradicate racism in all its forms, we have to eliminate mythology. This includes eliminating the symbol systems that create mythology. Any other starting point for the eradication of racism will prove to be futile unless we deal with the symbol systems that produce the behavior that makes racism a global practice.

The statements by Mac Ritchie emphasize the need to study the importance of the relationship of symbolism and mythology to the human condition. Consultants, as symbolic analysts, must study the dynamics of mythology; indeed, consultants must be students of mythology. Unfortunately, our traditional educational system is inadequate in providing the tools to solve problems in this highly technological environment. As stated several times in this chapter, we live out our lives in a mythological mode that we deem as the norm, no matter how ridiculous, absurd, and vicious that mythology is. That mythology is malignant, and as Max Müller stated, it can be found from one end of the globe to the other. This is what makes the job of the change consultant so critical — he/she must work in that environment and recognize the trend towards symbolizing every area of activity and mythologizing to justify that symbolization. Unless we understand those dynamics, change consultants will be ineffective.

We at Ridley & Associates use our concept, the Symptomatic Thought Process, as the key mechanism in our practice to provide management and productivity services worldwide. When asked, we offer preliminary suggestions on what is needed to solve the corporation's or country's particular problem. Not unlike W.E. Deming, we require total support from the highest echelons of management to implement our concepts. With that understanding, we provide education on the dynamics of symbolism and the use of the Symptomatic Thought Process in place of symbolism. We hold consultations, workshops, seminars, and training sessions. Our consultations last as long as the company feels necessary; sometimes our client relationship is long term. What we provide that other consulting firms do not is the creation and implementation of a concept that radically rearranges people behavior as never before. Because it advances a way in which people are able to make better decisions, both business and personal, and has such a direct effect on people behavior patterns, our Symptomatic Thought Process rearranges the structure of the world in a way that has never been experienced before.

Consultants who hope to render change must be clear: The operative business mode that has functioned since time immemorial has shown the results of a symbolic and mythological thought process. This is totally unacceptable, for it has wreaked havoc in every area of human activity. Unless that is changed, nothing will take place that can be deemed to be sane. By changing that mindset through the Symptomatic Thought Process, we can change those long-held assumptions that have castrated every area of business from one end of the globe to the other. Changing our mindset is a most difficult task, but there is no doubt we cannot continue as we are now, which is business as usual.

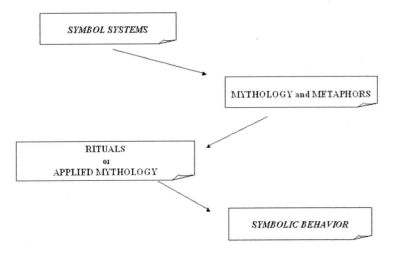

Figure 10:
The Passage of Symbol Systems into Symbolic Behavior

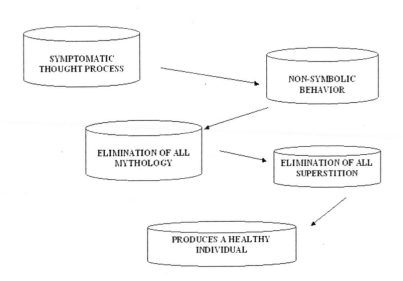

Figure 11: The passage of the Symptomatic Thought Process,
which results in a healthy individual

CHAPTER SEVEN

How Thought Processes Impact Technology for Productivity

It is maintained here that in order for globalization and productivity to be effective, in order for research and development to introduce new products that will qualitatively change our lives for the better, there must be a change in people behavior that will only occur when an attitudinal shift takes place. This attitudinal shift was emphasized by the former prime minister of Malaysia, Mahathir Mohamad, and was one of the main drivers for Malaysia's success in the Pacific Rim and in the world at large.

The engine that runs productivity is people. This chapter explores the reasons traditional thought processes have failed to produce behavior patterns that would allow effective decision making that would in turn enable people to drastically reduce or to completely eliminate problems. The most effective approach to problem solving is multidisciplinary, yet this approach has never been dealt with adequately. The attempt to solve problems has been one dimensional, and the resulting solutions have proven both inadequate and misleading. This applies to almost all disciplines but is especially applicable to the critical fields of the behavioral sciences. The late consultant W. E. Deming stated: "Transformation can only be accomplished by man. Not by hardware (computers, gadgets, automation, new machinery). A company cannot buy its way into quality."[1] Deming continued:

> In my experience, people can face almost any problem except the problems of people. They can work long hours, face declining business, face loss of jobs, but not the problems of people. Faced with problems of people (management included), management, in my experience, goes into a state of paralysis, taking refuge in formation of QC Circles and groups for Employment Involvement, Employment Participation, and Quality of Work Life. These groups predictably disintegrate within a few months from frustration, finding themselves unwilling parties to a cruel hoax, unable to accomplish anything, for the simple reason that no one in management will take action on suggestions for improvement. These are devastatingly cruel devices to get rid of the problems of people. There are of course pleasing exceptions, where the management understands their responsibilities, where the management participates with advice and action on suggestions for removal of barriers to pride of workmanship.[2]

I have often wondered why management and leaders find it so problematic to deal with the critical concern of people behavior which is at the core of management and leadership. The engine that runs productivity is people and their mode of behavior which dictates their decision making and creativity. To be sure, these two factors – people and their mode of behavior — are the lifeblood of technology, its effectiveness, and its impact on productivity.

I have come to realize that in solving people problems, you are dealing with the most critical area of human life. As a result, it is extremely difficult for managers and leaders to face the ultimate realities that accompany the problems associated with people, people behavior, and ultimately, a just and civilized civilization. Indeed, if one attempts to skip over these issues, then the critical research and development, along with an effective mode of technology transfer, will never be realized. The average procedures for problem solving in today's highly advanced, technological world are totally inadequate. Unfortunately, this deficiency begins with the basic assumption that the current thought processes that dictate human behavior are sound. Subsequent research and development, built on these same thought processes, drives a technology, again, assumed to be not only sound but also adequate for creativity and advancement of civilization.

Research is a crucial and critical part of productivity and its subsequent growth, since its function is to elicit knowledge and data to perpetuate a useful product. Development is essential for a product to reach its ultimate qualitativeness. Once these events have taken place, the transfer of that technology has to be accomplished or all work has been for naught. That is the reason why the thought processes that drive these events must be sound. The current use of technology does not emphasize this methodology simply because management and leaders do not want to confront uncomfortable, threatening issues.

A core problem affecting research and development is the tendency to proceed with isolated concepts that are unrelated to the multiple problems faced in today's society. Because of the one dimensional approach to problem solving, there is a disconnect. There is a fear derived from linking problem solving and research and development with the real problems of people taken in context with the cultural problems that emanate from real world experiences. We are all familiar with the critical problems evident in Africa, Asia, and the Middle East today. The problems of war, cultural conflict, and famine must be implicitly tied to technology and its development. Today's economic issues arising from globalization must be accounted for when conducting research, development, and technology transfer. Nothing can be done in isolation; all things are related. If that is not understood, then the methodologies used to advance technology and productivity will never be effective.

The point that I am making here is that people and their behavior drive the achievement of technology and its effectiveness. Deming stated, "The wealth of a nation depends on its people, management, and government, more than on its natural resources."[3] This is especially true when we look at Africa's problems as well as at other areas of the world that are rich in natural resources. When people behavior is ineffective and good management is lacking, people cannot take advantage of those natural resources. As noted by APO Secretary General Tajima, "The new development scenario in the region and the world, rapid advances in technology, new concepts in business, and new demands from society will require new perspectives and strategies in our productivity endeavor."[4]

SYMBOLS VS. SYMPTOMS

One point has to be made absolutely clear. The vast majority of scholars agree that there are two possible approaches to the problems and disturbances that life presents: a symptomatic approach or a symbolic one.

At this juncture, it is important to define symbolism and symptoms. Carl Jung gave a very good working definition of the symbolic when he stated: "A word or an image is symbolic when it implies something more than its obvious and immediate meaning."[5] This can also be the meaning of myth.

Conversely, a sign, in its concrete form, is a symptom. A good working definition of a symptom is a natural sign, as smoke is a symptom of fire. As Deacon says, "Laughter indicates something about what just preceded it as a symptom of a person's response to certain stimuli."[6]

There are two ways to use symptoms: One is technical, i.e., analyzing data (natural signs or symptoms) like genetic material or fossils "as a part of a greater event or a complex condition," as Langer states.[7] The other is behavioral, i.e., we use symptoms in our behavior when we see things as they really are without adding myth to what we see. We do not add more than its obvious and immediate meaning. A tree is a tree; there is no magic in trees. A stone is a stone; there is no magic in stones. We do not apply superstition to events or things. Even more basic, when we see someone from another culture or country who does not look like us, we do not add connotations that stem from individual idiosyncrasies or prejudices. We see each other as we really are; no more, no less. This is living without myth. Indeed, we experience the energy that creates whatever stimuli are present as symptoms of our experience. Living without myth is the ultimate experience as a nonsymbolic-behaving human. This is the engine that must be operable when we enter the phase of research and development and technology transfer, and any other starting point is fruitless and will lead to faulty results.

It has been traditionally understood that we think and live not only symptomatically, but also symbolically. This has been the problem. It is not possible to think symptomatically and symbolically at the same time and behave soundly. What this actually produces is a schizophrenic person who is very ritualistic and superstitious.

Traditional psychologists, especially Carl Jung, always turn symptoms into symbols. This produces a symbolizing attitude where humans make decisions based on myth and superstition, subsequently reversing symptoms into symbols. This phenomenon started in prehistory and continues today. It cannot be stressed enough that the critical interaction is a new, logical one that involves a dynamic relationship between symbols and symptoms. Everything must start from this. There is no other starting point.

It is essential to understand that whether a thing is a symbol or not depends chiefly upon the attitude of the observing person. For one person, an object can be a symbol; for another person, that same object can be a natural sign. Depending on the individual neurological process, anything can be a symbol. As Langer stated: "A natural sign is a part of a greater event or a complex condition, and to an experienced observer, it signifies the rest of that situation of which it is a notable feature. It is a symptom of a state of affairs."[8]

Although the traditional thought process has been to think symbolically, symbolic-behaving man cannot solve the problems that we face in today's world. Symbolic behavior has produced people who cannot deal with reality, so they mask that inability by mythologizing events and concepts. They then manipulate data in order to fit their own agenda. We experienced this with the meltdown of American firms such as Enron and Arthur Andersen. (See Figure 12).

Research and Development That Can Correct History

Symbolic thought is the engine that influences the effectiveness of research and development, and it eliminates any possibility of having an effective mode of technological transfer. Research that is approached with a

Figure 12: Cartoon Illustrating Accounting Errors

symbolizing attitude is accompanied by assumptions based on myths that seriously damage the research methodology. For example, a scientist educated in the West will in all probability have assumptions based on Western democratic principles, inclusive of history, anthropology, and other disciplines that formulate the complete educational network of the Western world. The scholar Martin Bernal states,

> In his Book II, Herodotus gives details of many cultic parallels between the Greeks and Egyptian religious systems and explicitly reasons that as they were closely far older in Egypt, that must be their place of origin (II:49). It is interesting to note that at the University of Oxford all books of Herodotus are required reading except for Book II. The situation is not so clear cut at Cambridge but there too Book II is omitted with some others.[9]

Institutions like Oxford and Cambridge do not encourage students to read Book II of Herodotus because of the emphasis Herodotus placed on Egypt's influence on Greece. Additionally, these institutions object to Herodotus' infamous passage, when he stated "that the

Egyptians had black skin and woolly hair." Herodotus was saying that the Egyptians were indeed black Africans.

This attitude of the Western world is compatible with the uproar over UNESCO's project to rewrite the history of Africa. As discussed in chapter 5, this objection to UNESCO's great work had a far-reaching impact on the organization's ability to achieve its goals in the areas of science and technology. UNESCO is the multilateral United Nations body responsible for education, culture, and science. In 1984, the United States pulled out of UNESCO, with Britain leaving a year later. Britain returned to UNESCO in 1997, when it was assured that the organization has been restructured; the U.S. finally rejoined in 2003. The withdrawal of the United States and Britain was driven primarily by their disagreement with UNESCO's then secretary general Amadou M'Bow, and his stated direction for the organization. UNESCO's science and engineering programs were cut by 37 percent due to its reduced budget.

In the process of challenging Western principles for the sake of research and development, Secretary General M'Bow had researched African history without mythologizing it. For *The General History of Africa Series,* he gathered eminent scholars to record an African history that was void of the paternalistic, racist ideas of the West. UNESCO's noble initiative would put to rest what the late Cheikh Anta Diop called the "most monstrous falsification in the history of humanity by modern historians." This point is important for it illustrates how UNESCO's seminal work was destroyed by a group of people who did not wish to see a fair interpretation of history. The mythologizing of historical research is taught in Western educational institutions perpetuating those assumptions that are borne into research. That mythologized research elicits ideas that fail to serve the interests of the entire population. Those ideas, developed without objective scrutiny, are geared to keep in place the prevailing status quo. Had Secretary General M'Bow's program been permitted to proceed, an accurate portrayal of world history would have demythologized previous false assumptions. This development would have led the way to the kind of sound research that would deliver an attitudinal change. The late physicist Cheikh Anta Diop stated:

> The attitude which consists of resorting to an insane misinterpretation of texts instead of accepting the evidence is typical of modern scholarship. It reflects the special state of mind that prompts one to seek secondary meanings for words rather than give them their usual significance. [10]

The late linguist, Max Müller, stated:

> What intellectual condition was our race when mythology originated? Was there a period of temporary insanity through which the human mind had to pass, and was it a madness identically the same in the South of India and in the north of Iceland? [11]

What I am saying is that the moment man started to symbolize, the human mind underwent a period of temporary insanity. That is what we call a neurological misadventure. Diop and Müller both were at a loss to explain the dynamics that created a situation where the human mind underwent a strange metamorphosis. Müller continued,

> Even if we take only that part of mythology which refers to religion, in our sense of the word, or the myths which bear on the highest problems of philosophy — such as the creation, the relation of man to God, life and death, virtue and vice — myths generally the most modern in origin, we find that even this small portion, which might be supposed to contain some sober ideas, or some pure and sublime conceptions, is unworthy of the ancestors of the Homeric poets, or the Ionic philosophers. [12]

These are the dynamics that produce the engine that directs research and development. There is an old technology saying that states, "garbage in - garbage out." If mythology is fed into research and development, the results will be more mythology. Products and ideas will be defective, will never stand the test of time, and will lapse into irrelevancy. Deming further stated,

> What is the world's most underdeveloped nation? With the storehouse of skills and knowledge contained in its millions of unemployed, and with the even more appalling underuse, misuse, and abuse of skills and knowledge in the army of employed people in all ranks in all industries, the United States may be today the most underdeveloped nation in the world. [13]

Although Deming wrote this over twenty years ago, I think it is the one of the most revealing statements ever made about the so-called superpower of modern history. Deming was actually describing symbolic behavior. The United States has mastered the manipulation of symbol systems which only reinforces its underdevelopment. Additionally, Deming's statement begs the question of why some of America's most talented and knowledgeable people are not being used in research and development. In fact, the predominance of underutilized members of society is people of color. Because of racism, poverty, unequal employment, and an unjust political system, people with the ability to solve problems are strongly discouraged. Contributions to research and development, when made by people of color, are resisted, due to myths, superstition and even physical force.

America's underdevelopment became most visible in the tragic bombing of the World Trade Center on September 11, 2001. It is well-documented that U.S. law enforcement agencies competed instead of cooperating with each other both in the months prior to as well as during critical, time-sensitive moments following the attack. Instead of allowing all its people to participate fully in the critical disciplines that could have avoided September 11, the United States spends zealous and time-wasting energy dividing and oppressing people of color. Notwithstanding our advanced technology, interdepartmental conflicts led to failure in technology transfer due to abhorrent people behavior. This is a symbolic behavior pattern that will ultimately cause not only destruction in the United States, but globally; and it must be eradicated wherever it is practiced.

Research and development are extremely important factors in making the world truly civilized. Objective research is not only critical for organizations but for life itself. Research scientists know that data can produce information that may or may not be desirable. There is an old saying: "You must be able to look truth in the face and not blink." When one is absorbed with one's personal agenda or in one's own prejudices, there is a tendency to manipulate the research findings, especially if those findings have a different outcome than expected. This is why it is imperative to perform research and development without a symbolizing mind-set. This would mitigate any desire to manipulate conclusions that do not coincide with what was expected.

The development of a product or idea is critical to the ultimate success of the product, whether material or intellectual. Development must reach established standards, and technology transfer can be successful only if it is free of mythology. When transferring technology, multidisciplinary data must be seriously considered, which means issues like religion, language, and other cultural differences must be carefully evaluated.

A principal illustration of the promises of research and development and technology transfer has to be the global quest to find a cure for AIDS. Pharmaceutical companies have done a splendid job fast-tracking this technology; in fact, breakthrough research has confirmed through clinical trials that generic AIDS drugs have as much efficacy as brand-name drugs. However, the implementation of generic drugs is being constrained due to lack of funds, as the Bush administration does not agree that the generic drugs have been proven to be as effective, even though they are chemically identical to the brand-name drugs. The U.S. bureaucratic system has prevented a method of distribution that will allow affected people to take advantage of these drugs. Let's be very clear about this: The technology is in place; but it is destructive people behavior that allows the HIV virus to continue its devastation, especially in poor areas of the world.

THE TECHNOLOGY OF FISH PRODUCTION

A study done by Dr. Ka He at Harvard's School of Public Health is an excellent example of the need for evolving research and development. Accepted wisdom over the last two decades has found that fish consumption, the more the better, reduces the risk of stroke and heart attack. The Harvard study found that men consuming seafood as seldom as once a month can cut their risk of the most common kind of stroke by more than 40 percent. The significance of this study illustrates that consuming even a low quantity of fish — one to three meals monthly – produced maximum benefit. Previous studies had dictated that fish had to be eaten at least once or twice a week, suggesting a correlation between additional fish consumed and the amount of benefit maximized. Comparatively, a conflicting Harvard study involving 8,000 female nurses found that women who ate fish five or more times weekly had a 50 percent lower risk of stroke than women consuming fish less than once a month. Dr. He could not explain why his study found a threshold level, while the women's' study found a progressive benefit.

Another mystery evolved out of Dr. He's research project. Science has concluded for years that the presence of omega-3 polyunsaturated fatty acids in fish wards off heart disease and stroke. This led to a consumer-based demand for fish oil capsules. However, Dr. He's study, like other recent ones, found no definitive connection that fish with larger amounts of omega-3 fatty acids conferred larger protection against stroke. This left experts to wonder whether the protection from stroke derived from some other components of the fish, some combination, or some other possibility. This does not mean that omega-3 fatty acids do not have other kinds of benefits.

What is exciting about Dr. He's study is that it can only reach a positive conclusion by symptomatic analysis. The long-standing assumption that omega-3 fatty acids are the entity in fish that protects against heart disease and stroke is called into question. Because of the resulting assumptions of the study, other components are being looked at besides omega-3. Because of the analysis of symptoms, the myth of omega-3 benefits is being rethought. Dr. He's study illustrates how a symptomatic approach is the only viable analytical tool for any research project. The Orientalist, Martin Bernal, states: "It is my contention that there is no scholarship that can stand outside the social and intellectual paradigms held by the community or communities to which the scholar belongs."[14] What is paramount here, and I want to emphasize this, is that no finding, no concept, can be viable unless it can be intrinsically tied and implemented within the cultural and global communities of the world. The Ivory Tower approach to scholarship is gone forever and should never raise its head again. All research and development has to be linked to the multiple issues that confront us today. Nothing can be separated.

What are the global implications of the technology of fish production? The overexportation of fish stocks might have disastrous consequences in developing countries. Global fish productions will probably not keep pace with population growth, and that might impact heavily on the developing world, where the demand greatly exceeds the supply.

European industrial fishing fleets are heading south to African borders, with European Union (EU) diplomats clearing the way with inequitable fisheries pacts. The EU is desperate to preserve the domestic fishing industries in European regions (Spain, Portugal, Britain, etc.) to save jobs dependent on employment in fishing. This gives the EU a technological edge against commercial challenges from the East. By and large, the diplomatic and technological infrastructures of developing nations are inadequate to effectively contest the European claim to fish in their waters.

This feeds right into the perception and reality that the so-called developed world cares nothing about the so-called developing world. This fits perfectly with what former Prime Minister Mahathir Mohamad meant when he commented on the West's devaluation of non-Westerners. "Dr. Mahathir believed this attitude was symptomatic of a new racism, reminiscent of that practiced by the British in Colonial times."[15]

We owe it to the global community to incorporate today's tensions and controversies into the results of research and development. We must have the objectivity and the courage to look at the results of our research — even if we dislike the outcome — and implement the data accordingly.

ANALYSIS OF SIGNS IN FOSSIL RESEARCH

A classic study reported in *Nature* magazine involved the discovery of the fossilized skulls of two adults and a child found in Ethiopia. Scientists claimed that for the first time they see the immediate ancestors of modern humans. There have been continuous debates on the origin of man and/or whether all humans derive originally from Africa or a multiregional approach, which states that there were several regional *Homo sapiens*.

All conclusive evidence from almost all disciplines rules out a multiregional approach. All evidence points in a direct line to Africa for all humans, and the recent fossil finds in Ethiopia prove without a doubt that the multiregional concept is null and void. The fossils found in Ethiopia must be considered as natural signs. In other words, they are symptoms that show that Africa is the cradle of humanity. The new fossils proved that *Homo sapiens*, with almost entirely human characteristics, had evolved in Africa before the Neanderthals evolved into their classic form. These fossils prove conclusively that the Neanderthals had no relationship with modern humans. The results of the finds and the evaluation of the symptoms concluded with the fact that we are all Africans. Only those with a symbolizing attitude will deny the results of the research, which is evident to all objective people.

Spencer Wells, an evolutionary scientist, began his research on the genetics of human population in Central Asia. Using DNA, Wells confirmed the African origin of humanity, and he was able to trace man's roots as he left Africa to populate the rest of the world. As we know, DNA is a natural sign, or symptom, of the dynamics of our genetic code. This phenomenon makes it possible for us to have a clear understanding of our past and the dynamics of the migration that humans embarked on. Wells' research was void of any mythology — the symptoms, or natural signs, were analyzed free of the flaws that mythological thinking would introduce.

Research and development carried out by individuals who do not think symbolically is free of superstition – unlike a project that starts from a symbolic base. A technology free of mythology can be effectively transferred, free of the conflicts that accompany a transfer that has symbol systems throughout.

The dilemma we face for effective technology transfer is whether to think symbolically or symptomatically. This is the all-encompassing issue here, and it cannot be escaped. In order for productivity to be effective, the engine that runs all technology must be driven by a symptomatic approach.

When a symbolic approach is taken, we end up with the situation in which the United States finds itself in Iraq. As is well known, it has been concluded by a U.S. Senate Intelligence Committee that the United States acted on deeply flawed data in going to war with Iraq. It was even suggested by former U.S. Secretary of State Colin Powell that the data was intentionally flawed. Whatever the case, the people of the United States were deliberately fed false information regarding Iraq. The study concluded that if Congress had known the real facts about the so-called weapons of mass destruction, it would never have sanctioned the war. This is indeed tragic. It demonstrates how the symbolizing attitude of the U.S. government mythologized facts and, based on those facts, developed a plan of action that was not only deeply flawed but totally incorrect and without merit. This led to the unnecessary death and injury of thousands of people and to the grief of untold thousands of families. The United States went into Iraq based on research data that was mythological in content and ritualistic in application. The final results were indeed horrific.

In my research, all evidence points to a barbaric civilization based on superstition and myth that is circling with no end in sight. The only way out of this circular pattern is to eradicate all symbol systems and replace it with a symptomatic approach that is thoroughgoing in every segment of civilization. This would produce a civilization where man is truly no longer *Homo symbolicus* but *Homo symptomaticus*.

CHAPTER EIGHT

Symptoms and Medicine

Medical procedures and methodologies have failed to adequately provide sound, effective medical care for the entire population due to symbolic thinking. This system of thought has led to the ineffective, circular practices that have caused the unacceptable disparities in healthcare distribution to the world's population.

In actuality, the global community is in a holding pattern that prevents qualitative change from taking place. This holding pattern is circular, and will remain so, as long as healthcare is delivered using mythology and superstition. This holding pattern originates in the educational system that trains our healthcare professionals. Our brightest, most creative minds are barred from the contributions that would help solve our most pressing medical problems, both nationally and globally. Heart disease, cancer, and AIDS would be more effectively dealt with, and possibly cured sooner, if we utilized our naturally given resources. I must repeat the statement by W.E. Deming:

> What is the world's most underdeveloped nation? With the storehouse of skills and knowledge contained in its millions of unemployed, and with the even more appalling underuse, misuse, and abuse of skills and knowledge in the army of employed people in all ranks in all industries, the United States may be today the most underdeveloped nation in the world. [1]

People behaving symbolically will never be able to enact medical procedures that would be beneficial to the global community. It is essential for the healthcare community to transition to a symptomatic mode of thought. We must remember that healthcare delivery should be total, mental and physical. More and more physicians and other healthcare professionals are recognizing that the approach to medicine must be multidisciplinary in order to better manage the complexities of modern medicine.

A good place to start would be with mental health and its implications to the health of the rest of the human body. Two of the most influential people in the mental health arena have been Sigmund Freud and Carl Jung. Both of these psychiatrists emphasized that symptoms and symbols are the key drivers that determine the mental health of *Homo sapiens*. Yet, their eventual professional parting of the ways was caused by their disagreement on how symptoms and symbols were to be used in psychotherapy. Freud stressed a symptomatic approach in conjunction with a symbolic one; conversely, Jung's therapeutic approach emphasized the importance of symbols and myth and the turning of symptoms into symbols. Freud failed to understand the uses of symptoms in relation to symbols, and he was also hindered by his sexual phobias in relation to human interaction. Jung, on the other hand, felt that symbolism and mythology were the binding factors in establishing effective psychotherapy. Jung emphasized that living mythologically was the only healthy way to live, both mentally and physically.

Unfortunately, mental health professionals have followed Jung's lead. Subsequently, that has laid the foundation for psychiatrists and psychologists to perpetuate symbolic thinking as the neurological process leading to a mental transference that perpetuates healthy decisions, both personally and professionally. What is problematic and complex about this is that the general populace in the medical field agrees and perpetuates this thought process. This dynamic severely complicates how we deal with issues such as racism. This symbolic mode of thought perpetuates harm and adds more devastation to people of color worldwide.

It is important to connect symptoms in our quest to solve problems. Medicine is at its best when it is connecting the symptoms to make accurate diagnoses. Three straightforward examples come to mind. First, the late George W. Thorn, a physician whose work helped transform the treatment of kidney diseases and other disorders, emphasized the importance of connecting the symptoms and naming diseases.

A second example is Surgeon Joseph Murray, a 1990 recipient of the Nobel Prize in Medicine, who partnered with Dr. Thorn for work in organ and cell transplantation, using the symptomatic approach in organizing successful kidney transplants at a time when it was not commonly performed.

A third example is a recent medical school case study regarding the complaints of a teenage girl. This story illustrates how critical it is to examine all information and to connect all the dots in order to reach the proper conclusions.

A fourteen-year-old girl complained of stomach pains with vomiting, but no fever. She had no pain with urination, but had occasional constipation. Physical examination revealed moderate pain when she was touched on her abdomen; yet the abdomen was not swollen or distended, and her liver and spleen were not swollen. However, her urine had a large number of red blood cells and no white blood cells – hence, urinary infection and appendicitis were ruled out, and the red blood cells attributed to menstruation. A first diagnosis was constipation, with a laxative prescribed.

Following a return visit to the emergency room a few days later, a new examination included an abdominal ultrasound to eliminate any surgical causes. The girl was admitted to the hospital and given intravenous fluids and morphine. Although there was some initial improvement, a CT abdominal scan suggested inflammatory disease of the bowel. Pediatric gastroenterologists planned an upper endoscopy and a colonoscopy.

The girl then developed a rash on her legs, four to six small lesions on each ankle. The endoscopy showed petechiae in her small intestine; small dark red marks that suggest damage to the blood vessels. The final diagnosis was Henoch-Schonlein purpura – a weakening and leaking of small blood vessels in the skin, leading to inflammation of the circulatory system. The girl was treated with corticosteroids to decrease inflammation, and her abdominal pain ceased. The blood in her urine was not from menstruation, as previously concluded, but from an infection in one of her kidneys.

An interesting side note to this extensive symptomatic analysis is the naming of the condition: Henoch-Schonlein purpura.

> Johann Lukas Schonlein, a 19th century German physician-scientist, described the association between

the skin rash and the joint problems as Schonlein's purpura. Eduard Henrich Henoch, a German pediatrician and Schonlein's student, described the skin lesions associated with abdominal pain as Schonlein-Henoch purpura. Currently the two eponyms will be used separately – Schonlein's purpura for skin and joint symptoms; Henoch's purpura for skin and abdominal symptoms – but in the most common term now used for the syndrome, the two names have switched position. In some cases, the eponyms are replaced with the name anaphylactoid purpura. Still, the two names, with the history they imply of piecing together the connections among a complex set of symptoms and tracing them to a common pathology, seem very appropriate for a disease that can still puzzle as it challenges us to connect the spots.[2]

One of the best methodologies for the detection of symptoms is the ultrasound technology that is now in use for predicting many potential health problems such as blocked arteries, which can lead to a stroke, aortic aneurysms, which can lead to a ruptured aorta; and hardening of the arteries in the legs, which are a strong predictor of heart disease. Advanced screening techniques with this ultrasound technology can detect symptoms before a heart attack or a stroke occurs.

Occasionally, the medical community will conclude that some diseases do not have symptoms. However, we should understand that symptoms occur in all disease states even if the first symptom is death itself.

I would like to emphasize the dynamics of how symptoms are turned into symbols. Verena Kast describes the dynamic very succinctly:

A sign, however, can assume the characteristics of a symbol. Take numbers, for example. A number is a sign. It is agreed that two is a sign for two units, and thus represents a quantity. But a number can also be considered qualitatively. The number thirteen is the sign for thirteen units, while — in terms of quality

— we might say thirteen is an unlucky number. It is assigned a content, or quality. Signs can easily evolve into symbols, particularly when we approach the world with a symbolizing attitude. [3]

Kast understands that the number thirteen is a sign that means thirteen units – it can only be seen as unlucky when we mythologize. Said another way, it is the height of superstition to believe that the number thirteen is an unlucky number. Kast goes further in her example of turning symptoms into symbols by depicting a tree and mythologizing that tree so that the tree takes on a human figure. [4] This is extremely important to understand, for it shows how the neurological misadventure takes place. The mythologizing of an entity or any single event produces a superstitious being with a symbolizing attitude. This event that we have just described lays the foundation for all the dynamics that occur in the human body.

That neurological process described above causes the behavior pattern that perpetuates an unhealthy lifestyle. Those same behavior patterns create the engines that drive the racism and greed reflected in all of the world's conflicts. These behavior patterns cause self-destruction as well as the destruction of others, as people are unable to deal with the realities of their existence, turning to drugs and other destructive outlets. These behavior patterns are described as thinking symbolically, and there is no redeeming factor. A symbolizing attitude causes people to indulge in behavior that is risky for themselves and others with whom they come in contact.

On the other hand, when one thinks symptomatically, one is led by the symptoms of one's experience. Instead of mythologizing, one reads the symptoms of their existence like a language, to which they respond accordingly. This means they do not mythologize the events in their life, nor do they approach their life with a symbolizing attitude.

One factor that needs to be looked at carefully is obesity. Obesity is prevalent in America due to the easy access to unhealthy and fattening foods, coupled with mental health issues. A diet of fruits and vegetables is recommended by health professionals, but these foods are rejected due to superior marketing and advertisement of unhealthy foods.

In previous chapters, we discussed the mythology of the foodstuffs fish and apples. It has been proven symptomatically that these foods are extremely healthful with the ingredients to prolong life. Research has proven that fish can actually enhance the health of the human brain, lowering the risk of Alzheimer's disease, heart disease, and some cancers. For example, a study conducted by Dr. George J. Miller, of the Medical Research Council in London, suggested that eating fish instead of steak sharply cuts the risk of a heart attack in the morning. In fact, a low-fat supper like broiled fish can lower the risk of heart disease. Dr. Miller looked at 170 men, ages forty to fifty-nine, and found that those with the highest fat intake had 12 percent higher Factor VII activity than those with the lowest fat intake. Factor VII, a blood-clotting substance, "...is a fuse that sets off an explosion of blood-clotting chemicals in the blood. The higher the level of Factor VII, the shorter the fuse and the larger explosion of clotting factors." [5] On the other hand, apples, which are mythologized as much or even more than fish, have been shown to improve general health overall, including lowering the risk of strokes and heart disease. As a matter of fact, an easy example of symbols turning into symptoms is the proverb of eating an apple a day keeps the doctor away. The health benefits of eating fish and apples are substantial and should be included in one's daily diet. The process of turning symbols into symptoms should be emphasized instead of turning symptoms into symbols.

Unfortunately, the lack of healthy diets in our society leads to dependence on multiple medications to correct disease states. The Symptomatic Thought Process completely revolutionizes the power of the pharmaceutical industry. The problems currently faced by the pharmaceutical industry are tied to symbolic behavior and mythological conclusions. Research and development fails to heed the negative side effects (revealed as symptoms) that costs lives and unnecessary suffering. The Symptomatic Thought Process creates an environment where greed and profit become secondary to product quality and safety. Pharmaceutical companies have great potential to alleviate suffering worldwide, however they are microcosms of the rest of society. Therefore, their problems are the results of the same behavior patterns that are endemic throughout civilization. We must remember that mythology is a dialect, an ancient form of language, and that language is a diseased language. Therefore, the drugs earmarked safe and effective are sometimes deadly, especially when a huge profit is foreseen by the pharmaceutical company. This is a result of a symbolizing attitude and, as we all have seen, the results can be disastrous.

There is now a temptation to develop medications for a specific race. First, it should be made clear that there is only one race, the human race. Dividing people into racial categories is mythological and, clearly, scientifically unsound. We share 99.99 percent of our genome with one another. The remaining .01 percent comprise nothing more than variations in skin color that are in fact biologically insignificant.[6] However, there are some scientists who would like to consider race when assessing drugs for specific diseases. For instance, the debate over the heart medication that is supposedly beneficial to blacks and not to whites has resurfaced the argument that race should be a factor in developing medications to treat diseases. A multidisciplinary approach to this debate proves conclusively that genes, not race, are important in understanding disease states. What must be made abundantly clear is that race is a myth, and applying metaphors to understanding disease states is futile and useless.

Howard University has been conducting an ongoing study in genetics and its relation to disease. The Howard University study concluded that there was no biological basis for race, and that the link between genes and disease should be made directly without taking race into account. Dr. George M. Dunston, founding director of Howard's Genome Center, stated, "By removing the barriers implied by the racial classifications we can more effectively study population differences in disease distribution." [7] Dr. Dunston is connecting the symptoms and discarding the mythological, racial categories. By applying the symptomatic approach, he is on the path to solving the problems caused by disease. It is important to connect the symptoms when analyzing and affecting a cure for disease states. Connecting the dots through symptoms is preferable to making mythological interpretations that lead to the traditional superstition of racism, presented when one starts with the premise that there are races of people. The simple fact that there are more variations within races than between them makes the concept of race a misnomer.

The Asian chapter with the Human Genome Organization has joined in the study of the human genome. The Asians begin from the premise that the gene pool is 99.99 percent identical, and they emphasize population rather than the race factor. This distinction is worthy of note, because the Asians will not be bogged down quarrelling about the mythology of different races. They are following the lead of Howard University's Dr. Dunston. By going directly to the underlying genetic causes of disease, without taking into account any possible correlation with race, Asian scientists are applying the symptomatic approach rather than the mythological one of race. The comparison of this Asian study to the Human Genome Project clearly shows that the only people that have continual problems with race are whites, who continually want to use the mythological argument of differences between the so-called races of people.

What has to be clearly understood is that racism is a disease. Notwithstanding an increasing minority of physicians and scientists that acknowledge racism as a disease, that recognition is not widespread. Those who refuse to face the reality that racism is a disease will continue to be in a state of denial that can only end in tragedy and ignorance. The only way to cure the disease of racism is to understand its dynamics. Those dynamics have their origin in symbol systems derived from a neurological misadventure that occurred in antiquity. When we read the literature and history of racism, it is understood by almost all scholars that racism is a mythological event that reveals itself as superstition. That is uncontested. It follows that superstition originates from a symbolic-behaving *Homo sapiens.* Refusing to understand racism as a disease is comparable to refusing to admit that HIV causes AIDS, smoking causes cancer and heart disease, or that an unhealthy diet causes serious health problems. The scientific community is inhibited from solving our most serious health problems because of its insistence on practicing racism. If we are to be liberated from the health problems that we experience, we must have the courage to face the reality that racism must be eliminated. The future of medicine rests on the understanding that symbolic behavior produces an unhealthy environment that is incapable of controlling disease, therefore forfeiting a healthy civilization that is free from the economic and environmental problems that we face today.

It is important that we understand the dynamics behind the statement that racism is a disease. The Orientalist F. Max Müller dominated the study of myth during the third quarter of the nineteenth century. His statements, that "Mythology is a disease of language" and that "the ancient symbolism was a result of something like a primitive mental aberration," caused a great uproar in the scholarly circles of his time. [8] Notwithstanding his opposition, Professor Müller was on target. Mythology is a disease of language. Since mythology is the result of symbolic thought, and symbolic thought produces superstition that results in racist thought patterns, it follows, then, that racism is a disease of the neurological processes of the human mind. We know that when people are in a disease state, it is extremely hard to face reality. Whites are in a state of denial when it comes to racism, and it has been that way since time immemorial. Since symbolism produced a neurological misadventure, and that neurological misadventure resulted in mythological, symbolic-behaving humans, Müller was correct in stating that it was "something like a primitive mental aberration." When language is infected by mythology, it is indeed a diseased language. That is one of the reasons why former Washington, D.C. health official, Dr. Watts, stated that they relied on symptoms instead of rhetoric during the SARS crisis. By connecting the dots symptomatically instead of depending on mythological rhetoric, a correct course of action could be taken for this unfortunate emergency.[9]

Scholars of all disciplines are unanimous that there are only two options that we have for living out our lives: a symptomatic or symbolic course of action. This is uncontested. It is up to us to choose which path to take. I maintain that living out our lives symptomatically is the foundation on which we can begin to solve all of the problems that we face in this universe.

PART THREE

CHANGING THE STRUCTURE OF CIVILIZATION

CHAPTER NINE

The Dynamics of Changing Civilization

P art 3 of this book is an attempt to show how the words *symptoms* and *symbols* are used and how superstition and myth are used in conjunction with symbols. Literature in all disciplines clearly demonstrates the impact of both symbols and symptoms on civilization.

Civilization as we know it today is based on myth. As we stated earlier, myth governed history and was at the same time responsible for justifying it.[1] That UNESCO declaration in *The General History of Africa* series underscores the importance of myth in civilization when it states:

The mythical approach in fact is common to all people. Every history starts off as religious history, but sometimes the mythical current overwhelms a nation's attitudes, opinions, or ideology.[2]

As a result of a neurological misadventure or, as Müller viewed it, a "primitive mental aberration," every history does indeed start off as religious history, which means that superstition was the engine that governed behavior from the beginning of time. That engine caused all the atrocities and difficulties that have plagued civilization from day one. Sir James Frazer (1854-1941), a Scottish classicist and anthropologist, wrote a pioneering study on the impact of religion and folklore on human development. In his study, Frazer spoke of a behavior driven by mythology and symbolism. This behavior determined the course that civilization followed throughout history.

> Frazer's original purpose was...to explain an ancient Italian folk custom. A runaway slave, if successful in pulling down a bough from a special golden tree, won the right to fight to the death the king of the sacred forest grove at Nemi and perhaps to become the next king of the woods....Frazer pondered the similarity of this golden bough of Nemi and the golden bough which, in Virgil's epic poem the *Aeneid*, allowed the hero Aeneas to enter the underworld and gave him access to its secrets.....[In analyzing the meaning of these events] Frazer opened up the whole world of myth and ritual, from the far reaches of the legendary past to the practices of primitive peoples of his day. It was an astounding revelation to Frazer's culture-bound world that the customs and superstitions of civilized society were in many ways comparable to the beliefs and practices of primitive people.[3]

Frazer's emphasis on the link between early civilization's mythology and superstition and those mythologies and superstitions commonly practiced in today's world caused quite a stir in academic circles. Theodore Gaster, editor of *The New Golden Bough,* dismissed Frazer's work as artistic and fanciful, not factual at all. Gaster, like other scholars, rejected the notion that the superstitions and folklore of so-called primitive societies were, in fact, prevalent in so-called civilized societies. Additionally, the fact that these rituals and myths came out of Africa did not help any.

Frazer's work is extremely important, because it shows how the myths and superstitions that came out of symbol systems controlled the behavior of man as he tried to make sense of his world. It is now understood by almost everyone that myth governed history, and that myth was created by a species in Africa that can be called *Homo symbolicus*.[4]

As stated before, we either must live out our lives symptomatically or symbolically. I maintain that we must live our lives out symptomatically. We must rid ourselves of all symbolic intent. Unfortunately, that has not been the case. We have become symbolic humans that have depended on the symbolic approach to solve our problems. Indeed, it has been a dual existence. We have been living our lives out both symbolically and symptomatically. The late psychiatrist, Edward C. Whitmont, stated:

> There are two possible approaches to the problems and disturbances which life presents. We can see them as symptomatic deviations from a desired normalcy of "what things should be like," caused by some wrongness and hence the expressions of trouble or illness. We can on the other hand suspect that the known facts may attempt to point further and deeper to a development still called for and a meaningfulness so far unrealized. Only then do we think or live not merely symptomatically but also symbolically. The realization of that meaning which has so far been missed might then point toward a cure.[5]

Whitmont's approach to life was a symbolic one He stated, "The whole of life can be seen as a symbolic quest."[6] He went on to state, "The world of myth has its own laws and its own reality."[7] If it were up to Whitmont, our whole existence would be nothing but a symbolic one without interference from symptoms. However, since symptoms are a natural neurological process rather than a symbolic one, which is indeed a neurological misadventure, it is indeed impossible to live a life without symptoms. So Whitmont, as stated earlier, said we must live our life both symbolically and symptomatically. Living our lives both symbolically and symptomatically leads to a troubled human species that is schizophrenic at best and superstitious throughout. It leads to a situation described by Terrence Deacon in his book *Symbolic Species*, where he states:

> The human case is difficult because we can neither rely on the logic of language to explain what happened to the brain, nor can we rely on some incremental increase in a general feature found in other species. Thus, when we use hindsight to analyze our own cognitive evolution – subtracting specific abilities or reducing overall thinking power – the simpler minds that we imagine as a result turn out to be both distorted images of ourselves and poor images of our ancestors and ape relatives. We end up misrepresenting other species' minds and not recognizing the oddities of our own. The result is an imaginary chimeric creature like those drawn in medieval bestiaries, half human, half animal, with a human head and an animal body like the Sphinx of ancient Egypt.[8]

Deacon was so taken by the overwhelming effect that symbolism had on the human mind that he called the human species *Homo symbolicus*.[9] The nineteenth-century Egyptologist Gerald Massey echoed Deacon's emphasis on the importance of symbolism when he stated: "Whether for good or ill, the symbol has proved all powerful. The hold of symbolism is in its way as strong in civilized society as in the savage world."[10] Massey went on to say, "Symbols still dominate the minds of men and usurp the place of realities."[11] Frazer, in his classic book, *The Golden Bough,* emphasized the symbolic, superstitious nature of humans in antiquity and in the modern world. His use of symbols and symptoms and their importance in civilization is uncontested. Curtis Church, in his foreword to *The New Golden Bough,* stated:

> It was an astonishing revelation to Frazer's culture-bound world that the customs and superstitions of civilized society were in many ways comparative to the beliefs and practices of primitive peoples.[12]

Frazer himself stated:

> Hence, every inquiry into the primitive religion of the Aryans should either start from the superstitious beliefs and observances of the peasantry, or should at least be constantly checked and controlled by reference to them.[13]

Frazer leaves no doubt that superstition that was created by symbolism made man a symbolic, superstitious human. He stated:

> But both in Babylon and in Egypt this ancient tool of superstition, so baneful in the hands of the mischievous and malignant, who also pressed into the service of religion and turned to glorious account for the confusion and overthrow of demons.[14]

Frazer stated further:

> Throughout the Malay region the rajah or king is commonly regarded with superstitious veneration as the possessor of supernatural powers, and there are grounds for thinking that he too, like apparently so many African chiefs, has been developed out of a simple magician.[15]

In addressing superstitions, Frazer went on to say:

Addressing some Australian blacks, a European missionary said, "I am not one, as you think, but two." Upon this they laughed. "You may laugh as much as you like," continued the missionary, "I tell you that I am two in one; this great body that you see is one; within that there is another little one which is not visible. The great body dies, and is buried, but the little body flies away when the great one dies." To this some of the blacks replied, "Yes, yes. We also are two, we also have a little body within the breast."[16]

Frazer emphasized the importance of primitive religion and the behavior patterns of early man. He believed that magic is the very foundation of religion. Frazer felt that magic preceded religion and was a source of the superstitious nature of religious worship. But what is important here is the realization that religion had a strong influence on the behavior of early man. That, in fact, led John Fiske to state: "The religious myths of antiquity and the fireside legends of ancient and modern times have their common root in the mental habits of primeval humanity. They are the earliest recorded utterances of men concerning the visible phenomenon of the world into which they were born."[17] Fiske gives an excellent description of the processes of myth and how they use superstition to affect man's behavior.

> Myths, like words, survive their primitive meanings. In the early stage, the myth is part and parcel of the current mode of philosophizing; the explanation which it offers is, for the time, the natural one, the one which would most readily occur to any one thinking on the theme with which the myth is concerned. But by and by the mode of philosophizing has changed; explanations which formerly seemed quite obvious no longer occur to any one, but the myth has acquired an independent substantive existence, and continues to be handed down from parents to children as something true, though no one can tell why it is true. Lastly, the myth itself gradually fades

from remembrance, often leaving behind it some ut-
terly unintelligible custom or seemingly absurd superstitious notion.[18]

It must be clearly understood that the superstition emanating from mythology causes extremely destructive behavior patterns of not only early man but in today's
contemporary civilization. Modern anthropologists feel
uneasy with Frazer's basic thesis because they feel
threatened by the notion that the behaviors of modern
people are affected by the same process of mythology
and superstition as early man. Superstitious mythology
has caused humanity to behave in the most bizarre ways
that one can imagine. Because that behavior is bizarre,
some of the most horrific tragedies of violence have been
caused by that same mythological behavior. They have
affected how we view civilization to such a degree that
the Egyptologist Cheikh Anta Diop has said that it has
created the most monstrous falsification in the history
of humanity by modern historians.[19] The degree to which
mythology and superstition has affected human behavior led Max Müller to claim that it has produced insane
results. That same attitude led Diop to state: "The attitude which consists of resorting to an insane misinterpretation of texts instead of accepting the evidence, [sic]
is typical of modern scholarship. It reflects the special
state of mind that prompts one to seek secondary meanings for words rather than give them their usual significance."[20] Both Müller and Diop are clear when they say
that mythology has not only affected people behavior
but how we see history.

University of Michigan anthropologists Joyce
Marcus and Kent V. Flannery found new ^{14}C dates from
Oaxaca, Mexico, that document changes in religious
ritual that accompanied the evolution of society from
hunting and gathering to the archaic state. These new
dates, which were determined by radiocarbon analysis,
showed how religion and ritual evolved in ancient soci-

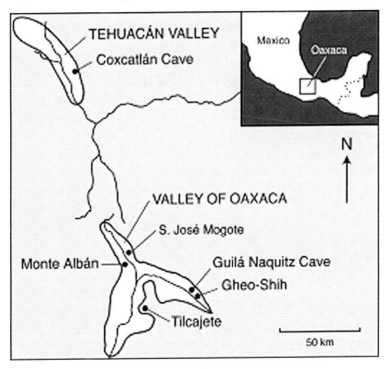

Figure 13: Valley of Oaxaca - National Academy of Sciences
Map courtesy of National Academy of Sciences (PNAS)
(Copyright 2004 National Academy of Sciences USA)

eties. The report by the anthropologists to the National
Academy of Sciences laid bare the religious impact on
the ancient culture of Mexico and how it impacted human behavior.

Marcus and Flannery state that: "Religious ritual
is one of the universals of human behavior. No society,
ancient or modern, is known to be without it."[21] The
work of Marcus and Flannery support the work of James
Frazer, especially when they describe the mythological
rituals that played such an important role in ancient
civilizations. The superstitious nature of man that
Frazer emphasized in his book, *The Golden Bough,* and
the ritualistic practices that come as a result of those

superstitions can be brutal and vicious, and indeed, makes no real sense at all. The University of Michigan anthropologists describe the results of rituals when they state:

> Additional evidence for Archaic ritual comes from Coxcatlan Cave in the Tehuacan Valley, 160 km to the northwest. Dating to *ca.* 7000 B.P., the evidence consists of individuals who appear to have been beheaded, cooked, and cannibalized before being buried in the cave, accompanied by baskets of harvested wild plants. Two conclusions to be drawn are that (i) the human sacrifice so common in later Mesoamerican cultures began in the Archaic, and (ii) such sacrifice may have been an ad hoc ritual associated with harvest seasons. Significantly, Coxcatlan Cave was large enough to accommodate a multifamily band.[22]

The viciousness that results from a symbolic attitude is apparent at every stage of human existence due to man's propensity for ritualistic activity. What is so important about *The Golden Bough* is Frazer's attempt to show how modern man's behavior is not qualitatively different from the savage's behavior; the reason being that modern man uses the same symbol systems and produces the same mythologies that have affected his behavior since he began to symbolize symptoms from his life experiences. When symptomatic thinking is turned into symbolic thinking, man becomes a ritualistic-behaving animal that is capable of the most damaging decisions and wretched behavior patterns. Frazer's illustrations of the behavior patterns of primitive people has been criticized as not being accurate, but the discoveries in Mexico prove without a doubt that humanity's symbol systems produce barbaric behavior in every area of human existence. Marcus and Flannery go on to state: "Ritual bloodletting, a form of autosacrifice, was carried out in the Structure 28 temple by using obsidian stilettos chipped to resemble stingray spines."[23] These barbaric thought processes have led Max Müller to emphasize the absurdity and sickness of mythology at every stage and age of human existence.

There have been many books written about civilizations. The standard textbooks that have given accounts of civilizations have been based on a mythological interpretation. The scholar Cheikh Anta Diop has written the definitive work on civilization. His two books, *The African Origin of Civilization* and *Civilization or Barbarism* have set the tone for corrective history. Diop makes sparing use of mythology and folklore in his works. By doing so, his work on civilization is void of the errors and mythological interpretations that have plagued the scholarly community from day one. Diop's work has been ignored by the white academic community worldwide because of his insistence on the black African origin of Egyptian civilization and the role Africa has played in world history.

What is so interesting about Diop is his vast multidisciplinary knowledge, to which he applies his writings on world civilization. In Diop's book, *The African Origin of Civilization*, he states that the historical account of world civilization that is given by modern scholarship is the most monstrous falsification in the history of humanity. Diop states over and over again how modern scholarship has distorted African history in general and Egyptian history in particular. Scholars have jumped through hoops to disprove an African origin of Egyptian civilization; they have mythologized historical accounts of early scholars who saw and claimed that Egyptians were a black African people.

To distort history, one has to mythologize history. It is important to understand that one cannot distort historical facts without mythologizing. Diop used a multidisciplinary approach and based his facts on solid evidence, using a symptomatic approach: i.e., his use of the melanin dosage test, where he could directly determine the skin color in the ethnic affiliations of the ancient Egyptians. He did this by microscopic analysis in the laboratory. A microscopic analysis is able to determine the signs, i.e., symptoms that indicate the color of the ancient Egyptians. These signs provide evidence that the ancient Egyptians were a black African people without a doubt. As Diop himself stated: "The evaluation of melanin level by microscopic examination is a laboratory method which enables us to classify the ancient Egyptians unquestionably among the black races."[24] Diop used methods adopted by physical anthropology, an analysis of blood groups to ensure that the conclusions reached were the proper ones. This is called a symptomatic approach to the issues prevalent in civilization. Any scholar using a symptomatic approach rather than a symbolic one would come to the same conclusion. For example, in Diop's writing on civilization, he has stated that Egyptian civilization has its origin in Nubia. He stated:

> During the reign of Psammetichus, when the Egyptian army was mistreated, some 200,000 of them, led by their officers, went from the Isthmus of Suez to the Nubian Sudan to place themselves at the service of King Nubia. Herodotus reported that the Nubian ruler settled the entire army on lands that it farmed, and its elements were finally assimilated by the Nubian people. That happened at a time when Nubian civilization was already several millennia old. Consequently, we are amazed when historians try to use this fact to explain Nubian civilization. On the contrary, all the earliest scholars who studied Nubia, even those to whom we owe the discovery of Nubian archeology (such as Cailliaud) conclude that Nubia had priority. Their studies indicate that Egyptian civilization descended from that of Nubia, in other words, Sudan. As Pedrals observes, Cailliaud bases this argument on the fact that in Egypt all the objects of worships (thus, the essence of sacred tradition) are Nubian. Cailliaud assumes then that the roots of Egyptian civilization were in

Nubia (the Sudan) and that it gradually descended the valley of the Nile. In this, he was merely rediscovering or confirming to some extent the unanimous opinion of the Ancients, philosophers and writers, who judged the anteriority of Nubia to be the obvious.[25]

Despite the quasi-unanimous testimony of the ancients, Diop felt that conclusive archaeological evidence was missing to prove decisively that Egypt has its origin in Nubia. But with the 1962 discovery by Bruce Williams of the University of Chicago of an engraved cylindrical censer, with particular patterns engraved on the censer, it was determined that these objects had preceded Egyptian monarchy by three generations. Diop stated: "The censer is the most ancient figure of a king found in the Nile Valley. Indecipherable signs of the hieroglyphic form prestaging the writing of the period close to the end of the fourth millennium also were noted."[26] Diop's phrase "indecipherable signs of the hieroglyphic form" is a symptomatic way of understanding the process of determining the value of the Nubian object. For Diop, the Bruce Williams discovery is the missing link that proves the Nubian origins of Egypt. When taken as a whole with the testimony of the ancients and the discovery, it leaves no doubt of the Nubian origins of the Egyptians. Diop goes on to state in a most compelling way:

> Diodorus of Sicily reports that each year the statue of Amon, King of Thebes, was transported in the direction of Nubia for several days and then brought back as if to indicate that the god was returning from Nubia. Diodorus also claims that Egyptian civilization came from Nubia, the center of which was Meroe. In fact, by following data provided by Diodorus and Herodotus on the site of that Sudanese capital, Cailliaud (circa 1820) discovered the ruins of Meroe: 80 pyramids, several temples consecrated to Amon, Ra, and so on. In addition, quoting Egyptian priests, Herodotus stated that of the 300 Egyp-

tian Pharaohs, from Menes to the seventeenth Dynasty, 18 rather than merely the three who correspond to the Ethiopian "dynasty" were of Sudanese origin.[27]

What I want to emphasize over and over again is the reason why Müller and Diop both emphasize this insane special state of mind, which is mythology that prompts one to seek secondary meanings for words rather than give them the usual significance. In fact, Müller states,

> Was there a period of temporary insanity, through which the human mind had to pass, and was it a madness identically the same in the south of India and in the north of Iceland? Even if we take only that part of mythology which refers to religion, in our sense of the word, or the myths which bear on the highest problems of philosophy — such as the creation, the relation of man to God, life and death, virtue and vice — myths generally the most modern in origin, we find that even this small portion, which might be supposed to contain some sober ideas, or some pure and sublime conceptions, is unworthy of the ancestors of the Homeric poets, or the Ionic philosophers."[28]

It is obvious that both Müller and Diop see the absurdity and indeed the sickness of mythological thinking. For instance, the late scholar St. Clair Drake describes how American anthropologist William Adams mythologized the racial identity of the Nubians. Adams stated:

> There is no longer, today, any satisfactory reason for believing that the modern Nubians are a different people from the Nubians of antiquity or of any intervening period. On the contrary, I think everything points to their being the same people. That their numbers have been swelled by immigration, warlike as well as peaceful, from the north and from the south, goes without saying. I have seldom referred to the Nubians as "black," not out of any racial sen-

sitivity, but because they have only intermittently been "black."[29]

The way Adams mythologized the racial identity of the Nubians shows you the length to which white scholars will go to distort African history. Modern Western scholars have stated that black scholars have spent too much time emphasizing the black Africanness of Egypt, and not enough time emphasizing the people of Nubia who are really black Africans. Now when the evidence points to the fact that indeed Egypt has its origins in Nubia, and that Nubian civilization predated Egypt, these white scholars want to deny the blackness of the Nubians. St. Clair Drake describes Adams as trying to "talk away the blackness of Nubians."[30] That translates to mythologizing Nubian people.

Another example of the insanity of mythological thinking is the tendency for the West to categorize some blacks that are of the Mediterranean as whites; but the same blacks, if they were to live in the West, would be categorized as Negroes. This crazy mythologizing of the racial identity of Africans is solely a mission of whites who just cannot come to terms with the achievement and the beauty of black Africans the world over. For indeed, black African people are a beautiful people, but all people can be a beautiful people, and there is no reason for whites to continue phobias about people of color. They must eliminate their symbolic thinking if they hope to return to sanity.

Some scholars have criticized Diop for what they perceive as treating folklore as fact. In fact, what Diop is doing is turning symbols into symptoms as he has done by turning the myth of Atlantis into historical science through radiocarbon analysis as was discussed earlier. As stated earlier, Diop makes very little use of mythology and folklore in his writings. Cheikh Anta Diop really has rewritten the history of the world in a most effective and thorough way. Diop did not realize that his approach in writing world history was a symptomatic one. I knew that for sure when we discussed his approach in his office at the radiocarbon laboratory.

Martin Bernal, in his work *Black Athena*, makes a sincere attempt to correct the distortion of world history. Bernal uses a vast amount of knowledge and evidence to debunk the notion that Greek history, viewed as European and Aryan, was the fountainhead of all knowledge, and that the Egyptian and Semitic cultural area played no role, or a very minor role, in Greek culture and achievement. Bernal's work is impressive because of the vast amount of sources that he references and because of his considerable knowledge of the ancient world. However, the main problem with Bernal's work is that he gets caught up in a mythological adventure from which he is unable to effectively extricate himself. But at one point Bernal uses natural signs that reveal symptomatic connections between Egypt and Greece. For example, he states: "However, it is not merely the symbolism of the plaques that shows the intimacy of contacts between Egypt and Greece at this time. An analysis of the lead in the glaze shows that it came from Laurion."[31]

It is important for Bernal to realize that the process of analyzing the lead in the glaze is a symptomatic method that authenticates the contacts between Egypt and Greece. To distort these findings is mythologizing the facts. To rely on the symbolism of the plaques is, in actuality, mythologizing, and that is always open to a falsification of history. Bernal, by using the symptomatic method, would not be challenged by the fact that the ancient Egyptians were a black African population. He would not hesitate to identify the Egyptians as being the genetic type of the earliest Egyptian, a Nubian. In his description of the pelasgians, who were among the earliest population of Greece, Bernal reveals no clear-cut idea of their origin. He admits the pelasgians pose a thorny problem to scholars, recognizing that they were the most widely known native population of Greece. It is very interesting to note that whenever a population presents an ongoing problem to academia in terms of their origins and identity, it is most likely due to their color and African origin. The scholar, François Dupuis, was certain that by the "authorities whom he could collect from monuments and from history, the pelasgians came originally from Ethiopia and were a powerful nation, spread over all parts of the ancient world and to which Greece, Italy, and Spain owed their civilization."[32] We must remember that Dupuis also stated that the "Ethiopians were the fathers of the Egyptians."[33]

Dupuis joins with the scholar Max Müller in displaying his utter contempt and frustration for the damage mythological symbolism has caused. Both of these scholars feel the absurdity and the insanity of mythology and the way it is practiced. The human sacrifices that have occurred throughout history are a result of such mythological thinking. Dupuis expressed the absurdity of the superstitions that mythology produced when he stated,

> The Manchoo Tartars sacrifice to Heaven at the least sign of an epidemic menacing to befall their horses. At the sacrifices made by Kublai-Kan to the Gods, he poured vases, filled with mare's milk on the ground, with the idea, that the Gods would come to drink it, and that the oblation would induce them, to take care of their herds. It will be said, that those customs are superstitious. But is there a single religion which has not superstitions very nearly equivalent to it, and which are not by its instrumentality chiefly, maintain in the mind of the people? Is it not a superstition, which makes millions of people believe that the Deity passes into a wafer, after pronouncing over it some mysterious words? That which a philosopher calls superstition, the priest calls a religious act and makes it the basis of his worship. Is it not the priest, who keeps up all the most absurd superstitions, because they are lucrative and keep

the people under his dependence, by making his
agency almost a necessary one in almost all the instances of our life?[34]

It is easy to see how the priest uses superstition as a
fear tactic to manipulate the behavior of his people. The
highest authorities of the nation sanction this. What
we see here is that the same savage and cruel practices
of antiquity by so-called primitive people is practiced
in today's' modern world by the highest authority. This
was Frazer's main point in *The Golden Bough*. We see these
practices implemented in the cultural conflicts around
the world in Africa, Asia, Europe, and Latin America.
No area of the world is exempt from this destructive
activity.

THE RELEVANCE OF RELIGION

The scholar Cheikh Anta Diop stated: "The idea of God
on his throne is a symbol. Osiris was the first god in the
history of religions to sit on the throne on judgment day,
to judge the souls of men."[35] Diop knew what we all
know; that God indeed is a symbol. He is in fact a myth
if he is a God that answers prayers, decides who lives
and who dies, and controls human behavior the world
over. The French scholar, François Dupuis, in an abridg-
ment of his larger work, the *Origins of All Cults*, gives a
courageous and accurate account of the theological dynamics that we face in the universe today. Dupuis realized that religion, along with race, is the most controversial and emotional subject that is discussed in the
world today. Religion has caused untold misery and
death and continues to be a focal point that we experience in the global conflicts that we see in the world today. Most importantly, Dupuis saw and understood the
symbolic, mythological and superstitious nature of the
universe in which we live. His abridged edition of *The
Origin of All Religious Worship* is an outstanding and courageous attempt to set the record straight on the dy-

namics of religion and its effect on humanity the world over. To get a feel of the religious environment in Dupuis' time, Dupuis wanted to destroy his original work, *The Origins of All Cults,* because he "feared that he would incite the religious community against him, he wanted to burn the manuscript but his wife took possession of it, and kept it from his sight, so long as she feared the loss of the work, the fruit of so many nights study."[36] Dupuis understood that religion is an ingrained superstition in humanity. He felt the impossibility of ridding the world of that superstition. That is clear in his statement:

> I am aware, that the mere proposition to examine, whether a religion is necessary or not, will revolt many minds, and that religions have struck too extended and too profound roots all over the Earth, that it would be a kind of folly, to pretend to day, to uproot the ancient tree of superstition, under the shade of which almost all men believe it to be necessary to repose. Therefore it is not at all my intentions to attempt it; because it is the same with religion as with those diseases, of which the germ is transmitted by the fathers to their progeny for a series of ages, and against which art has no remedy to offer. It is an evil the more incurable, as it makes us even fear the remedies, which might cure it.[37]

Dupuis goes as far as anyone can go in addressing a problem with religious thought as it is infected with mythology. His apparent hopelessness is a result of him not experiencing an alternative to his dire situation. Like Diop, he had not experienced...or more correctly...he did not recognize the dynamics of the Symptomatic Thought Process. He did not realize that there is indeed an alternative to the symbolic, mythological, superstitious world that he was encased in. It is interesting to note that the writings of Diop and Dupuis dealt in a thorough way with the two most important issues that have caused conflict and violence the world over, and both of their writings had to be buried. This tendency to destroy and bury literature that has a liberating effect on humanity will aid in a big way in destroying civilization itself. The refusal to allow important information to reach the masses of the people is totally inexcusable and must be stopped at all cost.

Frazer's *Golden Bough* is a true classic. Even his harshest critic, Theodore H. Gaster, stated,

> Indeed, what Freud did for the individual, Frazer did for civilization as a whole. For as Freud deepened men's insight into the behavior of individuals by uncovering the ruder world of the subconscious, from which so much of it springs, so Frazer enlarged man's understanding of the behavior of societies by laying bare the primitive concepts and modes of thought which underlie and inform so many of their institutions and which persist, as a subliminal element of their culture, in their traditional folk customs.[38]

Gaster goes on to say, that

> it was Frazer more than anyone else who first sought to classify and coordinate this vast body of material and to construct out of it an overall picture of how, at the primitive level, Man in general thinks and acts, and of how that primitive mentality persists sporadically even in the more advanced stages of his development. It is in this attempt to *construe* the data in universal terms, just as much as in its unparalleled coverage of them, that the distinctive significance of *The Golden Bough* really lies; and this it is that has earned for it the status of a classic. What, in effect, Frazer did was not only to enable us to see more clearly "the rock whence we were hewn," but also to provide a broad, psychological frame of reference within which the phenomenon of particular cultures, ancient and modern alike, might be more adequately interpreted and understood.[39]

Gaster is absolutely correct in his two statements about Frazer. Frazer laid bare the phenomenon of the forces that led man to be a truly symbolic animal. And it is these symbolic forces that must be made symptomatic to usher in a true civilized world. Frazer saw the golden bough as mistletoe, but the late A B. Cook suggested that it "may have been an apple tree, since apple trees are still to be found at Nemi, and mistletoe grows on them."[40] As noted by J. Rendel Harris, Cook suggested that

> The religious or mythological transition from oak tree to apple tree corresponds to an actual advance in prehistoric civilization. Tribes that were once content to subsist upon acorns and wild fruits in general learnt gradually the art of cultivating the more edible varieties of the latter, and so came in the course of many centuries to keep well-stocked orchards....The apple in particular, the oldest cultivated fruit-tree in Europe, is felt to be the equivalent to the oak.[41]

Because of Cook's suggestion above, and since mistletoe grows on apple trees, it could be that the golden bough was in reality a golden apple. For instance, a legendary myth of the golden apple is that it was the cause of the Trojan War.

> Although the apple symbolized fertility and eternal life, it also bore a dangerous, even diabolical dimension. In the blending of Christian, Celtic, and Greco-Roman myths, there emerged two apples: the good apple and the bad apple, a dualism that has followed the fruit into the late twentieth century and found its origins in the ancient Greco-Roman myths. The tragedy of the Trojan War, after all, was set in motion by the rolling of the golden apple.[42]

Out of the mythological symbolic syndrome came apple tree wassailing, a ritual involving drinking to the health of the apple trees.

Figure 14: Apple Wassailing. Mark Rosenstein: *In Praise of Apples*, Lark Books. Used with Permission of Lark Books.

Apple wassailing, a form of which is still practiced in some rural areas of England on Twelfth Night, is an ancient ritual in which the apple is celebrated as a symbol of fertility. Some English men and women, in fact, still believe that wassailing is their best assurance of a successful apple crop.

In older forms of this ritual, villagers gathered beneath the largest tree in the orchard and suspended pieces of cider-soaked toast from its branches. The toast, it was thought, would attract robins, once believed to be good spirits. To prevent evil spirits from wending their way to the huge apple tree, strategically placed villagers fired shotguns into the air throughout the orchard.

Singing participants would dance around the tree, dousing its trunk and roots with hard cider and quenching their own thirst as well. As time passed, the wassailing ceremony – heretofore a solemn tribute to the deity of the apple tree – took on an extraordinarily jolly tone, possibly due to the quantity of cider consumed. Wassail, made from cider and ale, is still a traditional English drink and is frequently consumed on Twelfth Night and Christmas Eve. It is usually served in a bowl, with roasted apples floating on its surface.[43]

As stated earlier, mythology enables the manipulation of facts and phenomena that is unparalleled in the history of the world. Just as mythology allows oak trees to be apple trees, it allows Black people to become white people at the whim of a symbolizing attitude. That symbolizing attitude is solely the possession of *Homo sapiens*. Unfortunately, as scholarship has done with the treatment of the Egyptians, mythology allows academia to classify people's racial identity to fit their racist agenda, to initiate, according to Diop, "the most monstrous falsification in the history of humanity."[44]

SIGNS AND SYMPTOMS

As stated earlier, it is very important to understand and to realize that the word *sign* is synonymous with the word symptom. Again, as stated earlier, we agree with the late scholar Edward Whitmont that there are two approaches to the problems that life presents, a symptomatic one and a symbolic one. However, unlike Whitmont, I see that the only possible way to live in a healthy way is a symptomatic existence, free of symbols. In other words, to live a life without a symbolizing attitude. The histories of the world as written in our textbooks are those that have been reduced by those with a symbolizing attitude. Which means that the evidences we find in a symbolizing civilization are interpreted and examined from a mythological point of view that leads to a falsification of history as it is taught in much of the so-called civilized world. Any reading of history must take into account how the symbol systems mutilated symptoms that were indicators of what occurred throughout the whole of civilization. "Unlike symbols, indices are part of what they refer to and this makes them reliable in ways that symbols are not."[45] This is very important, for it shows that symptoms are much more reliable than symbol systems. Because these symptoms carry their original stuff to which they point, they are much more reliable than the mythological symbols that are continually used to interpret our history throughout civilization. Symptoms are a language that is void of myth. Unlike symbolic languages, they are disease free. They are free of being placed in a category designated by Max Müller when he stated that mythology is a disease of language. When reading history and interpreting it from a nonsymbolic mode, it opens up a whole new world that has truth at its core. That status can never be attained by those who have a symbolizing attitude.

Symptoms have been with humans from their genesis. The same cannot be said of symbols; for, which I stated before, symbols came out of a symptomatic environment, and that occurrence we have labeled a neurological misadventure of primordial man. The signs of civilization that present themselves as symptoms have been a prevalent and natural and also necessary part of this universe. When we read history with a symptomatic attitude, a qualitatively different story emerges from the one that we get from a symbolizing attitude. With the advent of molecular biology, we are privy to an understanding of the phenomenon of history and what has taken place. As the scholar Spencer Wells states, "Myths fail to account for the spectrum of cultures, shapes, sizes and colors we see when we look at people around the world."[46] Wells goes on to state, "Herodotus, the 5th century B.C. Greek historian, provided posterity with far more than a description of Greco-Persian wars. He also gave us our first clear description of human diversity, viewed through an idiosyncratic classical lens."[47]

171

Allen Wilson, the late Australian biochemist, was an expert in molecular biology. By using DNA and proteins, he was able to track the path of humans as they left Africa. His methods were those of using signs and analyzing the symptoms that resulted from his DNA research. His partner, Rebecca Cann, aided him in studying the pattern of DNA variation in humans from around the world. The results were that all humans came from a woman in Africa who lived approximately 200,000 years ago. But the important thing to remember about the research of Wilson and Cann is that they used a symptomatic approach. They did not mythologize the results from their research. By not mythologizing the results of their painstaking work, a true understanding of our human past took shape. There are scholars who insist upon mythologizing science. Some have even gone so far as to say that science itself is a myth, and that the results of scientific inquiry are mythological. They want the mythological element to remain so that they can manipulate scientific findings to fit their particular idiosyncrasies and whims. In his book, *The Star of Deep Beginnings*, the scholar, Charles Finch, states: "It is impossible not to think mythically, indeed, be mythical, for the mythic impulse is innate to humanity, suffusing all human endeavor, including science."[48] The above represents the typical approach of traditional scholarship. However, if it is impossible not to think mythically, then we have to say that it is impossible to solve our problems. There is no question that the mythic mentality is the source of our problems throughout the universe. I refuse to believe that the problem of racism will not be solved; the problem of cultural conflict will not be solved; and the problems of war will not be solved. And that is exactly what it means by stating that it is impossible not to think mythically. For humanity must realize once and for all that the symbolic thought processes that produce mythology and superstition must be eliminated if we are to be a civilized universe. A science that is based on myth is a science that distorts history to the fullest. It is an event that creates, as Diop states, a "monstrous falsification of history." And to think mythically continues this falsification of history. By thinking symptomatically, we eradicate the falsification of history and open up opportunities to solve the problems of the world. It is now commonly stated in the scientific community that a large number of Y polymorphisms indicate an African origin of modern humans. The key terms in that statement are "Y polymorphisms" and "indicate," both of which are signs that are symptomatic of an African origin of modern humans. The word symbols has no place in that assertion, as using it in that statement would be, according to Müller, "a disease of language." Symptoms are so natural in human existence that the word symptom itself does not have to be uttered. For all the events that happen in human life, we experience as signs of our interaction and experience that which comes from being alive and functioning in the world. To add a mythological and symbolic content to that activity is not only unnatural; it is the beginning of a neurological misadventure that will cause conflict and death to those who participate in that farce. Any reading of human history will show the dynamics of what mythologizing symptoms will do.

There is a marked difference when using symptoms instead of symbols. Frazer, for instance, says, "The first signs of purity show themselves."[49] He follows that up by stating: "Symptoms of puberty appeared on a girl for the first time."[50] Frazer is using signs and symptoms interchangeably. He would not use symbols instead of symptoms, for the symbols have no actuality in the event that he tries to describe. If he had used symbols in his language, it would be indeed a disease of language, as Müller stated. By using the word symptom in language to describe our everyday activity, we are in contact and a part of the actual dynamics that we describe. Symbols, which produce myth, can never be an adequate expression of participation in the actual event that we describe. Symbols produce a mythological setting that has no part in the original or real drama that we partake in and describe to the people with whom we want to communicate. In another statement, Frazer states, "Yet despite the great heat they were everywhere signs of autumn."[51] The signs of autumn were symptoms that one experiences as they anticipate the beauty of autumn. That is decisive, for autumn could never be experienced symbolically because there is no reality of a symbolic description. It is only through a symptomatic approach that we can experience and participate in the reality and become a part of the reality that we point to and describe. By thinking symptomatically, we behave in such a way that leaves no room for the falsehoods that symbols produce. Using the Symptomatic Thought Process, the possibility of entering into superstitious behavior is zero. Because the symbolizing attitude no longer exists, being superstitious is obliterated. Throughout the reading of history, it is quite clear that authenticity and sanity take place when symptoms are used instead of symbols by virtue of the fact that the absurdity of mythology is eliminated. The insanity that comes from mythology was called a mythic period when everything was mythologized to such an extent that it later caused

Figure 15: Incense burner from Tomb L24 - known as a Censer
Reprinted courtesy of the Oriental Institute
of the University of Chicago

a barbaric civilization. That barbaric civilization has created an absurd existence based on absurd ideas that only a mythological and symbolic attitude could produce.

Cheikh Anta Diop, in his remarks on the Censer that was discovered in Nubia by Keith Steele of the University of Chicago, and that was made public by a researcher named Bruce Williams, states: "The Censer is the most ancient figure of a King found in the Nile Valley. Indecipherable signs of hieroglyphic form presaging the writing of the period close to the end of the fourth millenium also were noted."[52]

What is important in this statement is the "signs of hieroglyphic form." These signs are symptoms that will show, and they are the reality of the Censer and its relation to Egyptian history. Signs are symptoms and always will be symptoms. These symptoms will provide information that otherwise would never have been obtained. By following the symptomatic approach, we no longer will get bogged down with the superstitions that make up religion. As Diop stated, "The idea of God on his throne is a symbol. Osiris was the first God in the history of religions to sit on a throne on judgment day to judge the soul of man."[53] Similar to the view of François Dupuis, the fact that God is a symbol follows that all the gods are mythological beings that spread throughout the world as symbol systems. Dupuis is very telling when he said:

> I am aware, that the mere proposition to examine, whether a religion is necessary or not, will revolt many minds, and that religions have struck too extended and too profound roots all over the Earth, that it would be a kind of folly, to pretend to day (sic), to uproot the ancient tree of superstition, under the shade of which almost all man believed it to be necessary to repose. Therefore it is not at all my intention to attempt it; because it is the same with religion as with those diseases, of which the germ is

transmitted by the fathers to their progeny for a series of ages, and against which art has no remedy to offer. It is an evil the more incurable, as it makes us even fear the remedies, which might cure it.[54]

Dupuis realized the sensitivity and tension that arises when one talks about religion and its theological attributes. Dupuis realized that one always inquires about a substitute when there is a serious call for the elimination of any entity. There is always anxiety about the remedies that take the place of what has traditionally been held as sacred. So one can imagine, as Dupuis stated above, the revulsion that occurs when one talks about the elimination of religions, and what takes their place. In my many lectures and talks on symbolism, the question of what will take its place is always raised. As stated throughout this book, symptoms would replace symbolism and would be the cure for all the problems that exist because of symbolism. When one understands the uses of symptoms and how they interplay with human existence, and reveal themselves as signs, one will come to a clear understanding of how symptoms supercede symbols and provide us with information and a dynamic that allows not only reeducation to take place but a qualitative change in human behavior. The goal is always to go from the symbolic to the healthy state of the symptom. That occurs whenever there is a symbolic situation at hand. One example could be illustrated in the following article from London's *Financial Times*:

> A committee of senior executives from Sony Music and Bertelsmann Music Group will meet shortly to decide the future organization and cost structure for the world's second-largest recorded music group.
>
> Nevertheless, the green light for the 50-50 merger of the recorded music arms of Sony Corporation and Bertelsmann, the German media group, represents a *symbolic* victory for the industry's dominant operators. They have persuaded regulators to waive con-

cerns over apparent price collusion and potential market abuse, arguing that the competitive landscape has been transformed by the growth of mass market retailers and the onset of internet piracy. Rival music companies such as EMI of the UK and US-based Warner Music, which abandoned their own merger four years ago in the face of regulatory opposition, will monitor the deal for *signs* that the enlarged company can increase sales and develop new artists.[55]

This article clearly shows the dynamics of symbols and symptoms that take place in a merger between two music giants. It is noted that the European Commission's acceptance of the merger was categorized as a "symbolic victory" for the industry's dominant operators. But the most important and necessary dynamic was the monitoring of the signs that will show that the enlarged company can increase sales and develop new artists. Those signs are symptoms that will catapult the company to profitability. The dynamic here is to show how symbols will be turned into symptoms so that a successful transaction and conclusion can occur.

Symptoms override symbols in all instances. That has to be understood and experienced if the dynamics of today's world are to be dealt with and understood at all. We return to Cheikh Anta Diop's suggestion that Egyptians had a symbolic conception of the world: "The last meaning they gave to things, which was a symbolic meaning, was not meant for everyone to understand or bear the weight of."[56]

That statement about the ancient Egyptians is relevant for our lives today. When businesses operate in a symbolic vein, deception is usually the mode of the day. Business practices often become inaccessible not only for the chief executive involved but for the workforce of the company — and that is an ingredient for financial disaster. In that case, the company is mired in mythology that is so confusing that no one really knows what they are doing or what goals they want to achieve

It is essential to understand that practically every entity can be symbolized. That is understandable because it is understood that humans are symbolizing animals. As Herbert Read states, in *Sirlot's Dictionary of Symbols*,

> Man...is a symbolizing animal; it is evident that at no stage in the development of civilization has man been able to dispense with symbols. Science and technology have not freed man from his dependence on symbols; indeed, it might be argued that they have increased his need for them. In any case, symbology itself is now a science...[57]

So it is essential to understand that every word we use must be symptomatically applied. The following are words that must lose their symbolic inference and become symptoms: The word color refers to the "conception of black and white as diametrically opposed symbols of the positive and negative."[58] The color black, for the most part, has been a negative symbol that has always been inferior to the color white. "When two colors are contrasted in a given symbolic field, the inferior color is feminine in character, and the superior is masculine."[59] So, to take the black/white relationship, black is inferior and feminine; while the color white is always represented as superior. Of course, there have been instances where the color black and the color white have had other symbolic inference. But the overriding factor is that the color black has had negative connotations that have always been inferior to the color white – and that phenomenon is entirely due to symbolism, which when applied results in mythology and superstition. This superstition becomes ingrained in civilization as fact. When color loses its symbolic intent, it becomes a symptom of an entity that is liberated from all negative characteristics. There are, indeed, no negative characteristics involved in the color black. The word loses all evil connotations and becomes a productive entity. Then, and only then, can it become symptomatic in its use and be used as a symptom of any situation that it finds itself in.

Table 1 illustrates the symbolic intent of words opposed to the symptomatic content of words.

It is crucial that we understand how symptoms should be used as opposed to symbolic intent. Our whole existence should be an exercise of reading the signs and symbols of the universe, which means reading the symptoms and, by doing so, living our lives symptomatically and turning symbols into symptoms wherever we find them. We must completely understand that symptoms supersede symbols in every area of human existence. Symptoms are a language that must be read and understood. Whether the actual word symptom or the word symbol is mentioned in literature itself does not mean that the entity is not present. In reality, there are only two ways to read literature, and those two ways are symptomatically or symbolically, like life itself, which is lived either symptomatically or symbolically. The prevailing assumption is that we must live symptomatically and symbolically, along with reading literature symptomatically and symbolically, but that creates a schizophrenic individual who is void of any productivity and healthy behavior patterns. The healthy approach is to read and to write literature from a wholly symptomatic viewpoint. When reading literature, one must discard the symbolic intent or the symbolism in the literature; one must read and digest the literature symptomatically. Two articles written in 2006, one in the *Financial Times* and the other in *The Wall Street Journal*, illustrate my point. The one in the *Financial Times* is as follows:

"Darfur is a Disturbing Symptom of a Wider Problem"

We have got to know Darfur as Africa's "hidden war," the "unseen tragedy," the "forgotten crisis". Well, not any longer it isn't.

Table 1: Word Table Illustrating Symbols vs. Symptoms

WORD	SYMBOLIC INTENT	SYMPTOMATIC
Black	Negative; evil; feminine	A sign pointing to color
White	Positive; superior; masculine	A sign pointing to lack of color
Cat	Associated with the moon; black cat; color associated with darkness and death	Small animal of the feline family
Darkness	Associated with the principle of evil; related to mystic nothingness	Absence of light
Island	Isolation; solitude; death	A small body of land surrounded by water
Fox	The devil; base attitudes;	A wild mammal of the canine family
Footprints	Symbolize the way of gods, saints or demonic spirits	A natural sign that something was or is present
Climate	Interplay between space, situation, the elements and temperature	Natural signs of the weather
Rope	General symbol for binding and connection; expressing the sacred, inner path that binds man's intellect with his spiritual essence	A continuous chain
Room	Individuality; private thoughts; closed room with no windows symbolizes virginity and/or other kinds of non communication	A partitioned space within a larger dwelling
House	Repository of all wisdom; representation of the different layers of the psyche	A dwelling constructed of various materials for habitation
Fire	Flame; life; health; superiority; control– symbol of transformation and regeneration	A chemical result of burning elements that release heat and light
Egg	Immortality; seed of generation;	Reproductive cell of female animals, frequently found in a hard shell
Earth	Light and darkness; Yin/Yang	Ground or soil; third planet from the Sun
Eagle	Height; sun spirit; father; associated with the gods of power and war; equal in the air to the lion on earth	Powerful bird of prey with strong wings and soaring flight
Bee	Work; obedience; diligence; eloquence;	Hairy insect skilled in extracting nectar and pollen from flowers
Angel	Symbol of invisible forces; of powers ascending and descending between the source-of-life and the world of phenomena	A symptom of mythological thinking
Stone	Symbolizes unity, strength, cohesion, harmonious reconciliation with self	A rock; compacted earth; mineral matter
Steps	Ascension; gradation; communication between different, vertical levels	Structure used to ascend or descend
Sun	Purification; tribulation; source of supreme riches; Its positive symbol — glory, spirituality; illumination; idealism incompatible with reality	The star around which other planets of the solar system orbit its negative symbol — vanity;
Treasure	Sublimated form of the symbolism of the color gold – work and suffering contribute to progress in its profoundest sense of self-awareness, virtue, and superiority	Hidden riches; something of value
Tree	Life of the cosmos; Inexhaustible life; immortality	Tall woody plant, typically with a single trunk

The gathering disaster in the western outback of Sudan has, belatedly, grabbed the world's attention. But by the time the "forgotten war" claimed the headlines it was officially over with a ceasefire of sorts already agreed between the government and Darfur-based rebels.

Near silence throughout the whole of a year-long conflict in the region has given way to alarm. Darfur has become a world cause, combining elements of the Rwanda catastrophe 10 years ago and the Ethiopian famine 10 years before that. But how long will this attention be sustained? And will it go any way towards remedying the core problems that brought about the present crisis?

Emergency aid is badly needed, in larger quantities and more quickly than has been coming up to now. What immediate aid can do is save lives and buy time for Darfur. But let's have no illusion that it will solve Sudan's problem.[60]

The title of White's article, "Darfur Is a Disturbing Symptom of a Wider Problem," shows how symptoms are used in a way that symbols could never be used. It also shows the overall superiority of symptoms over symbols. In White's description of the conflict, he states that "Darfur has become a world cause combining elements of the Rwanda catastrophe ten years ago and the Ethiopian famine ten years before that." In White's phrasing, i.e., "combining elements of the Rwanda catastrophe...and the Ethiopian famine," the word *element* is a sign or symptom of the catastrophe. Symbols can never be used in that case because symbols are disconnected with reality. In other words, symbols, which are synonymous with myth, can never be involved in the reality that is actually taking place, but are totally divorced from it; whereas symptoms are a necessary and total part of the reality that is in question. In this case, it is "Darfur has become a world cause combining elements of a Rwanda catastrophe and the Ethiopian famine." White goes on to say that the distinctions are more tribal than cultural, that "the tragedy is that the conflict does not stem from an ethnic confrontation but has become one created by the rebellion and the brutal response to it." White is describing the dynamics of symptoms within this conflict, and he is totally correct in labeling both groups as black Africans, as both groups are black, both are Muslim. The symptoms reflect the reality of the situation, and to mythologize these symptoms is to create further problems and complications that will lead to further conflict and death.

The traditional viewpoint that places symbols as an indispensable part of human interaction and experience is totally false. In fact the symbolic dynamic is the direct cause of the rebellion and violence in Darfur. By reacting to the symbols, and to the symbolic behavior that caused the conflict in the first place, there will be no end in sight but an increase in the loss of lives. An understanding of the symptomatic dynamics of the tragedy in Darfur is the only way to remedy the problem.

Another illustration of the dynamic of symptoms and symbols and their uses appeared in a 2002 article written by Stephen Kinzer in the *New York Times*:

> A Clash of Symbols: Defining Holy Sites on Faith – Hatred and violence are hardly new in the Holy Land, but the battle raging around the Church of the Nativity in Bethlehem is especially heart-rending for many religious believers. Few events symbolize the tragedy of the current conflict more poignantly than the military siege at the place where the Prince of Peace was born. But was he?

> "It's very doubtful that Jesus was born in Bethlehem, " said Hershel Shanks, editor of the magazine *Biblical Archaeology Review*. "He's always referred to as the Nazarene, not the Bethlehemite. But there were very clear reasons for putting him in Bethlehem. He was supposed to be the scion of David who came back

and gave us salvation, and since David was born in Bethlehem, there was a desire to put Jesus there. This doesn't reduce the power of symbolic stories, but it's not historic reality."

Archaeologists have made discoveries that challenge fundamental traditions of Judaism as well as those of Christianity and Islam. One who teaches at Tel Aviv University, Ze'ev Herzog, published an article in 1999 asserting that historical evidence about the emergence of the Jewish people tells a story "radically different" from what most Jews are taught to believe.

"There is certainly a tremendous gap between archaeological knowledge and what people want to believe from tradition," Professor Fears said, 'but there are also gaps in what archaeologists think they can prove. Even when they can prove something or make it more likely, that does not in any way undermine the deep attachment that people have to these places."[61]

The previous article demonstrates clearly the dynamics of symptoms and symbols. The symptomatic results of archaeological research demonstrate how symbols and symptoms clash in a search for reality. The first and second paragraph of the above article shows the power of symbolic stories. These symbolic stories are the tradition on which civilization bases its faith. However, as the article states, "These symbolic stories are not historic reality," simply because these symbolic stories become myths and superstition, which, in fact, all religions are. The unavoidable clash occurs when the symptoms reveal truths that are at odds with the myths that have endured for centuries. Unfortunately, the overwhelming majority of people have lived their lives based on these symbolic assumptions, which has culminated into a superstitious tradition that has created an environment where a permanent state of conflict, war, and deep-seated racism have been allowed to flourish, as if indeed, that were the norm. Even when faced with the truths that symptoms have revealed, there has been a tendency to mythologize the symptomatic findings that have corrected the historical inaccuracies.

Unless we make an earnest attempt to face the realities of civilization, we can expect to continue on a path of barbarism and destruction. Nowhere is that more evident than the struggles in the Middle East, in Africa, and in the conflicts throughout the world. Former Prime Minister Mahathir Mohamad of Malaysia couldn't have said it better, when he stated in *New African,* "We still think that might is right, that the strong must dominate, and the weak must submit. Frankly, I don't think we have progressed much from the Stone Age. They used clubs, but we have nuclear weapons."[62] Dr. Mahathir believed that this new attitude was symptomatic of a new racism. Indeed, it is imperative that we decide to discard symbols and live a symptomatic existence. Only then can there be any hope for a civilized world.

Civilization or Barbarism

The two scholars who challenged the basic assumptions of civilization were Cheikh Anta Diop and Charles François Dupuis. Dupuis, as stated earlier, was known for his great work, *The Origin of All Cults.* The abridged edition in English came out as *The Origin of All Religious Worship.* Dupuis argued that all religion has its origin in Egypt, and that the ancient Egyptians were a black, African people. Dupuis was of the opinion that the Ethiopians were the fathers of the Egyptians. For Dupuis, all religions were mythological and had their base in the mythological system of the Egyptians. As Martin Bernal mentioned in his book, *Black Athena,* Dupuis' work had to be buried, for his honesty and scholarship was a threat to those who use religion as a means to confuse and create fear in the minds of people.

Dupuis also saw all religions as superstition, and he took the responsibility to state that all religions interfered with the productive behavior of people and caused superstition to be rampant in the decision making and mental processes of human beings. Dupuis stated:

> I am aware, that the mere proposition to examine, whether a religion is necessary or not, will revolt many minds, and that religions have struck too extended and too profound roots all over the Earth, that it would be a kind of folly, to pretend to day, to uproot the ancient tree of superstition, under the shade of which almost all men believed it to be necessary to repose. Therefore it is not at all my intention to attempt it; because it is the same with religion as with those diseases, of which the germ is transmitted by the fathers to their progeny for a series of ages, and against which art has no remedy to offer. It is an evil the more incurable, as it makes us even fear the remedies, which might cure it.[63]

Dupuis understood very clearly that religion was a superstition and nothing more. He felt all religion had to be eradicated and, importantly, he equated religion with disease, which is easily understood once we appreciate, with Max Müller; that indeed, religion is a disease of language and, in actuality, is a mental aberration. Dupuis understood how symbolism was ingrained in the neurological processes of humans. Unfortunately, he thought it was almost impossible for man to rid himself of his superstitious nature, which therefore would cause all religions to continue to flourish throughout civilization.

Dupuis eloquently described how religion causes superstitious in every area of life. The rituals caused by religion have caused damage that is unparalleled in world history. The idea of praying to a deity for assistance that is denied to another is not only absurd but is insane in all its manifestations.

Cheikh Anta Diop, the Senegalese scholar, was not far behind, when he stated, "The idea of God on his throne is a symbol. Osiris was the first God in the history of religions to sit on a throne on judgment day, to judge the souls of men."[64]

Diop also understood clearly that the idea of God as a symbol played an important part in the behavior of man throughout civilization. Diop understood that it took a special state of mind to produce a symbolic, mythological framework that would be the guide to man's relationships. Indeed, the behavior patterns that have their origins in symbol systems caused civilization to become barbaric. Diop, following Max Müller's observation that "mythology is a disease of language," stated: "It takes a special state of mind that prompts one to seek secondary meanings for words rather than give them their usual significance."[65] Diop went on to state, quite candidly, "This special state of mind arises from an insane misinterpretation of texts,"[66] which he saw as typical of modern scholarship.

It is extremely important to understand that the symbol systems that created religion are so destructive that it is imperative that we find an answer to their elimination, and that we do not fear where the search will take us. That search has been completed with the Symptomatic Thought Process, which eliminates any need for symbols and their resulting rituals and superstition.

The debate between Max Müller and Gerald Massey was an interesting one, for it showed the basic misunderstanding of the role of mythology in language. Müller's statement that "mythology is a disease of language" was challenged by Gerald Massey in his book, *Gerald Massey's Lectures*, where he stated that "instead of mythology being a disease of language, it may be truly said that our theology is a disease of mythology."[67] Massey is mistaken when he says that theology is a disease of mythology, for theology is in itself mythology.

Theology is but an element of mythology and, in reality, it cannot be separated from mythology. For all of Massey's writing on religion, symbolism, and myth, and its distortions, Massey failed to realize the destructive nature of mythology and its symbolic content. That is the one serious flaw in his massive writings: his inability to understand the true nature of mythology and its symbolic origins. But that is understandable when we see the traditional assumptions that have been held about symbolism by scholars of all disciplines. Massey was on target when he stated "the simple realities of the earliest times were expressed by signs and symbols."[68] That statement was repeated in 2001 by African-American artist David Hammons, when he indicated that he developed inspiration for his art by "reading the signs and symbols of the street" while sitting on a bench on a summer evening. These statements show that beginning from time immemorial, man's thought process, behavior, and motivation have always stemmed from an approach dictated by symptoms and symbols, which produces what we call a very schizophrenic human, for as stated earlier, we must decide whether to act upon our signs or symbols, although remembering that signs and symptoms are synonymous. So in order to free ourselves from our schizophrenic behavior, we must behave symptomatically without symbolic input. Symbols must be completely eliminated from our thought processes.

CHAPTER TEN

The Symptomatic Thought Process and the Future

To properly understand how symptoms evolve, it is necessary to realize that the human brain, although complicated, is part of the whole physical process of the human body. The brain itself is not a symbol, but a vital part of the physical makeup of humans. Out of the human brain comes stimuli that affect the behavior of all mankind, resulting in speech, which is the origin of human language. The stimuli produce vibrations, or waves, that are symptomatic of the neurological processes in the human brain. How we react to these stimuli determines our behavior and our decision making in all human activity. With these neurological processes, we begin to understand and to question everything that we see and come in contact with. If we symbolize or mythologize what we see and come in contact with, that creates a neurological misadventure. When man began to mythologize his environment, he became a symbolic-behaving being. In other words, it can be stated that when man began to symbolize the stimuli that he received from his environment, he began to think mythically. As stated before, this has caused all the problems that we face in civilization today. If humans had begun from a symbolic base instead of a symptomatic one, there would be no neurological misadventure.

The scholar Max Müller spoke of how language was produced by the vibrations that came from the human brain and how they formed the vowels that made up the words that produce language. He stated,

> We know now what vowels are made of. They are produced by the form of the vibrations. They vary like the *timbre* of different instruments, and we in reality change the instruments on which we speak when we change the buccal tubes in order to pronounce *a, e, i, o, u* (the vowels to be pronounced as in Italian).[1]

However, when we begin to symbolize the energy, or the stimuli that arise from vibrations, language indeed becomes a disease. Müller stated, "By a kind of negative reasoning, it had long been supposed that, as quality could neither arise from the amplitude nor from the duration, it must be due to the form of the vibrations."[2] So it must be clearly understood that natural and healthy language is symptomatic. Language is not symbolic. When it is symbolic, it indeed becomes a disease of language. Müller is confused about the processes that make up a disease state for language. For example, he stated that metaphor is one of the most powerful engines in the construction of human speech. And without it, we can hardly imagine how any language could have progressed beyond the simplest rudiments. Then he goes on to state:

> Whenever any word, that was at first used metaphorically, is used without a clear conception of the steps that led from its original to its metaphorical meaning, there is danger of mythology; whenever those steps are forgotten and artificial steps put in their places, we have mythology, or, if I may say so, we have diseased language, whether that language refers to religious or secular interests.[3]

Müller does not seem to understand that metaphor is indeed mythology. Critics have accused him of keeping in place the mythology that he is trying to destroy, or, in fact, remythologizing the myths and rituals that he attempted to eliminate. That is understandable when you realize that Müller had no alternative for his symbol systems. He did not have the luxury of implementing a Symptomatic Thought Process in place of a symbolic one. So it is easy to understand why Müller never did accomplish what he set out to do – and that is how to make a diseased language healthy again. What Müller did accomplish was to understand that there was something very wrong in the neurological processes that created symbolism. Unfortunately, he got caught in the circular dynamics of the myths and the language that he sought to analyze and understand.

What is extremely important for us to understand here is that the stimuli we encounter are symptomatic of the events around us. Following are descriptions of two separate examples of symptomatic dynamics:

> A long table in front of the stage was decorated with oversized red, black and green candles and other symbols of Kwanzaa. Vendors' booths created an indoor African market and the air was scented with incense and the delectable aroma of fried fish and sautéed onions.[4]

Walking down West 43rd Street the other day, I was drawn to an old haunt by the seductive aroma of baking apples, cinnamon and butter. It was emanating from sour-cream apple walnut pies.[5]

Although the Kwanzaa event was marked by a conglomeration of symbols that are evident in all rituals, the aromas described in both settings are truly symptomatic of the actual dynamics taking place. The experience of scent and aroma are symptomatic of a condition. When we follow the symptoms of our condition instead of the symbols, we have a reality that is existentially connected. The symbols of a condition can never be connected in any existential way to our condition.

Max Müller made an attempt to turn what can be described as a mythological and allegorical event into a symptomatic one:

> According to Herodotus, an equally orthodox writer, the two black doves from Egypt which flew to Libya and Dodona, and directed the people to found in each place an oracle of Zeus, were in reality women who came from Thebes. The one that came to Dodona was called a dove, because, he says, speaking a foreign tongue, she seemed to utter sounds like a bird, and she was called a black dove on account of her black Egyptian colour. This explanation he represents not as a guess of his own, but as founded on a statement made to him by Egyptian priests; and I count it therefore as an historical, not as a merely allegorical interpretation. Similar explanations become more frequent in later Greek historians, who, unable to admit anything supernatural or miraculous as historical fact, strip the ancient legends of all that renders them incredible, and then treat them as narrations of real events, and not as fiction.[6]

This method of stripping the supernatural or miraculous from historical events is called demythologizing. It can also be described as turning symbols into symptoms, which is restoring a diseased language to a healthy state.

That is the reason why Müller said he could accept the event as historical fact rather than allegorical interpretation. What is symbolic must be eradicated and turned into symptoms.

The process of mythological change, as it addresses each situation, is truly unique. Nowhere is that better demonstrated than in classical antiquity with Celtic legends. The dynamic of the mythical god, Apollo, is one case in point. J. Rendel Harris believes that the great god, Apollo, the Lord of Light and Healing, was only an apple in disguise.[7] A.B. Cook believed that since the mistletoe is found growing on the apple tree, that the apple and its mistletoe are the original sacred symbols.[8] Harris also believed that Apollo, in the Greek religion, had its origin in the northern regions (the name Apollo is not Greek, but a name that came from a northern tribe). Gerald Massey believed that the god Apollo had its origin in Africa, and particularly Egypt, where Apollo was known as a God of healing and light, related to the sun, but not the sun itself. The Greek Apollo is the same solilunar personification as is the divinity Thoth. It is understood that the myth of the Greek god Apollo has its origin in Egypt.

Mythology is at the discretion of the mythmaker. It is the sole product of symbolizing humans. It is the product of a symbolic species – symbolic-behaving humans with a symbolic attitude. Myth-making man is a very superstitious man, which in turn makes him a religious human. The famous statement by Max Müller, that "mythology is a disease of language," has been ridiculed widely by scholars. Massey believed that instead of mythology being a "disease of language," it may truly be said that theology is a disease of mythology. Massey failed to realize that theology is not a disease of mythology; in fact, theology is mythology itself. You cannot say mythology is a disease of mythology; but Müller is correct, mythology is a disease of language. Massey is just plain incorrect in quoting Max Müller's statement on mythology. As I said earlier in previous chapters, the reality of antiquity was expressed by signs and symbols. This means the interplay of symptoms and symbols was the most fundamental and profound way of communication. This very fundamental way of communication and behavior is being used in today's world.

LIVING OUR LIVES OUT SYMPTOMATICALLY

It is very important to show how symptoms form the natural ingredient of the behavior process. Symbols are not only inferior to symptoms, but are an unnatural part of the neurological process that is the engine that dictates human behavior. Symptoms are sometimes thought to be used only when describing the medical conditions of people. But symptoms, as Marjorie Garber points out, were first used in nonmedical cultural exchanges:

> Most experts agree that the exodus of workers from poor countries is a symptom of deep economic, social and political problems in their homelands, and can prove particularly crippling in much-needed professions in health care and education.[9]

This statement shows how symptoms are concrete signposts that provide obvious clues to the intricacies of situations that arise that need to be confronted and addressed. The predominance of situations within which signs and symptoms are disregarded can have life-threatening effects. For example, another salient area that requires a focused response to signs presents itself when business and industry do contingency planning in the event of a business disruption.

> One of the bedrock characteristics of disruptions is that they are almost never the result of a single failure. A large-scale disruption is usually the result of a confluence of several factors. Furthermore, there are typically many *signs* that a disruption is about

to take place. Like the tremors that precede a volcanic eruption, these tell-tale *signs* point to an impending catastrophe. Such *signs* are often missed or ignored by managers. But when the conditions for a disruption are present and not addressed, the likelihood of a disruption – even a low-probability one — is not very low anymore. When the telltale *signs* start to appear, a disruption may be imminent even though its timing, place, and exact form may be unknown. (Italics mine)[10]

Well-known business interruption events with significant indicators appear in Table 2.[11]

It is quite clear that by ignoring symptoms, catastrophic events can take place at any time and with a huge loss of life. The failure to heed signs or symptoms is caused by two issues that humans refuse to acknowledge – the first being the inability to confront and deal with reality because of insecurity and fear; the second being, because of that inability to deal with reality, a symbolic attitude becomes operable where mythologizing becomes the answer to solving any problem. Mythologizing a symptom is the sole characteristic of a symbolizing attitude, which makes it easier for a person who refuses to deal with reality to find an exit. Unfortunately, this phenomenon is prevalent in civilization today in every discipline, particularly race and religion. A failure to heed these symptoms will have tragic consequences for our civilization as a whole.

We seek additional examples of the act of connecting myths to symptoms in antiquity. Folklorist Adrienne Mayor has one primary objective, which was to connect the myths of ancient people with the bones buried in their land. Mayor was actually examining the natural signs, a practice that is symptomatic of the activities and life of ancient people. What is so important here is the turning of myths into symptoms, therefore eradicating the myth.

Table 2: Business Interruption Events

EVENT	SIGNS
1984 - pesticide leak in Bhopal, India worst industrial accident in history killed 4000, ½ million lingering injuries	Temperature/pressure gauges were so inaccurate that employees never referred to them The refrigeration unit to chill the MIC was shut off. The gas scrubber which neutralized escaping MIC had been shut off for maintenance. If the gas scrubber were operative, its capacity was 1/4 of the pressure reached in the explosion The flare tower was turned off awaiting repair. If the flare tower had been operative, its capacity was 1/4 of the volume of gas released. The water curtain could not reach the top of the flare tower. The storage tank alarm failed. One storage tank was filed beyond recommended capacity A reserve storage tank was filled already.
1986 Challenger Shuttle Explosion	Severe pressure on NASA scientists to deliver a quota of missions Manufacturer owed incentive pay for each successful flight Highly-publicized "teacher in space" Mission was cancelled the night before
2000 Firestone Tire/Ford Explorer Rollovers 20 million tires recalled after 148 deaths 525 injuries due to tread separations and blowouts	Shoulder pocket tire design led to cracking United rubber process led to lower tread adhesion Explorer's higher center of gravity increased rollovers after blowouts at high speed Ford recommended under-inflation for improved ride
1986 Chernoby Nuclear Accident Besides deaths and injuries, entire cities and villages had to be resettled - cancer rates remain high in the region 20 years later	Reactor had several design flaws Reactor safety systems were disabled Construction/safety weaknesses detailed seven years prior

This is significant, because the common assumption in today's civilization is to dissolve the symptom after we have *symbolized* its meaning. However, if the symptom is dissolved, the subject itself disintegrates. If we follow myths instead of symptoms, we lose the very foundation on which we stand. Because civilization is the victim of a symbolizing attitude, we have experienced unending wars, destruction, and a behavior pattern that has caused populations to create a barbaric world instead of a civilized one. That is why the former prime minister of Malaysia, Mahathir Bin Mohamad stated: "We still think that the strong must dominate and the weak must submit. Frankly, I don't think we have progressed much from the Stone Age. They used clubs, but we have nuclear weapons."[12]

By adopting a symbolizing attitude, man has not progressed qualitatively from the Stone Age. By acting out mythologically, the progression from clubs to nuclear weapons has resulted in the killing of millions upon millions of people. I emphasize that this is the result of a symbolizing attitude leading to mythological behavior, which is the state of being of humans today.

Gerald Massey quoted Emerson as saying, "A good symbol is a missionary to convince thousands."[13] Massey went on to state: "When Europe was converted to Christianity, it was by making use of the same symbols that were hallowed in the pagan cult. Whether for good or ill, the symbol has proved all-powerful."[14] The hold of symbolism is in its way as strong in civilized society as it is in the savage world. Massey's statement is applicable to the actions of Bruce Wilkinson, a U.S. preacher who migrated in 2002 to the African country of Swaziland. Wilkinson's intent was to establish a massive tourist-orphan-industrial complex to house 10,000 Swazi orphans, on 32,500 prime acres near two of the country's best game reserves. Wilkinson, who insisted that God had plans for Swaziland, proselytized his own brand of Christianity in an attempt to convince the Swazi government to give him a ninety-nine-year lease on the land and control of both game parks. The government of Swaziland rebuffed Wilkinson's proposal, because like most white Westerners, he wanted to come over and take over not only the project but the country itself.[15] Wilkinson wanted to imbue the country with a white Western Judeo-Christian ethic and worldview, and make as much money as he could at the expense of Africans. This is the traditional way religious leaders in the Western world behave towards Africa. These symbolic-behaving people mythologize what Africa truly needs to conjure up ways that will bring wealth to the Western world and its tentacles.

The symbol system that we call religion is just that, a symbol system that is used to manipulate and create havoc worldwide. Once again, we turn to the scholar, François Dupuis; in his book *Origins of All Religious Cults*, where he brilliantly sets an agenda of what religion does to the individual in civilization. Dupuis stated:

> What an absurdity is it not, to admit that a God of infinite goodness, who however does good only so far as he is urged to do it, should be solicited and determined to it by prayers and offerings! How much more I prefer those nations, which address no prayers at all to a God of goodness, because they suppose his nature to be such, that he will do all the good he can, without any solicitation on our part being required! What a contradiction, to admit a God, who sees and knows everything, and who notwithstanding wants to be notified and enlightened by Man about his necessities! A God, whose decrees are framed by eternal wisdom, and who yet modifies and changes them every instant, according to the interests of him who prays.[16]

Dupuis made clear the fact that to pray to a personal God and expect that prayer to be answered is pure superstition. Dupuis went on to say: "Since the duties, which religion imposes, are sacred, if that religion is absurd or atrocious, then the most ridiculous superstitions and the most horrible crimes become duties."[17]

Dupuis had the courage to state the obvious: All religions are indeed superstitions that are built on a symbolic foundation. This foundation reveals itself as myth and rituals. The missionary who tried to bring his act to Swaziland was rebuffed because the African officials realized his agenda was not in their best interests. It was couched in a deception that was based on the superstition that we call religion. This is very important. Whenever we eradicate symbolic intent, i.e., religion and superstition, we are thinking and behaving symptomatically naturally, whether we realize it or not. This is all important, for it forces us to raise the question: Can religion be eradicated at all? Dupuis states:

> I am aware, that the mere proposition to examine, whether a religion is necessary or not, will revolt many minds, and that religions have struck too extended and too profound roots all over the Earth, that it would be a kind of folly, to pretend to day, to uproot the ancient tree of superstition, under the shade of which almost all men believed it to be necessary to repose. Therefore it is not at all my intention to attempt it....[18]

It is understandable that Dupuis found it a kind of folly to uproot superstition, because he realized how deeply ingrained mythology and superstition are in cultures around the world. However, in fact, at this point in civilization, we have no choice. We either eradicate the symbol systems that produce religion and racism, or we destroy ourselves as we stumble like drunken idiots to solve the crucial problems that will inevitably reduce our civilization to ashes. The situation in Swaziland is symptomatic of the dynamics that occur when a people confront the power of symbolic thought and reduce it to symptomatic behavior. All of Africa should respond the way the leaders of Swaziland responded to Preacher

Wilkinson. The question often arises, How do you live out your life symptomatically? The answer is, you live out your life symptomatically by living it without a symbolic attitude that produces a nonsymbolic behaving people. Once you get rid of all symbols as decision-making factors in your life, then you automatically make your decisions symptomatically, as Table 3 demonstrates.

Table 3: Living Symptomatically vs. Symbolically

Living Symptomatically	Living Symbolically
Longer, healthier lifespans	Shortened lifespans
People judged on their abilities	Greed
Elimination of racism	Permanent drug culture
Exploitation of creativity	Permanent state of chaos
Elimination of Illnesses due to	Racism
poverty and inadequate research	Disease
Higher standard of living for all	

That is how natural symptomatic thought works. Symbolic thought is a neurological misadventure. The sole reason for a symbolizing attitude is to create the ability to mythologize. One mythologizes to escape from facing reality and to create a situation and an environment that will be compatible with whatever motives one decides will be beneficial to him and in whatever situation one finds oneself. We see this attitude at work in the wars and in struggle for power worldwide.

The idea that symbolic thought is a neurological misadventure is supported by the fact that "symbolic thought does not come innately, built in"[19] Nowhere in the brain are symbols found to be represented.

For this reason, they cannot be located in any single neural substrate; rather, as each supportive representational relationship is brought to play in the process of producing or comprehending a word, each corresponding neural substrate is activated in different phases of the process.[20]

That is the reason why symbols are not a natural neurological occurrence. So it can be rightly called a disease of language. So Max Müller, who was vilified for saying that mythology is indeed a disease of language, is indeed correct. For not only is mythology a disease of language, language is a natural ingredient of the dynamics of the human brain. It is a symptom of a natural, neurological process that enables humans to interact with each other in a forceful, productive way. It only becomes problematic when the symbol systems kick in that produce mythological, linguistic expression, which then produces a diseased language. Symptoms, on the other hand, are an innate ingredient of the human brain.

Symptoms are ways of speaking. And the analysis of symptoms is a reading practice. Jacques Lacan made the link between symptom and language explicit in one of his most famous utterances: "the symptom resolves itself entirely in an analysis of language, because the symptom is itself structured like a language." "Enjoy your symptom!" enjoins the latter-day Lacanian theorist Slavoj Zizek, using the word "symptom" precisely in a wider, cultural, sense.[21]

The idea that all creativity comes from symbolic thinking is a true misnomer, for symbolic thinking stifles instead of enhancing creative thinking. What symbolic thinking does create is a mode of superstition that makes humans victim of their symbolic thought. As Gerald Massey stated, "Modern popular superstition to a large extent is the ancient symbolism in its second childhood."[22] Herbert Read stated: "Humans are a symbolizing animal. At every stage of civilization, people have relied on symbolic expression, and advances in science and technology have only increased our dependence on symbols."[23] On the other hand, Terrence Deacon states:

The history of the twentieth century, like all those recorded before it, is sadly written in the blood that irreconcilable symbol systems have spilt between them. Perhaps this is because the savantlike compulsion to see symbols in everything reaches its most irresistible expression when it comes to the symbolization of our own lives' end. We inevitably imagine ourselves as symbols, as the tokens of a deeper discourse of the world. But symbols are subject to being rendered meaningless by contradiction, and this makes alternative models of the world direct threats to existence.[24]

It is quite evident that throughout the whole of history, symbolic-behaving humans have created civilizations that have continually been taken over by barbarism. And that is continuing to this day, as we see in the conflicts and wars throughout the world. Anyone who reads a newspaper knows where these conflicts are taking place: in the Sudan, in Iraq, and in the Middle East, as well as in Asia and in Latin America. We see wars and conflict that threaten the very existence of all humans and any resemblance of civilized life. This is all due to a symbolic thought process that guarantees a mentality of war and destruction. According to Massey:

> Misinterpreted mythology has so profoundly infected religion, poetry, art, and criticism, that it has created a cult of the unreal. Unreality is glorified, called the ideal, and considered to be poetry, a mocking image of beauty that blinds its followers, until they cannot recognize the natural reality.[25]

What has happened is the insane condition of our world where what is real has become the unreal. What is unreal has become a cult that is considered the real. Massey was correct in his statement, which leads us to the conclusion that this long-standing idea that what separates humans from other animals is our ability to symbolize. That has been the prevailing assumption by anthropologists and other scientists, but that is also a misdemeanor. As evidence by the genocide, murder, and vicious acts perpetrated throughout civilization since time immemorial, we have not progressed from the behavior of our animal cousins.

I realize that the idea of discarding all symbols is a great cultural shock, but as stated before, that cultural shock had led scholars like Dupuis to state,

> That it would be a kind of folly, to pretend to day, to uproot that ancient tree of superstition, under the shade of which almost all men believed to be necessary to repose. Therefore it is not at all my intention to attempt it; because it is the same with religion as with those diseases, of which the germ is transmitted by the fathers to their progeny for a series of ages, and against which art has no remedy to offer. It is an evil the more incurable, as it makes us even fear the remedies, which might cure it.[26]

We have been so used to living under the assumption that symbolic thought is the norm that it is inconceivable to us to live without symbolizing. But what has to be very clear is that to live a symptomatic existence is to live without symbolizing. And that indeed can be very scary, especially for a people who've been living a mythological existence since almost the dawn of life itself. But it must be thoroughly understood that we really do not have a choice. Either we rid ourselves of symbolic behavior and live our lives symptomatically, or we perish.

It must be emphasized and understood, for the questions most asked are What does it mean to live a symptomatic life? How indeed do we live our lives out symptomatically? Since symptoms are innately ingrained in the human brain, and symbols are not, when we automatically eradicate symbols from our thinking processes, we automatically begin to follow our symptomatic impulses. That creates humans that do not make decisions out of mythological assumptions, which eradicates the need to act barbarically. Gerald Massey, in his book, *Ancient Egypt*, described this scene:

> The present writer once had a cat before which he placed a sheet of polished tin. The cat saw herself reflected as in a mirror, and looked for a short time at her own image. So far as sight and appearance went, this might have been another cat. But she proceeded to apply the comparative process and test one sense by another, deliberately smelling at the likeness to find out if any cat was there. She did not sit down as a non-verifying visionary to formulate hypotheses or conjure up the ghost of a cat. Her sense of smell told her that as a matter of fact there was no other cat present; therefore she was not to be misled by a false appearance, in which she took no further interest. That, we may infer, was more like the action of Primitive Man, who would find no human likeness behind the phenomena of external nature.[27]

Massey's statement illustrated very clearly from the cat's sense of smell that the animal was able to ascertain what was real and what was not. This is symptomatic of the reality that was confronted by the cat. Her sense of smell told her that as a matter of fact there was no other cat present. Therefore, she was not misled by a symbolic presence. This animal actually performed in a way that the overwhelming majority of humans have not. If modern man had responded like that cat, then we would have civilization instead of barbarism. So it is an entire falsehood to state that what separates humans from animals is our ability to symbolize. Here is Terrence Deacon's take on the ability to smell as a symptom:

> Consider the example of a symptom, like the smell of smoke. When I smell smoke, I begin to suspect that something is burning. How did my ability to treat this smell as an indication of fire arise? It likely arose by learning, because I had past experiences in

which similar odors were traced to things that were burning.[28]

Deacon recognizes the act of smell as a symptom and the dynamic of how symptoms occur. But like other traditionalists, he assumes that the great difference between humans and animals is the symbolizing abilities of *Homo sapiens*. And this is a misdemeanor that must be corrected if we are indeed to go on being creative and productive human beings.

Two questions asked over and over again is how do we live a symptomatic life, and what does it mean to live a symptomatic life? As stated before, and it must be emphasized, symptoms are a natural neurological process of the human brain. Symptoms are a truly natural outcome of all phenomena; whereas symbols are not an innate part of the neurological process or in fact any process at all. Since symptoms are a natural and irrevocable process of all of life, when one behaves in a nonsymbolic way, one automatically lives out one's life symptomatically. This is indeed very important for one ceases to be a mythic creature. That understanding opens the door to a whole new knowledge of the world we live in and the solving of problems. As stated earlier, two of the phenomena that come from symbolic thinking and behavior are religion and race. We, again, turn to François Dupuis, as he brilliantly attacks the minefield that we call religion.

> I feel that I should make myself ridiculous, if I should proceed further with these reflections on the absurdity of a system, which places the Deity so to say at the orders of a mortal, creating as many Gods as man has passions and wants, even unto imagining a God Crepitus.[29] ....Is truth then so heavy a load to carry? Should its light be more dreaded than the darkness of error?[30]

What Dupuis is saying is that there was a tendency to avoid truth because facing reality is the hardest thing for humans to do. But that is the reason mythology has been used so predominantly in civilization. To avoid facing the truth, man has mythologized his existence and his decision making. Dupuis is correct in his assessment of religion. Religion is not necessary and is in fact a hindrance as man attempts to live a civilized existence. Dupuis goes on by stating,

> Every day it is repeatedly said, that a religion is necessary to the people, and by religion is meant that one, which has priests, ministers, temples, altars, formulas of prayers, and which lulls Man into falacious hopes, by persuading him, that the Deity hears him, and that she is ever ready to fly to his assistance, if he only knows, how to say his prayers.[31]

Religion is not necessary to the people, and in fact it is a superstitious entity that not only dehumanizes but is one of the prevalent forces used to go to war and to usher in conflicts throughout civilization. Professor Yosef ben-Jochannan stated:

> Was it not a very sad day indeed when the originators of the disgusting term – "RACE" – introduced it to mankind as a "scientific explanation" for the apparent physical, mostly facial, variations between the various so-called "ETHNIC" groupings within the human family? Between the terms – "RACE" and "RELIGION" – mankind has created the abyss which will certainly help to destroy civil living itself. This will certainly come to pass, should sanity fail to prevail over the pathological RACISTS and RELIGIOUS BIGOTS who write history for their colleagues – the conquerors – to gloat over, while the conquered languish in cultural deprivation and physical torture until death [through genocide] finally makes its long awaited appearance.[32]

It must be understood that race and religion are mythological phenomena that were created by a symbol system. In other words, if symbols did not exist, race and religion would not exist. This has been borne out in multidisciplinary research that is beyond dispute. The fact that racism is a superstition, and that superstition is a disease of the human mind, has not been accepted by a white population that is in self-denial. Albert Einstein, the great German physicist, has stated that "racism is not a disease of Black people but of white people."[33] Yosef ben-Jochannan stated that "racism is a disease of a sick and fearful modern man."[34]

I realize that these statements will be extremely difficult for the white population globally to accept. But it is even harder for the whole global population to accept the fact that symbols are a misadventure that must be eliminated in order for civilization to continue in a productive and peaceful way. This goes against the grain of academic and nonacademic thought, from antiquity up to the modern age. But we have no choice. We must stop living a life where we make decisions based on a mythological framework that has been deemed sacred. That framework has forced us to live a life that is totally unreal, one that leads to the basic destruction and conflict that we see operating around the world. The scholar Cheikh Anta Diop makes a profound statement, when he states:

> The attitude which consists of resorting to an insane misinterpretation of texts instead of accepting the evidence is typical of modern scholarship. It reflects the special state of mind that prompts one to seek secondary meanings for words rather than give them their usual significance.[35]

Diop is not only describing a symbolic state of mind, he is actually defining what mythology means, which also is the definition of symbol systems. Max Müller stated that that special state of mind is indeed an insane mind. It is becoming increasingly clear that to think symbolically causes a state of human behavior that is indeed insane. As stated by Albert Einstein and Max Müller, it is a product of a diseased mind.

The idea that symbolism is a neurological misadventure of primordial man, and that symbolism must be eradicated and replaced by a Symptomatic Thought Process is a new concept that understandably will cause a lot of ink to flow. Because of the reality that it turns around every assumption that has been held about man and his existence, it will be very controversial and difficult for many to accept, especially those who have benefited from racism and religious practices that continue to destroy civilization as a whole.

As stated before, anything can become a symbol, depending on the symbolizing mind of the user. Since symptoms, unlike symbols, are an innate phenomenon of the human mind, and of life itself, the eradication of symbolic thought automatically releases the phenomenon of symptomatic thinking. To visualize how extensive symbolic thinking is, one only has to go through a dictionary to see that every word, every entity, is a potential symbol depending on the symbolizing attitude of the user. For example, *Day of Rest* is thus defined:

> Like so many other aspects of existence — both in customs and in utilitarian activities — the concept of the Day of Rest does not arise from material or empirical necessity (even leaving aside the religious implications). According to Erich Fromm the observance of the Sabbath amongst the Hebrews does not denote mere repose for reasons of health, but rather something much more profound. In effect, because work implies a state of change - of war - between man and the world around him, it follows that rest designates peace between him and Nature. One day a week – a day which, by virtue of the analogy between time and cosmic space, corresponds to the idea of the centre implicit n the position of the sun among the planets or the location of the earth according to the geocentric system – must be set side for experiencing the spontaneous, perfect harmony of man in

Nature. By not working, the human being can break away from the order of change which gives rise to history, and thereby free himself from time and space to return to the state of paradise. This symbolism provides the explanation, furthermore, of what Bell called "the fiery restlessness of the rebel": the instinctive hatred of all forms of rest characteristic of the man of warlike spirit who challenges all Nature and the world as it appears to the senses.[36]

The term, the *Day of Rest*, when rid of its symbolic connotations, becomes what it is, a day when one's main objective is to rest from his usual activities – nothing more and nothing less. Any religious or secular connotations that imply anything more is essentially mythological and should be eliminated. This should be applied to all words and entities that are used universally in today's world. A word or entity can never be a symbol or sign simultaneously; it must be one or the other.

We should remember Zizêk's statement, "a symptom dissolves after we have symbolized its meaning.[37] This is what Deacon means when he states:

> The near synchrony in human prehistory of the first increase in brain size, the first appearance of stone tools for hunting and butchery, and a considerable reduction in sexual dimorphism is not a coincidence. These changes are interdependent. All are symptoms of a fundamental restructuring of the hominid adaptation, which resulted in a significant change in feeding ecology, a radical change in social structure, and an unprecedented (indeed, revolutionary) change in representational abilities. The very first symbols ever thought, or acted out, or uttered on the face of the earth grew out of this socio-ecological dilemma....[38]

It is extremely important to understand that the elimination of symbols in human existence allows the symptomatic process to flow unaltered and uninterrupted.

Dupuis gives an excellent example of what it means to take symbols and metaphor out of linguistic expression:

> Let us therefore take up Isis at the epoch of the death of her husband, and let us follow her steps from the time she is deprived of, until that, when she is again restored to him on his return from the infernal regions, or in order to speak without metaphor, from the time, when the Sun has passed in the austral or lower regions of the World, until he repasses as conqueror in the boreal regions or to the upper hemisphere.[39]

Dupuis uses the example of Isis and the death of her husband to show the mythological content of the fabled story that influenced the Egyptians and their behavior so drastically. By taking out the metaphor of the story of Isis and Osiris, he speaks of the natural phenomenon of an astronomical event. Taking symbolic content out of literature automatically reveals the symptomatic content, which translates into what really happened. This is earth shattering, for it knocks out the confusion and the inaccuracies that are caused by myths and their metaphorical meaning. It returns language back to its basic symptomatic origin. This is one of the most important values of Dupuis' works on myth and religion and their origins. As we experience the religious wars and the friction between different cults that are occurring throughout the world, it is obvious that there is a missing piece in our approach to solving these conflicts. What has happened is that unfortunately all our dialogue and efforts to intervene and to solve these global conflicts have been hampered by our continual use of a symbolic base that is the engine that decides our therapies and answers to these complicated and stressful problems? Using our present methods, we are not solving any problems but actually adding more fuel to the fire by continually using symbolic extensions to solve problems that are created and fueled by symbolic-behaving humans. We have not understood the basic problems of humanity: man is a symbolic-behaving species, and that it becomes extremely difficult and problematic to have the courage to advocate the eradication of those symbolic inferences that would mean the elimination of all religions and religious thought as we know it now. That is a tremendous cultural shock that few are willing to bear. As indicated earlier, Dupuis states:

> I am aware, that the mere proposition to examine, whether a religion is necessary or not, will revolt many minds, and that religions have struck too extended and too profound roots all over the Earth, that it would be a kind of folly, to pretend to day, to uproot the ancient tree of superstition, under the shade of which almost all men believed it to be necessary to repose.[40]

Dupuis thought it would be a kind of folly to eradicate mythological superstition because of the depth of its entrenchment in the human brain. He states further:

> Therefore it is not at all my intention to attempt it; because it is the same with religion as with those diseases, of which the germ is transmitted by the fathers to their progeny for a series of ages, and against which art has no remedy to offer. It is an evil the more incurable, as it makes us even fear the remedies, which might cure it.[41]

This reminds me of a young banking executive from the Middle East who once told me that even though she knew something was terribly wrong with the myths and superstition that kept her people tied to a religious assumption that was doing great harm, she was too afraid to think of and participate in anything that might cure the disease state that her people are in.

Traditionally, symptoms are used in a way that not only show their necessity, but their far-reaching superiority over symbols. In a *Time* magazine article about U.S. troop withdrawal from Iraq, the headline was "Symptoms of Withdrawal." The article showed how various activity and situations were signs of a need and a desire to withdraw troops from Iraq. It would be totally inappropriate to use the term *symbols of withdrawal* because the symbolic has no substance or reality to initiate an activity except in a totally mythological setting. Symptoms, which have always since the beginning of time been innate in human activity have always been the engine that not only dictates activity but enables one to scrutinize and to analyze all activity that takes place. We must always keep in mind this very helpful statement of Susanne Langer:

> A natural sign is a part of a greater event or of a complex condition, and to an experienced observer, it signifies the rest of that situation of which it is a notable feature. It is a symptom of a state of affairs....But natural signs too may be misunderstood. Wet streets are not a reliable sign of recent rain if the sprinkler wagon has passed by. The misinterpretation of signs is the simplest form of mistake."[42]

What we are saying here is that error and mistakes will always be made as long as humans are involved. How we see and interpret symptoms are not only natural but must take place if any progress is to be made. It has often been stated by anthropologists and behavioral scientists that symbolic thought was necessary to create all the sciences and the creativity that we have in civilizations past, present, and future. But that has been the big mistake of all time. The difficulty arises when we mythologize the symptoms and launch a path of ritual and superstition that has basically made humans insane, as we see in the atrocities that are occurring all over this world, and the justification of these atrocities, which are built on a foundation of racism and religion.

An additional example of how symptoms can be misunderstood, other than the wet street example given by Langer, is how physicians misdiagnose symptoms that present themselves in patients. Notwithstanding the dozens of diagnostic tests typically run on the average patient presenting symptoms, physicians commonly err in their ultimate diagnosis.

> Under the current medical system, doctors, nurses, lab technicians and hospital executives are not actually paid to come up with the right diagnosis. They are paid to perform tests and do surgery and to dispense drugs.... There is no bonus for curing someone and no penalty for failing, except when mistakes rise to the level of malpractice. So even though doctors can have the best intentions, they have little economic incentive to spend time double-checking their instincts, and hospitals have little incentive to give them the tools to do so.[43]

Symbolic activity equates to doing things for the wrong reasons. When symbolic intent and mythology are introduced, human behavior and decision making are impacted. As noted above, nowhere is this more prevalent than in the practice of medical diagnosis.

We know that symptoms, even though popularly understood to be linked with medicine and a disease state, were first used culturally. As we emphasized earlier, symptoms are innate to the human condition, whereas symbols are not. To further show the absurdity of symbolic thought and its resulting mythology and superstition, we only need look at the preference for light skin in many cultures throughout the world. For instance, India's approach borders on the cruel when we consider how their darker-skinned population is treated. Notes Alex Perry in *TIME*,

> India's desire [for pale skin] is a national obsession. [Their] fairness-cosmetics market has grown 67% to

an annual $250 million. Indians are motivated to change their ethnicity [by lightening their skin].[44]

Perry goes on to quote: "Indians are more racist with other Indians than any American ever was with his slaves. The desire for whiteness has very little to do with beauty."[45] Whether Indians are more racist than any American was with his slaves is doubtful to me. But the problem is once we begin to mythologize our symptoms, always realizing that symptoms are innate to the human condition, we do ourselves a disservice that will have tragic consequences, not only for ourselves but also for civilizations to come.

Terrence Deacon states that humans are symbolic savants. Deacon maintains that other species were never subject to selection for symbolic capacity. Because other species lacked the evolved neurological supports, it is difficult for other species to acquire rudimentary symbolic abilities. It is important to note that it is not impossible for other species to acquire symbolic abilities; it just requires human support! What is so interesting about Deacon's labeling humans as symbolic savants is that illustrates the uniqueness of the human ability to symbolize practically everything they come in contact with. Humans as symbolic savants are indicative of the problems of human behavior in all areas of activity. Symbolic savants have created conflicts globally that point to decisions based on mythology and superstition. This is why Dupuis is so forceful in his indictment of all religions and the resulting superstitions that keep humans enslaved. This is the reason why Dupuis explains in despair:

> It would appear almost an act of folly in pertaining to uproot that ancient Upas-tree of religious superstition under the poisonous shade of which mankind has been for ages accustomed to repose, and the roots of which are so widespread and profound.[46]

214

Various disciplines have used mythology and incorrect assumptions for so long that it is ingrained in the pedagogy. The general assumption is that it is almost impossible to get rid of those superstitious beliefs that make humans a deeply religious group. Dupuis continued:

> It was not only a consequence of the philosophical opinion, which constituted the soul a portion of the matter of fire, circulating eternally in the world — it was in its application, one of the great springs which are employed in order to rule men by superstition.[47]

Modern man is ruled by superstition. Because that superstition is a result of symbolic thinking, it is difficult to rid modern man of the type of behavior that has caused and is causing the conflicts we see in the world today. The majority of us do not realize the resulting superstition of symbolism, because most of us think of superstition as being a problem of antiquity. We feel that modern, sophisticated man, for the most part, has liberated himself from the superstitions that were prominent in the past. People who view themselves as intelligent, sophisticated, and knowledgeable do not refer to superstitions in their behavior. They do not see racism as a product of superstition. They do not see religious belief as a product of superstition. Indeed, they will tell you that they do not believe in the practices they would label as a predominant behavior of the savages that roamed the earth in the past. They would indeed call that behavior barbaric. However, Frazer has shown that the behavior of modern man is not qualitatively different from the behavior of the populations in the past known as savages.

It is only when we eradicate our penchant for symbolizing what we fear, what we do not want to face, that we are able to eradicate the superstitions from our thought process and behave in a way that would make our world a civilized one instead of a barbaric one. So when you read about the religious riots in India, the religious and racist conflicts in Darfur, and the hypocrisy and racist terrorism that is a product of the United States, we attribute that to the manipulation of symbols and the application of superstitious behavior and decision making. You cannot attribute that to anything else. If man is to survive, he must immediately begin to eliminate symbolic thought. Despite what some people would call an impossible task, we must keep in mind that symbolizing is not an innate product of the neurological system — but symptomatic thought is. By thinking symptomatically, our language becomes free of metaphor. By thinking symptomatically, we rid ourselves of symbolic behavior.

Thinking symptomatically exposes myths that have been taken literally and acted upon as the truth. Some of these myths have become sacred in the minds of people that have been held captive by them. Egypt's so-called Mysteries System is one of the myths that have had an enormous effect on civilization since antiquity. The scholar, George G. M. James, was a modern proponent of the Egyptian Mysteries System. We must remember that the Egyptian Mysteries System was a complex religious system that was at the same time a secret order into which members were initiated and bound by pledges of secrecy. The Egyptian Mysteries System was a symbolic system wrought with superstition, as are all religious systems. Dupuis stated:

> Truth ignores mysteries; they are the attributes only of error and imposture, and the offspring of the necessity to deceive, if such a necessity could possibly be admitted to exist. It is therefore beyond the limits of reason and truth that we must look for their origin. Hence their dogmas have always been surrounded by darkness and secrecy. Children of the night, they are afraid of light. We shall however attempt to carry it into their gloomy recesses. Egypt had her Initiations, known under the name of mysteries of Osiris

and Isis, of which those of Bacchus and of Ceres were mostly a copy.[48]

We must always remember that exploding myths for the sake of truth will harm no one. As Dupuis stated, "Is truth then so heavy a load to carry? Should its light be more dreaded than the darkness of error?"[49] We can no longer deceive ourselves, for deception binds us to a false history and a disastrous future. That is why we must continue to think symptomatically so that our language and behavior are free of symbolic intent. Diop knew that something was very wrong when he stated:

> We have said earlier that a people without an historical conscience are a population. The loss of national sovereignty and of historical conscience following a prolonged foreign occupation engenders stagnation, or even sometimes regression, disintegration, and the partial return to barbarism: This was the case with Egypt under the Romans, if we can believe Juvenal. Because of the continuing loss of national sovereignty from the time of the arrival of the Persians in 525 B.C., Egypt, which had civilized the world, with tall ships toward the country of Punt, only knew how to build clay barges under the Romans in the second century A.D.

> Worse, she fell back into superstition and barbarism. Juvenal describes tribal wars between two groups, Denderah and Hombos, whose totems are inimical and who are supposed to have destroyed each other through cannibalism. This event is to have taken place under the consulate of Iuncus, in A.D. 127.[50]

Diop knew that a people without a correct understanding of the dynamics that shaped their history were prone to be a very superstitious population. George G. M. James was also on target when he stated:

> The practice of teaching the doctrines of religion to people under the guise of myths originated from the

Egyptians and was adopted by the Phoenicians and Thracians, and subsequently introduced to the Greeks.

> According to Strabo, it was not possible in ancient times to lead a promiscuous multitude to religion and virtue by philosophical harangues. This could be effected only by the aid of superstition, by prodigies and fables. The thunder bolt, the aegis, the trident, the spear, torches and snakes were the instruments made use of by the founders of States, to terrify the ignorant and vulgar into subjection. These references must speak for themselves.[51]

It should be very clear to all that all religions are superstitions that derive from a symbolic thought process. These superstitions have affected the behavior of people in a way that has never been fully chronicled until now. These superstitions that the ancients practiced are the reason why we went to war in Iraq. It's the reason why we have racism and conflict globally that will never cease until symptomatic thinking becomes a reality to us all. Always remembering that the elimination of symbolic thought automatically releases symptomatic thought.

Because religion is so absurd and atrocious, the most ridiculous superstitions and the most horrible crimes drive human behavior globally. That is why Dupuis added:

> This is the foundation of all religions. This is "that" religion, which is reproduced everywhere, and which I maintain to be at least useless to Man; it is the same, which has procured immense wealth and such an enormous power to the priests of all countries; which has covered the globe with temples and altars, and which has originated all the superstitions, which dishonor mankind.[52]

This lends credence to the attitude of the West in their dealings with international conflict. A 2002 article in the *Financial Times* quoted Malaysia's former prime minister, Mahathir Mohamad:

> It is a question of injustice. It seems that it is all right for Palestinians to die and Afghans to die. Thousands of Bosnians died, 200,000 died, and the world watched on TV and did nothing. But if you kill anybody else that is wrong.

The article continues:

> Dr. Mahathir believed this attitude was symptomatic of a new 'racism' reminiscent of that practised by the British in colonial times. "The feeling is that a western life is much more valuable than anybody else's. It is all right for others to die but don't you dare touch westerners."[53]

What is important to understand here is that the same dynamics that Frazer described in *The Golden Bough* and Dupuis emphasized in the *Origin of All Religious Worship* – these dynamics that have their origin in symbolic behavior and mythology — are in effect in a thoroughgoing way in the modern world. These dynamics cause havoc and are so ingrained in our behavior that the task of ridding man of his superstitions is a daunting one. The classics have been mythologized to such an extent that the disciplines have become hopeless because of the prevalent racist overtones. It should be emphasized repeatedly that a connection must be seen between how symbolism operated in antiquity in the affairs of the ancients and how it continues to operate in the affairs of man in the modern world. That is why Mahathir Mohamad was correct in his assertion:

> We still think that might is right, that the strong must dominate and the weak must submit. Frankly, I don't think we have progressed much from the Stone Age. They used clubs, but we have nuclear weapons. Labeling people as Satan or part of an axis of evil provokes; it does not resolve anything.[54]

219

This, I think, is the value of Frazer's work. He constantly shows how symbols and superstition interact in the behavior of primitive people. In his *Golden Bough*, he gives example after example of the ritualistic superstitious behavior of man as he encountered the dynamics that shaped his existence. Those dynamics have not changed since the beginning of time. Dupuis backs up Mahathir Mohamad's statements, offering:

> I cannot see, that civilized people differ a great deal in point of religion from a savage one. The only difference there, is in the forms; but the object remains always the same, in other words: to engage Nature and the Genii, which are presumed to preside over her operations, to be at the disposal of all the wishes of mankind. This is the object of all worship. Take Hope and Fear away from the people, and its religion vanishes.[55]

All evidence points to the fact that religion is a superstition, and that the idea of a God is a symbol that is the engine of that superstition. Diop understood that, when he stated:

> The religious conceptual apparatus, essentially forged during the monarchial phase of human evolution, bears the imprint of that period. Thus, in the language of the revealed religions, the relationship between God and humanity is one of master and slave: "Lord, we are your slaves." The idea of God on his throne is a symbol. Osiris was the first god in the history of religion to sit on a throne on Judgment Day, to judge the souls of men.[56]

It is obvious, if we continue to go down these same mythological roads that we have taken in the past, we will reap the consequences, which are continual wars, destruction, and hopelessness.

Forecasting has become a popular way of analyzing the present to forecast the future. Economic forecasting has been a useful way to foresee how long poor nations will continue to be poor; and how long rich nations will continue to dominate the poor. The financial institutions of the world depend on economic forecasting to realize their continual profit and stability for years to come. Unfortunately, the area of forecasting is built on a foundation that is symbolic and superstitious from the ground up. Frazer realized the danger of entities and institutions built on superstitions and superstitious behavior. He stated:

> But the comparative study of the beliefs and institutions of mankind is fitted to be much more than a means of satisfying an enlightened curiosity and of furnishing materials for the researches of the learned. Well handled, it may become a powerful instrument to expedite progress if it lays bare certain weak spots in the foundations on which modern society is built – if it shows that much which we are wont to regard as solid rests on the sands of superstition rather than on the rock of nature.[57]

It is important to understand the critical nature of our predicament. Symbolic behaving *homo-sapiens* produced civilizations that are built on mythology. These civilizations produced institutions that are built on superstition. These institutions have been regarded as sacred by the masses of the people. The masses of people do not recognize the destructive nature of these superstitions in their daily lives. Frazer continued:

> The Menace of Superstition: In civilized society most educated people are not even aware of the extent to which these relics of savage ignorance survive at their doors. The discovery of their wide prevalence was indeed only made last century, chiefly through the researches of the Brothers Grimm in Germany. Since their day systematic inquiries carried on among the less educated classes, and especially among the peasantry, of Europe have revealed the astonishing, nay, alarming truth that a mass, if not the majority, of people in every civilized country is still living in a

221

state of intellectual savagery, that, in fact, the smooth surface of cultured society is sapped and mined by superstition. Only those whose studies have led them to investigate the subject are aware of the depth to which the ground beneath our feet is thus, as it were, honeycombed by unseen forces. We appear to be standing on a volcano which may at any moment break out in smoke and fire to spread ruin and devastation among the gardens and palaces of ancient culture wrought so laboriously by the hands of many generations. After looking on the ruined Greek temples of Paestum and contrasting them with the squalor and savagery of the Italian peasantry, Renan said, "I trembled for civilization, seeing it so limited, built on so weak a foundation, resting on so few individuals even in the country where it is dominant."[58]

The superstitions that plagued Egypt are exemplified by symbolic action. One prominent practice was that of beheading enemies and placing the heads at the feet of the dead (see Figure 16).

Removing the head and setting it by the feet or thigh is an age-old prophylactic against the deceased

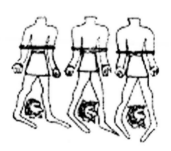

Figure 16: Decapitated Enemies
Decapitated enemies lying with their heads placed between their feet, on the victory palette of Narmer, possibly the first king to unify Egypt, ca. 3100 B.C.
Elizabeth Wayland Barber: *When They Severed Earth from Sky,*
Princeton University Press. Reprinted by permission of
Princeton University Press.

Figure 17: Clay sculpture of Narmer, first Pharoah of Egypt
From Cheikh Anta Diop, *The African Origin of Civilization: Myth or Reality* (1974). Used with permission of Lawrence Hill Books.

coming back, represented already on an Egyptian battle monument of 3100 B.C.

So it is easy to understand why we have the situation that exists now in the Middle East, in Darfur, and the perpetual greed and dysfunction that continues to plague Europe and the Americas. This is the reason why Diop's question – "Will we have civilization or barbarism?" — is so important. As of now, we seem to be satisfied with a civilization whose foundation is weak and full of symbolic intent, which will lead to total destruction if symbolism is allowed to reign as the fundamental engine that runs a civilization that is quickly turning into barbarism. Our failure to face reality only enhances the speed of our destruction.

There are periods when attempts are made to express ideas without metaphor — which means to think without myth. Thinking without myth means that the foundation of our thoughts is not mythological. As I alluded to in my previous book, *Symbolism Revisited: Notes on the Symptomatic Thought Press,* the *London Financial Times* published two articles that revealed a demythologized understanding of the superstition we call religion.

In *Death is Outwitted by Gods Reborn in Spring*,[59] it was stated:

> Universal symbols far more ancient than Christianity and their recurrence in the myths and folklore of the world is arresting and fascinating. Osiris of Egypt was imprisoned by his wicked brother, Seth, in a coffin. It was thrown into the Nile but was washed ashore and came to rest inside the trunk of a tamarisk tree. He was released from the tree, dying again and then being reborn, and a pillar of wood with four crossed branches – the Djed column – was raised upright as the sign of his life everlasting.

> Perhaps the drawing of parallels, in symbol and ritual, between Christianity and other mythologies might not have to be greeted, so many centuries later, with cries of outrage and apostasy from the literalists. Christian theology is, understandably, committed to the premise that earlier rituals were only anticipations of the coming of Christ, who was their apotheosis. Inevitably, it interprets other traditions in this light.

> When Mary, the mother, and Mary Magdalene are shown sorrowing on either side of the cross, they can be compared with the sisters mourning Osiris. And, as the Djed column was raised in ancient Egypt, after the Nile's life-giving inundation, the people cried "Osiris is risen," just as tomorrow, we proclaim: "Christ is risen."

> Why, though, should either festival be *lessened* by comparison with the other? And, more than this, might not our own celebration – with our advantage of the knowledge of both – be enlarged by an awareness of the other? Not least on the ground that one way of loving our neighbors is to include their humanity within our own?

Even though Gerald Massey and Charles François Dupuis are not quoted in this article, the article states what both men have argued over and over again: the Egyptian origin of Christianity.

The *Financial Times* also printed an article called *Religion: Are We Better Off Without it?*[60] about the age-old dispute between science and religion. Their conclusion is that science has the higher moral ground. As I stated in *An African Answer: The Key to Global Productivity*, religion has caused untold conflict and harm in the world because of its symbolic, mythological origin. Whether in Africa, India, Bosnia, or Ireland, hundreds of thousands of people have been slaughtered and murdered over religious mythology. As the *Financial Times* article stated:

> [These people who do such acts] find their support from their myths and texts, among their priests and their silent co-religionists, because retribution is part of religion. In some devious way they are convinced that they are carrying out their god's will.
>
> Therein lays the moral advantage of science. Its morality is incompatible with such imperatives; scientific principles and logic cannot be construed as incitement to mass killings, or even individual murder. Science has had its backsliders: a few scientists have shown themselves capable of murder in the name of research, as happened in Nazi Germany and Japanese prison camps during the second world war...but today religion, with its backbone of retribution, jihad crusade and battle, presents a threat to mankind that is quite as serious as any of the environmental and social perils attributed to science, and much more immediate.

A couple of years ago, I remember a scholar of Byzantine history saying he hoped that 'mankind will soon learn that religion is too important a matter to kill each other about.' It took me two days to realize how tragically mistaken that thought was. I wished him to say 'if

225

only mankind would learn that religion is too *unimportant* a matter to kill each other about.[61]

CHAPTER ELEVEN

The Golden Apple

Never has the impact of symbols and their resulting mythology on civilization been more evident than as it is shown in UNESCO's *General History of Africa* series. Former director general of UNESCO, Amadou-Mahtar M'bow, stated:

> For a long time, all kinds of myths and prejudices concealed the true history of Africa from the world at large. African societies were looked upon as societies that could have no history. In spite of important work done by such pioneers as Leo Frobenius, Maurice Delafosse and Arturo Labriola, as early as the first decades of this century, a great many non-African experts could not rid themselves of certain preconceptions and argued that the lack of written

sources and documents made it impossible to engage in any scientific study of such societies.

Although the *Iliad* and *Odyssey* were rightly regarded as essential sources for the history of ancient Greece, African oral tradition, the collective memory of peoples that holds the thread of many events marking their lives, was rejected as worthless. In writing the history of a large part of Africa, the only sources used were from outside the continent, and the final product gave a picture not so much of the paths actually taken by the African people as of those that the authors thought they must have taken. Since the European Middle Ages were often used as a yardstick, modes of production, social relations and political institutions were visualized only by reference to the European past.

In fact, there was a refusal to see Africans as the creators of original cultures which flowered and survived over the centuries in patterns of their own making and which historians are unable to grasp unless they forgo their prejudices and rethink their approach.[1]

It is evident that former Director General M'Bow understood the impact that mythology has had on Africa and its people. It shows the extent of how whites have manipulated symbol systems to create a damaging image of Africa that is perpetuated by all disciplines. This is especially true, as M'Bow stated further:

Furthermore, the continent of Africa was hardly ever looked upon as a historical entity. On the contrary, emphasis was laid on everything likely to lend credence to the idea that a split had existed, from time immemorial, between a "white Africa" and a "black Africa," each one unaware of the other's existence. The Sahara was often presented as an impenetrable space, preventing any intermingling of ethnic groups and peoples or any exchange of goods, beliefs, customs, and ideas between the societies that had grown up on either side of the desert. Hermetic frontiers were drawn between the civilizations of ancient Egypt and Nubia and those of the peoples south of the Sahara.

It is true that the history of Africa north of the Sahara has been more closely linked with that of the Mediterranean basin than has the history of sub-Saharan Africa, but it is now widely recognized that the various civilizations of the African continent, for all their differing languages and cultures, represent to a greater or lesser degree, the historical offshoots of a set of peoples and societies united by bonds centuries old.

Another phenomenon that did great disservice to the objective study of the African past was the appearance, with the slave trade and colonization, of racial stereotypes that bred contempt and lack of understanding and became so deep-rooted that they distorted even the basic concepts of historiography. From the time when the notions of "white" and "black" were used as generic labels by the colonialists, who were regarded as superior, the colonized Africans had to struggle against both economic and psychological enslavement. Africans were identifiable by the colour of their skin, they had become a kind of merchandise, they were earmarked for hard labour and eventually, in the minds of those dominating them, they came to symbolize an imaginary and allegedly inferior *Negro* race. This pattern of spurious identification relegated the history of the African peoples in many minds to the rank of ethno-history, in which appreciation of the historical and cultural facts was bound to be warped.[2]

So we see the huge effect that mythology has on Africa. Race and religion has been and continues to be the two entitles that have caused the most pain and destruction throughout the world. The *General History of Africa* series makes some of the most relevant and provocative statements on the issue of race. It is understandable

why the racist Western world did everything to destroy
UNESCO, due to the organization's efforts to stymie
the Eurocentric view of the nonwhite world. For instance,
UNESCO stated:

> Race is not so much a biological phenomenon as a
> social myth. What better illustration could there be
> of this claim than the fact that in South Africa a
> Japanese is regarded as an "honorary white" and a
> Chinese as "coloured," where as a man who is con-
> sidered to be white in Brazil is considered black in
> the United States. The truth is that all the peoples
> of the world are of mixed blood, and are likely to
> become increasingly mixed.

> Even so, the myth of race continues to do untold
> harm. Since Hitler asserted that between the Aryan
> "Prometheus of Mankind" and the black "half ape
> by descent" there was the intermediate Mediterra-
> nean type, the racial myth is still very much alive.
> In the objective development of peoples, two factors
> contribute to the typical profile of a group: the ge-
> netic heritage (heredity) and the environment.[3]

It is a fact that myth governed history and justified it at the same time. Despite all the evidence that
Egypt has its origins in Nubia, white scholars continue
to put forth the myth of an Egypt that is non-African
and of the Middle East. That is because of the superstitious racism that is always prevalent in a world dominated by mythology. That is why people who have an
agenda that is built on a system that will tolerate fairness to all people emphasize the necessity of mythology.
Let us be very clear: the genetic type of the Egyptians
were as Diop states, Nubian. They were black Africans.
Any other statement to the contrary is built on denial
and a racist attitude. Symbol systems and their carri-
ers, mythology and superstition, have led to the continual destruction of civilization. As we know, superstitions that are ingrained in the symbol systems are in-

deed worldwide. This is what makes the statement of UNESCO even more relevant, when it says:

> The mythical approach, in fact, is common to all peoples. Every history starts off as religious history, but sometimes the mythical current overwhelms a nation's attitudes, opinions or ideology. Under the Nazi regime, for instance, the myth of race, substantiated in rituals that went back into the remote past, led mankind into one of the most terrible periods in all its history.[4]

That statement, from UNESCO's *General History of Africa,* shows the effect of the neurological misadventure that took place when man began to symbolize. It demonstrates the depth of the problem: that, indeed, history has been dictated by its mythology. Mythology has completely overwhelmed the attitude and behavior of civilization. That is why Dupuis stated that it would be almost impossible to uproot that ancient tree of superstition. I can understand Dupuis' feelings of helplessness; he wanted to burn the manuscript of his book, *The Origin of All Religious Cults*, for fear of being ostracized and ridiculed to the fullest extent for his views on the effect of religion on the people of the universe. François Dupuis' great value was that he exposed how religious cults caused tremendous damage in every area of people activity in every age of civilization. As stated before, Dupuis' masterful work on religious cults exposed how myth-making man was affected by the superstitions that come naturally from mythological religions. As Rendel Harris states, in the *Origin and Meaning of Apple Cults:* "We see through it down a long vista across which many shadows are cast, the reasons which made man a religious animal, and not merely the superstitions that keep him so.[5]

Harris' statement is extremely important: in order for humans to practice religion, they indeed must be superstitious, because all religions are superstition. And that is because of symbolic-behaving humans. We had briefly skimmed over before Rendel Harris' essay, *"Origin and Meaning of Apple Cults."* Harris' thesis was that the great god Apollo, who was known for his healing virtues, had solar attributes of the mistletoe. And the mistletoe grows on the apple tree. So therefore, the apple is Apollo's original sacred symbol. In fact, Apollo was an apple tree spirit. That is why the apple has been called the symbol of the sun god, Apollo. Once again we turn to the scholar, A.B. Cook, when he suggests that

> ...the religious or mythological transition from oak-tree to apple-tree corresponds to an actual advance in prehistoric civilization. Tribes that were once content to subsist upon acorns and wild fruits in general learnt gradually the art of cultivating the more edible varieties of the latter, and so came in the course of many centuries to keep well-stocked orchards.[6]

Apples play a tremendous important part in the mythology of civilization. The scholar, Benjamin Foster, states,

> The stories of the Garden of the Hesperides and the wooing of Atalanta suggest at once the importance of the apple in ancient mythology; but the extent to which superstitions of various kinds about apples are current to this day, and even in our own country, may perhaps not be so generally realized. These modern folk-notions about the apple have to do chiefly so far as I am acquainted with them, with love or fruitfulness. A girl removes the peel of an apple in one long strip, throws it back over her head, and, turning round, tries to discover, in its twists and curves, the initial of her sweetheart. Or the seeds of an apple are placed on the palm of the hand, which is then clapped to the forehead, and, from the number of seeds sticking there, certain valuable conclusions are drawn. H.F. Tozer says that in modern Greece throwing an apple is a sign to express love, or to make an offer of marriage. Frazer, in *The*

232

Golden Bough, tells of a custom among the Kara Kirgiz, in accordance with which barren women roll upon the ground under a solitary apple-tree, in order to obtain offspring.[7]

Greek and Roman myths are full of stories about the apple. It is said that the apple was the cause of the Trojan War, ca.1200 B.C. The war has its roots in the marriage between Peleus and Thetis, a sea-goddess. Eris, the goddess of discord, angry at not being invited to the wedding, stormed into the wedding banquet and threw a golden apple onto the table, stating that the apple belonged to whoever was the fairest. Chaos ensued as Hera, Athena, and Aphrodite each reached for the apple. Zeus appointed Paris as the judge (since he was the prince of Troy and thought to be the most beautiful man alive). The three beauties approached Paris: Hera promised him power; Athena promised him wealth; and Aphrodite promised the most beautiful woman in the world. Paris chose Aphrodite, and she promised him another man's wife: Helen, wife of Menelaus. Although the twin prophets Cassandra and Helenus, as well as his mother, Hecuba, tried to talk him out of it, Paris left for Sparta to capture Helen and make her his wife. When he got to Sparta, Menelaus, Helen's husband, treated Paris like royalty. As soon as Menelaus left Sparta to attend a funeral, Paris kidnapped Helen (who was no doubt attracted to Paris in the first place) along with Menelaus' riches. Paris took Helen back to Troy, where he married her. This myth of the Trojan War has been retold for millennia. Browning states,

> Among the Greeks the golden apples of immortality grew on a tree in an orchard hidden on Mount Atlas beyond the ocean at the end of the world, likely the Canary Islands. They were protected by the three nymph daughters of Atlas from great giants who continuously sought to steal them. Simple possession of

the apples guaranteed immortality, which the gods, of course, reserved for themselves.[8]

But what is important and needs to be emphasized is the superstitious nature of man, as he mythologizes the apple to make it a cult. And that same superstitious nature that produced apple cults is the same behavior pattern that produced all the religions of the world, and that has dictated the decision-making and behavior patterns of *Homo sapiens*. *The Origin and Meaning of Apple Cults* by J. Rendel Harris fits perfectly into Dupuis' *The Origin of All Religious Cults*, as Dupuis tries to make sense out of the symbol systems that created all religions.

As we have shown in previous chapters, the statement of Max Müller, that mythology is a disease of language, has caused an uproar in academic circles. Scholars had shown great respect for his work on mythology up until he made his statement on the origins of myth. For instance, the scholar, John Fiske, stated in his book *Myths and Myth-makers*:

> No earnest student of human culture can as yet have forgotten or wholly outlived the feeling of delight awakened by the first perusal of Max Müller's brilliant "Essay on Comparative Mythology," a work in which the scientific principles of myth-interpretation, though not newly announced, were at least brought home to the reader with such an amount of fresh and striking concrete illustration as they had not before received. Yet it must have occurred to more than one reader that, while the analyses of myths contained in this noble essay are in the main sound in principle and correct in detail, nevertheless the author's theory of the genesis of myth is expressed, and most likely conceived, in a way that is very suggestive of carelessness and fallacy.[9]

Even Gerald Massey, the British Egyptologist who has always been considered outside the mainstream of

Figure 18: Atlas Bringing Apples to Heracles
Sculpture showing Atlas (right) bringing the Apples of the
Hesperides to Heracles, who, with a cushion and a little help
from Athena, holds up the sky. Metope from Temple of Zeus,
Olympia, Greece, ca. 460 B.C. Elizabeth Wayland
Barber, *When they Severed Earth from Sky,* Princeton University
Press. Reprinted by permission of Princeton University Press.

academia, criticized Müller's "disease of language" statement, when he stated:

> Mythology was a primitive mode of *thinging* the early
> thought. It was founded on natural facts, and is still
> verifiable in phenomena. There is nothing insane,

235

nothing irrational in it, when considered in the light
of evolution, and when its mode of expression by
sign-language is thoroughly understood. The insanity lies in mistaking it for human history or Divine
Revelation. Mythology is the repository of man's most
ancient science, and what concerns us chiefly is this
– when truly interpreted once more it is destined to
be the death of those false theologies to which it has
unwittingly given birth! [emphasis Massey's][10]

I would have to put the same description on Massey
that scholars have put on Müller. Massey has done a
great job in describing the dynamics mythology played
in human history, especially in Africa and in all areas of
religion. But the conclusions Massey reached on mythology are the conclusions of the so-called mainstream
scholars. And this is interesting, since Massey is considered outside of the mainstream. But the reason why
Massey is considered outside the mainstream is because
of the importance he placed on Africa in the making of
civilization and his insistence that the Egyptians were a
black people. As a matter of fact, when any scholar comes
to those conclusions, they are considered outside the
mainstream. Because in truth, the mainstream is basically racist.

Be that as it may, Massey's conclusion on symbolism and its resulting mythology gave rise to later scholars such as Carl Jung and their preoccupation with the
role of mythological symbols on human behavior. Professor Max Müller believed mythology was really a
primitive mental aberration; mythology is a disease that
springs up at a particular stage of human culture. He
called that stage the Mythic Period. And Müller wondered whether that period was a time of temporary insanity through which the human mind had to pass. But,
unfortunately, that period was not temporary. And it
has lasted throughout history. And it is very important
to remember that symbol making is not an innate characteristic of the neurological process, but is caused by a

neurological misadventure of primordial man. Diop has stated that mythology is an insane misinterpretation of fact. What is so interesting is the fact that the psychiatrist, Carl Jung, and others, have stated that mythology is the norm, and a natural process of the human mind. We know that there is nothing further from the truth. What disturbed Müller the most were the outrageous superstitious acts that were based on mythological assumptions that were believed to be actual truth by primitive man. Now what has been unanimously agreed upon by all scholars is the fact that early man based his whole life and behavior patterns on myth. That has been documented by Carl Jung, Frazer, and most other scholars in various disciplines. But also, it is understood that Africans and all other nonwhite people are considered to be the most symbolic and the most superstitious people on earth. This statement by Marimba Ani is worth repeating:

> The African world-view, and the world-views of other people who are not of European origin, all appear to have certain themes in common. The universe to which they relate is sacred in origin, is organic, and is a true "cosmos". Human beings are part of the cosmos, and, as such, relate intimately with other cosmic beings. Knowledge of the universe comes through relationship with it and through perception of spirit in matter. The universe is one; spheres are joined because of a single unifying force that pervades all being. Meaningful reality issues from this force. These world-views are "reasonable" but not rationalistic: complex yet lived. They tend to be expressed through a logic of metaphor and complex symbolism.[11]

Also, the psychiatrist, Francis Cress Welsing, states in her book, *The Isis Papers*:

> Carl Gustave Jung was the major European behavioral scientist to emphasize the importance of sym-

bols, their production and their meaning in the brain's total process and behavioral output. Nevertheless, his massive volume of work has taken a lesser place to that accorded Sigmund Freud in the late 19h and 20th centuries of Western (white) thought.

However, it should be remembered that the understanding and use of symbols (including the interpretation of dreams), reached their highest development in African and Asian cultures and was of major significance in these cultures dating back to the earliest time (prehistory) – long before there was any European cultural development.[12]

It is commonly known that you can present black people with symbols and they will be satisfied. The superstitious nature of African people and all people of color will lead to their total destruction. African scholars, whether they are actually from the continent or the diaspora, do not get it. The more they stress the need for symbolic behavior, the harder it will be for us to solve our problems.

Two illustrations that I highlighted in my book, *An African Answer: The Key to Global Productivity*, are so important that they need to be emphasized here also. One is the effect of symbolism and its resulting superstition on the behavior of Africans. The cartoon by Gary Larson illustrates the highly superstitious nature of African people. (See Figure 19.)

Herodotus asserted that the Egyptians were the most superstitious of all people. He stated, "They are religious to excess, far beyond any other race of men". The translator, George Rawlinson, stated in his footnotes, "The extreme religious views of the Egyptians became at length a gross superstition and were naturally a subject for ridicule and contempt."[13]

The second illustration describes how anthropologists saw former president Ronald Reagan's "view of history as 'mythological from day one.' The Iran-Contra

"With a little luck, they may revere us as gods."

Figure 19: Cartoon of white hunters
From "The Far Side" by Gary Larson, reprinted by permission
of Chronicle Features, San Francisco, CA

affair was described as a crisis of 'sympathetic magic', which was a phrase used by anthropologist James Frazer in his classic work, *The Golden Bough*. Reports of Ronald Reagan's reliance on astrology only reinforced his reputation for basing decisions on myth. As President, Ronald Reagan was America's chief mythmaker, and the fact that he was elected at all shows the extent to which mythology exists in the American psyche. Apparently, not everyone was fooled. A nationally syndicated cartoon portrayed Reagan criticizing the so-called voodoo practices of his nemesis, Manuel Noriega, without himself (Reagan) realizing that he was the victim of these same neurological processes. (See Figure 20.)[14]

Figure 20: Ronald Reagan voodoo visit
Auth © 1988 The Philadelphia Inquirer.
Reprinted with permission of Universal Press Syndicate,
all rights reserved.

That same symbolizing attitude is apparent today in the Bush Administration's policies, particularly in how we were led into the war with Iraq, and its subsequent atrocities. Unfortunately, African American scholars continue to express the need and importance of symbolic thought. As the scholar, St. Clair Drake, said, "Diop makes very sparing use of mythology and folklore, but some students of the Black experience lean heavily on this type of material." Any initiative that an African takes to think nonsymbolically and to go directly to the issues that affect not only Africans but the global population will be met with scorn and efforts to intimidate and eliminate. Such a case was made of the UNESCO initiative to rewrite African history. It was spelled out literally in a piece by the *London Financial Times*. This article did not mythologize the events that occurred with UNESCO and the Western world, and the author should be given credit for saying exactly what happened with the initiatives of UNESCO that threatened the Western world. (See Figure 21.)

Figure 21: Laura Bush at UNESCO Headquarters in Paris
Reprinted with permission of Reuters/Philippe Wojazer

President's Wife Brings U.S. into UNESCO's Fold after 19-year Stand Off by Robert Graham in Paris — America's 19-year stand-off with UNESCO, the United Nations body responsible for education, culture and science, ended yesterday when Laura Bush, wife of US President George W. Bush, attended the organization's annual conference.

The first lady of America, a one-time librarian, declared before a big international audience, including several heads of state, that the US was ready to become actively involved again in UNESCO as of October 1. She also stressed the importance of UNESCO's mission in the world.

UNESCO is the multilateral organization with which the US has had one of its most difficult relationships, dating back to a walk-out in 1984. This was when the Reagan administration concluded that UNESCO was wasting public money and was betraying its impartial mandate, endorsing projects that attacked US 'imperialism'.

The US administration had taken exception to Amadou M'Bow, the long-serving Senegalese secretary-general of UNESCO, who had acquired an increasingly tight grip on the organization's agenda. In particular, the US had objected to Mr. M'Bow's plans to use UNESCO funds to establish a third world news agency to offer an alternative to the dominant Anglo-Saxon news agencies.

The US also believed Mr. M'Bow was being tacitly encouraged by his French hosts at UNESCO to challenge so-called American cultural imperialism. These views were shared by the Thatcher government in Britain, which pulled the UK out of UNESCO a year after the US.

Britain only returned to UNESCO in 1997, long after the departure of Mr. M'Bow and when assured that the organization had been restructured.

The US move to return to active membership of UNESCO, now embracing 189 countries, was signaled by Mr. Bush in September 2002.

The US move will have an immediate impact on the organization's weak finances. It will pay a $60m (Euro52.4m, £36.2m) re-entry fee and then become the biggest contributor to the budget again.

This means the next two-year budget covering 2004-5, shortly to be approved at $610m, will be 22 per cent underwritten by the US.

Since 1999 the organization has been run by Koichiro Matsura, a senior Japanese diplomat who has slimmed down staff, reorganized overseas offices and begun to focus more on linking UNESCO ventures with company sponsorship.

Even though the organization lost prestige and lacked financial resources during the US absence, one of the organization's most successful activities has been declaring monuments and natural sites as the 'heritage of mankind'. Since 1974 some 750 such sites have been classified.

However, UNESCO's impact on the international education scene has been hampered by low budgets.[15]

It is obvious that the U.S. and the West are threatened by the African presence at the U.N., particularly any thrust towards revising the racist, pedagogical dominance held universally by people who classify themselves as white. The United States' opposition to UNESCO's new convention on cultural diversity is another excellent example. After two years of debate among member states, UNESCO adopted the convention (with a vote of 148—2) encouraging governments to promote their culture, providing subsidies and quotas as incentives. In its resistance, the U.S. was in denial regarding the saturation of American culture overseas. Stated France's cultural minister, "Hollywood movies account for 85 % of movie tickets sold worldwide. In the U.S., only 1% of shown movies come from outside the U.S."[16]

The UNESCO convention on cultural diversity is a symptom of the rejection of United States imperialism. It has been stated that "many experts believe its principal importance is symbolic."[17] Those threatened by the truth will turn symptoms into symbols, castrating any potential for creativity that would lessen Western cultural arrogance.

The event of the U.N. convention brings into focus Marjorie Garber's introduction to her book, *Symptoms of Culture*. I personally felt totally alone in my books and writings on symptoms until I read Garber's book. On reading her book, I immediately felt that someone else also saw the light in the importance of symptoms and culture. Her introductory chapter applies very well to the UNESCO convention, when she states,

> One of the most striking symptoms of culture in our time has been the phenomenon of the so-called "culture wars," a conflict that might be located precisely in the clash between the timeless, ahistorical, universalizing, decontextualizing function of the "symbol" and the historically contingent, specific, and overdetermined function of the "symptom."[18]

Symptoms are a reading and cultural practice. Symptoms are a language, a way of life. When we live life out symptomatically, we live it out authentically. It is only when we symbolize our life that we live a mythic experience that is full of superstition, racism, and religious folly that destroys our culture and civilization as a whole.

THE DYNAMICS OF SIGNS AS SYMPTOMS — MYTH AS SYMBOL

It is very important to understand that signs are indeed symptoms. Signs and symptoms are synonymous. We read articles every day that talk about signs and what they reveal. A 2006 article appearing in the *New York Times* titled *"Astronomers Find the Earliest Signs Yet of a Violent Baby Universe,"* traced the cosmos back to its first trillionth of a second.[19] This shows how symptoms are the true revealers of what happened in the past and what is happening in the present. That is something that symbols can never do.

Terrence Deacon stated, "Unlike symbols, indices are part of what they refer to, and this makes them reliable in ways that symbols are not."[20] That statement is extremely important, for indices are symptoms, and symptoms are always a part of what they refer to. That is what makes them so reliable. Symbols can never be a part of what they refer to, and that in part makes them unreliable. Deacon goes on to say, "We can invariably imagine ourselves as symbols, as the tokens of a deeper discourse of the world. But symbols are subject to being rendered meaningless by contradiction. And this makes alternative models of the world direct threats to existence."[21] This statement is very important, for it describes why alternatives to symbolic behavior are a threat. Replacing symbols with symptoms is feared because we have been living our lives out symbolically for so long, and superstitions are hard to give up. This is why François Dupuis stated, "It would be a kind of folly, to pretend today, to uproot the ancient tree of superstition, under the shade of which almost all men believe to be necessary to repose."[22] But indeed, we must uproot that ancient tree of superstition if we are to survive as a species. This is extremely important. As we look at the world today and see wars and trouble spots globally, it is evident that we must give up our symbolic existence, which produces the very destruction that is threatening civilization. We must, and I repeat, we *must* live out our lives symptomatically, instead of symbolically, if we are to survive as a human species. That needs to be emphasized over and over again, and, if I possibly could, I would say it a million times over and over again. All of the problems we have faced in the past and in today's world are caused by our symbolic behavior and resulting superstitions. This is why we must revisit the statement by sculptor David Hammons of Harlem, New York, when he said, he "reads the signs and symbols of the street" for inspiration for his work.[23] Hammons' statement is supported by Gerald Massey, who stated, "The simple realities of the earliest times were expressed by signs and symbols."[24] We must choose whether to live out our lives symbolically or symptomatically, and the choice must be symptomatically. This makes null and void Whitmont's statement that we live our lives out symptomatically and symbolically at the same time. This produces a schizophrenic individual with behavior problems that are present in the conflicts we see globally.

In *The Golden Bough,* Frazer interchanges signs and symptoms. In one passage, he states,

> Among the Zulus and Kindred tribes of South Africa, when the first signs of puberty shew (sp.) themselves while the girl is walking, gathering wood, or working in the field, she runs to the river and hides herself among the reeds for the day, so as not to be seen by men...she remains at home until the symptoms have ceased, and during that time she may be fed by none but her mother."[25]

Frazer goes on to say, "When symptoms of puberty appear on a girl for the first time, the Guaranis of Southern Brazil, on the border of Paraguay, used to sew her up in her hemlock, leaving only a small opening in it to allow her to breathe."[26] Frazer shows without a doubt that, indeed, signs and symptoms are synonymous. The crucial and most damaging effect on symptoms is the turning of symptoms into symbols, which begins the damaging effect of mythologizing, which as I have stated over and over again, is a neurological misadventure. This dynamic is supported quite succinctly by Verena Kast, when she states:

> A sign, however, can assume the characteristics of a symbol. Take numbers, for example. A number is a sign. It is agreed that two is a sign for two units, and thus represents a quantity. But a number can also be considered qualitatively. The number thirteen is the sign for thirteen units, while – in terms of quality – we might say thirteen is an unlucky number. It is assigned a content, or quality. Signs can easily evolve

into symbols, particularly when we approach the world with a symbolizing attitude.[27]

Kast's statement is extremely important, for it shows how mythology begins and its resulting superstition. In this case, the statement that "thirteen is an unlucky number" is a myth becoming superstition.

The damage that symbols have caused in the world is immense. We see the damage of symbolic behavior played out in the Middle East, Africa, Europe, and Asia, indeed, the whole world. When events and behavior are mythologized, things change at a frightening pace, bringing utter, thoroughgoing confusion. Only someone totally detached from the world will deny this. This can be documented by various articles and statements in the news media as they try to describe people behavior in a world gone mad. One such article in the *New York Times,* called "In a World of Symbols, One Brings Confusion," written by Patricia Leigh Brown, in 1992, states:

> We live in an age of icon overload. The profusion of symbols is everywhere: in ever-obliging male silhouettes that indicate the location of the nearest trash receptacle, and in magazine articles that end in a flourish with a little square....Look no further than the local supermarket. The mere act of buying a soft drink has become a semiotic exercise....Symbols, which are as ancient as the cross, the star, the crescent, and other religious iconographics have proliferated in recent years, due in part to the search for a common language in a mobile world.[28]

What has to be understood here is that the original language was a symptomatic one, which is what makes symptoms a reading practice. As Max Müller has stated, "mythology is indeed a disease of language." The fact that we have bought into a diseased language is a product of our symbolic, or diseased, behavior. That behavior was brilliantly exhibited in the Rwanda conflict, where genocide was committed on scores of people due to friction between the Hutus and Tutsis. The antagonists were the Europeans, who played on the mythological dynamics of physical characteristics. English explorer John Henning Speke articulated the European point of view, when he stated that

> The tall, elegant people with Caucasian features migrated from Ethiopia and are descended from King David. The shorter people with flat noses are Negroid and come from the South. The tall ones have 5,000 years of civilization in their blood, the short ones, a timeless history of backwardness.[29]

The tall, elegant people are supposed to be the Tutsis, and the short, backward people are supposed to be the Hutus. This mythologizing of people and linguistic characterization is indeed a diseased language resulting from symbolic behavior. This led to the tragic genocide of one group over another, perpetuated by a European, racist attitude resulting from mythological, superstitious behavior. This shows the irrational and barbaric behavior pattern that has been the historical makeup of a people who classify themselves as white. Kast was correct when she stated, "Symbols can indicate what the future holds in store, but tend to do so far too subtly to state in linear terms what might be good about a situation."[30]

As we stated earlier, a symbol can never be reliable, for it is not a part of that which it originated; while symptoms are always a part of their original source. This is what makes symbols undesirable at every level.

As we look at the world around us, we see the destruction of lives and the environment in such a way that it is hard to envision its recovery. However, a behavior pattern initiated by the Symptomatic Thought Process will allow us to experience every relationship in a qualitatively new way. That qualitatively new way will eradicate the barbarism that we find ourselves in today; and instead would bring about a just civilization that will endure forever.

Endnotes

INTRODUCTION

1. This phrase was coined by the author and registered with the U.S. Copyright Office, May 4, 1984.

CHAPTER ONE

1. *Herodotus: The Histories,* Book II (New York: Alfred A. Knopf, 1997), 140.
2. George Rawlinson, translator of *Herodotus: The Histories,* Book II (New York: Alfred A. Knopf, 1997), 140.
3. John Thornhill and John Burton, "Mahathir Warns US on Iraq Attack," *The Financial Times,* September 17, 2002.
4. Friedrich Max Müller, *Comparative Mythology* (New York: Arno Press, 1977), 12, 14.
5. Diop, *African Origin,* 242.
6. Friedrich Max Müller, *Comparative Mythology,* 70.
7. Friedrich Max Müller, *Lectures on the Science of Language* (New York: Scribner, Armstrong & Co., 1878), 21.
8. Edgar J. Ridley, *The Neurological Misadventure.*

9. Cheikh Anta Diop, *The Cultural Unity of Black Africa: The Domains of Matriarchy and of Patriarchy in Classical Antiquity* (London: .Karnak House, 1989), 146.
10. John Fiske, *Myths and Myth-makers: Old Tales and Superstitions Interpreted by Comparative Mythology* (Boston: Houghton, Mifflin & Co., 1901), 16.
11. *Ibid.*, 70.
12. *Ibid.*, 21.
13. *Ibid.*, 88.
14. Müller, *Comparative Mythology*, 16.
15. David Mac Ritchie, Ancient and Modern Britons Volume I (South Dakota: Pine Hill Press, 1991), 91.
16. Charles François Dupuis, The Origin of all Religious Worship (New Orleans: 1872, reprinted by University of Michigan Scholarly Library), 315.
17. M.M. Arnault, Biographie nouvelle des Contemporains, as part of Charles Francois Dupuis' The Origin of all Religious Worship (New Orleans: 1872, reprinted by University of Michigan Scholarly Library), 12.

Chapter Two

1. Benjamin O. Foster, Notes on the Symbolism of the Apple in Classical Antiquity (Cambridge, MA: Harvard Studies in Classical Philology, 1911), 39.
2. Sir James George Frazer, *The Golden Bough*, The Roots of Religion and Folklore (New York: Avenel Books, 1981), 73.
3. Frank Browning, *Apples* (New York: North Point Press, 1998), 87.
4. *Ibid.*, 76.
5. *Ibid.*, 86-87.
6. *Ibid.*, 68.
7. Mark Rosenstein, *In Praise of Apples: A Harvest of History, Horticulture and Recipes* (Asheville, NC: Lark Books, 1996), 7.
8. Edith Hall, "When is a Myth Not a Myth? Bernal's 'Ancient Model'," *Black Athena Revisited*, Lefkowitz and Rogers, Ed. (Chapel Hill: University of North Carolina Press, 1996), 343.
9. J. Rendel Harris, *Origin and Meaning of Apple Cults*, The John Rylands Library, date and place unknown.
10. *Ibid.*
11. Müller, *Science of Language*, 22.
12. Müller, *Comparative Mythology*, 12.
13. Gerald Massey, *Natural Genesis* (Baltimore: Black Classic Press, 1998), 124.

14. Martin Bernal, *Black Athena: The Afroasiatic Roots of Classical Civilization*, Volume I (New Brunswick: Rutgers University Press, 1987), 128.
15. *Ibid.,* 128.
16. Gerald Massey, *Ancient Egypt,* Volume I (Baltimore: Black Classic Press, 1992), 333.
17. *Ibid.,* Ancient Egypt, 343.
18. Geraldine Brooks, "Eritrea's Leaders Angle for Sea Change in Nation's Diet to Prove Fish Isn't Foul," *The Wall Street Journal,* June 2, 1994.
19. Nick Karas, *Brook Trout: A Thorough Look at North America's Great Native Trout – Its History, Biology, and Angling Possibilities* (New York: The Lyons Press, 1997).
20. *Nova: Ancient Creature of the Deep,* WGBH Boston Video, 2003.

CHAPTER THREE

1. St.Clair Drake, *Black Folks Here and There: Volume I* (Los Angeles: University of California at Los Angeles Centre for Afro-American Studies, 1987), 323.
2. Jacqueline DeWeever, *Mythmaking and Metaphor in Black Women's Fiction* (New York: Palgrave Macmillan, 1992).
3. Toni Morrison, *Playing in the Dark: Whiteness and the Literary Imagination,* Cambridge, MA: Harvard University Press, 1992), 63.

CHAPTER FOUR

1. Susanne K. Langer, *Philosophy in a New Key: A Study in the Symbolism of Reason, Rite and Art* (New York: Mentor Books, 1948), 57.
2. J.E. Cirlot, *A Dictionary of Symbols* (New York: Philosophical Library, 1962).
3. Marjorie Garber, *Symptoms of Culture* (New York: Routledge, 1998).
4. Edgar J. Ridley, *Symbolism Revisited: Notes on the Symptomatic Thought Process* (Trenton, NJ: Africa World Press, 2001), 3.
5. Terrence A. Deacon, *The Symbolic Species: The Co-Evolution of Language and the Brain* (New York: W.W. Norton & Co., 1997), 401.
6. Garber, 14
7. Kenneth Chang, *ABCNews.com, What the Hominid Ate* (1999).
8. CNN.com, *Skull May Redefine Human Ancestry,* March 21, 2001.
9. Malcolm W. Browne, "Researchers Call Rare Fish Evolutionary Link to Human Race," *New York Times,* date unknown.
10. John Noble Wilford, "Skull Details Suggest Neanderthals Were Not Humans," *New York Times,* January 27, 2004.

11. Brenda Fowler, "Scientists Explore Ancient Lakefront Life, in the Sahara" *New York Times*, January 27, 2004.

12. Ed Stoddard, "Kissing Cousins: Hominid Fossils 1.5 to 2 Million Years Old," *ABCNews.com*, April 26, 2000.

13. Kenneth Chang, "New Human Ancestor? Hominid Fills Gap in Fossil Record," *ABCNews.com*, April 22, 1999.

14. *Ibid.*, "Evolution of the Skull: One Bone Moves the Face," *ABCNews.com*, May 13, 1998.

15. Christine Soares, "Hominid Fossil Says Plenty: Rediscovered Fossil Rustles Family Tree," *ABCNews.com*, September 6, 1999.

16. *Ibid.*,

17. William K. Stevens, "Dust in Sea Mud May Link Human Evolution to Climate," *New York Times*, December 14, 1993.

18. Nicholas Wade, "Neanderthal DNA Sheds New Light on Human Origins," *New York Times*, July 11, 1997.

19. Karen Foerstel, "New Black History Unearthed in City," *New York Post*, August 4, 1997.

20. Langer, 94-95.

21. John Noble Wilford, "Ancient Bird Had a Brain Built for Flight, Research Says," *New York Times*, August 5, 2004.

22. Dupuis, *Origins of all Religious Worship*, 301.

23. Cheikh Anta Diop, *Civilization or Barbarism: An Authentic Anthropology* (Brooklyn, NY: Lawrence Hill Books 1981), 69.

24. *Ibid.*, 83.

25. St. Clair Drake, 326.

26. Martin Bernal, *Black Athena*, Volume 2, 291.

27. Gerald Massey, *Gerald Massey's Lectures* (Brooklyn, NY: A&B Publishers, 1998), 143.

28. Deborah Solomon, "The Art World is Coming to Harlem: That May Not be a Good Thing for Harlem's Art," *New York Times Magazine*, August 19, 2001

29. Gerald Massey, *Natural Genesis*, 14.

30. Ngugi wa Thiongo, "Decolonising the Mind," *New African* (February 2004), 23.

31. *Ibid.*, 23.

32. Dr. Randall White, as quoted by John Noble Wilford, *New York Times*, "When Humans Became Human," February 26, 2002.

33. Dr. Edward Whitmont, *The Symbolic Quest: Basic Concepts of Analytical Psychology* (Princeton, NJ: Princeton University Press, 1969), 76.

34. J. Ki-Zerbo, Editor, *General History of Africa, Volume I, Methodology and African Prehistory* (London: James Currey Publishers, 1989), 16.

35. Whitmont, 136.

36. J. Ki-Zerbo, 18.

37. St. Clair Drake, 62.
38. Frantz Fanon, as quoted in Drake, St. Clair, *Black Folk Here and There*, Volume I, 63.
39. Slavoj •i•ek, *Enjoy Your Symptom* (New York: Routledge, 1992, 154).
40. St. Clair Drake, 107.
41. *Ibid.*, 114.
42. Garber, 5.
43. Carl Jung, *The Basic Writings of C. G. Jung* (New York: The Modern Library, 1993) 19.
44. Friedrich Max Müller, *Comparative Mythology*, 14.

CHAPTER FIVE

1. John Thornhill and John Burton, "Mahathir Warns US on Iraq Attack," *The Financial Times*, September 17, 2002.
2. Rollo May, *The Cry for Myth* (New York: Dell Publishing, 1991), 92.
3. Ridley, *Symbolism Revisited*, 5.
4. Thornhill and Burton.
5. Joseph E. Stiglitz, *Globalization and Its Discontents* (New York: W.W. Norton & Co., 2002), 120.
6. *New York Times*, November 1, 2003.
7. Stiglitz, 122.
8. Eric Pooley, "Mayor of the World," *TIME*, December 31, 2001.
9. Pooley.
10. *Ibid.*
11. James Harding, "Preaching to the Converted," *Financial Times Weekend*, January 4-5, 2003
12. Ridley, *An African Answer.*
13. Helen Epstein, "The New Ghetto Miasma," *New York Times Magazine*, October 12, 2003.
14. Mireya Navarro, "Going Beyond Black and White, Hispanics in Census Pick 'Other'," *New York Times*, November 9, 2003.
15. E. Ablorh-Odjidja, "Black Power Loses Political Base," *New African*, December, 2003.
16. Ridley, *Symbolism Revisited*, 69.
17. Tina Rosenberg, "Have Not: A Way to Make Globalization Work for Everybody Else," *New York Times Magazine*, August 18, 2002.
18. J. Ki-Zerbo, Ed.
19. Nelson Mandela, quoted by Swarns, Rachel L., in "Mandela Rebukes Bush Over Crisis With Iraq, *New York Times*, February 1, 2003.

20. James G. Frazer, *The Golden Bough: The Roots of Religion and Folklore,* reprinted New York: Macmillan by Avenel Books, 1981).

21. Max Müller, *Lectures on the Science of Language* (New York: Scribner, Armstrong & Co., 1878).

22. Slavoj Zizek, *Enjoy Your Symptom* (New York: Routledge, 1992), 23.

23. Joseph E. Stiglitz, *Globalization and Its Discontents* (New York: W.W. Norton & Co., 2002), 3.

24. W. Edwards Deming, *Out of the Crisis* (Cambridge, MA: Massachusetts Institute of Technology Center for Advanced Engineering Study, 1982), 6.

CHAPTER SIX

1. Thabo Mbeki, "Addressing the Backlash Against Globalisation: A Southern Perspective of the Problem," *paper presented at the World Economic Forum,* Davos, Switzerland. January 28, 2001.

2. Robert Reich, "Are Consultants Worth Their Weight," *Financial Times,* February 24, 1995, 1-2.

3. Max Müller, as cited by Gerald Massey in *Gerald Massey's Lectures* (Brooklyn, NY: A&B Books Publishers, 1998), 165.

4. Edgar J. Ridley, "The Neurological Misadventure of Primordial Man," *Journal of Black Male Female Relationships* (San Francisco: 1982).

5. Susanne K. Langer, *Philosophy in a New Key,* as cited in Ridley, Edgar J., *An African Answer: The Key to Global Productivity* (Lawrenceville, NJ: Africa World Press, 1992).

6. Edgar J. Ridley, 1992, 27.

7. Marjorie Garber, *Symptoms of Culture* (New York: Routledge, 1998), 7.

8. *Ibid.,* 9.

9. Thabo Mbeki, "Briefing: Millennium Africa Renaissance Program: Implementation Issues," *paper presented at The World Economic Forum,* Davos, Switzerland, January 28, 2001.

10. Mark Sappenfield, "Harassment: New Race-Bias Issue: The Workplace Climate," *Christian Science Monitor,* August 17, 1999, 1.

11. James P. Miller, "Bias Complaint Put In New Light," *Chicago Tribune,* September 10, 2000.

12. *Ibid.*

13. Kimberly Blanton, "Massachusetts Cases Raise Questions of Subtle Forms of Workplace Bias," *Boston Globe,* October 15, 1999.

14. Judge Sandra Lynch, as cited by Blanton, Kimberly, "Massachusetts Cases Raise Questions of Subtle Forms of Workplace Bias," The *Boston Globe*, October 15, 1999.
15. David Segal, "Denny's Serves Up a Sensitive Image," *Washington Post*, April 7, 1999, A2, E1.
16. John Romandetti, Denny's CEO, as quoted by David Segal, April 7, 1999.
17. Richard J. Herrnstein, and Charles Murray, *The Bell Curve: Intelligence and Class Structure in American Life* (New York: The Free Press, 1994).
18. Mary Lefkowitz, *Not Out of Africa: How Afrocentrism Became An Excuse to Teach Myth as History* (New York: BasicBooks, 1996).
19. Michael Dixon, "The Missing Measures of Practical Promise," *Financial Times*, December 7, 1990.
20. David Olson, as cited by Robert Sternberg and Richard Wagner, Ed., *Practical Intelligence* (London: Cambridge University 1990).
21. George Soros, *Open Society: Reforming Global Capitalism* (New York: Public Affairs, 2000).
22. Joseph Jett, with Sabra Chartrand, *Black and White on Wall Street* (New York: William Morrow & Co., 1999), ix.
23. Keith H. Hammonds, "Invisible in the Executive Suite," *Business Week*, December 21, 1998.
24. Jo Bolig, as cited by Jonathan Kaufman, "Trading Places: Where Blacks Have More Than Whites, Racial Tension Erupts," *The Wall Street Journal*, February 8, 2001.
25. Lloyd G. Trotter, President and CEO, *GE Industrial Systems*, as cited by Mary Williams Walsh, September 3, 2000.
26. Mary Williams Walsh, "Where G.E. Falls Short: Diversity at the Top," *New York Times*, September 3, 2000, 3-1, 3-13.
27. Chad Glover, "Ancient Tablets Bolster Idea Egypt was First Civilization," *Philadelphia Tribune*, December 17, 1998.
28. Marc Bendik, as quoted by Janita Poe, "African Americans Plaintiffs Seek Full Rewards of Corporate Workplace," *Atlanta Journal and Constitution*, October 15, 2000.
29. *New York Times*, December 16, 2000, B11.
30. Edgar J. Ridley, 1992.
31. Jonathan Kaufman, "Odd Couple: How Omar Green, 27, Became the Point Man and Protégé for a CEO," *Wall Street Journal*, as cited by Edgar J. Ridley, in Symbolism Revisited: Notes on the Symptomatic Thought Press (Africa World Press).
32. Ridley, *Symbolism Revisited*.
33. Andrew Lang, as cited by David Mac Ritchie, *Ancient and Modern Britons*, 1884, reprinted 1991.
34. David Mac Ritchie, 1884, reprinted 1991.

255

CHAPTER SEVEN

1. W. Edwards Deming, *Out of the Crisis,* Massachusetts Institute of Technology Center for Advanced Engineering Study, 1982, 18.
2. *Ibid.,* p. 85.
3. *Ibid.,* p. 6.
4. APO Secretary General Takashi Tajima, *45th Session of the APO Governing Body Meeting,* 3-5 September 2003, Korolevu, Fiji.
5. Carl G. Jung, Ed., *Man and His Symbols* (New York: Doubleday, 1964), 20.
6. Terrence W. Deacon, *The Symbolic Species: The Co-Evolution of Language and the Brain* (New York: W.W. Norton & Co., 1997), 57.
7. Susanne Langer, *Philosophy In A New Key, A Study in the Symbolism of Reason, Rite and Art* (New York: Mentor Books 1948), 94-95.
8. *Ibid.*
9. Martin Bernal, *Black Athena: The African and Levantine Roots of Greece, from African Presence in Early Europe,* Ivan van Sertima, Editor (New Brunswick: Transaction Books 1985), 80.
10. Cheikh Anta Diop, *The African Origin of Civilization Myth or Reality* (Westport, CT: Lawrence Hill & Co., 1974), 243.
11. David Mac Ritchie, *Ancient and Modern Britons Volume I* (South Dakota: Pine Hill Press, 1991), 90-91.
12. Friedrich Max Müller, *Comparative Mythology* (New York: Arno Press, 1977), 14.
13. W.E. Deming, 6.
14. Bernal, 66.
15. John Thornhill and John Burton, "Mahathir Warns US on Iraq Attack," *Financial Times,* 9/17/02.

CHAPTER EIGHT

1. Deming, *Out of the Crisis,* 6.
2. Perri Klass, M.D., *New York Times,* September 21, 004.
3. Verena Kast, *The Dynamics of Symbols: Fundamentals of Jungian Psychotherapy* (New York: Fromm International), 11.
4. *Ibid.,* 118.
5. Dr. George J. Miller, quoted in "Fatty Meals Pose Risks Within Hours," *New York Times,* January 20, 2004.
6. Robin Marantz Henig, "The Genome in Black and White (and Gray)," *New York Times Magazine,* October 10, 2004.
7. Nicholas Wade, "Articles Highlight Different Views on Genetic Basis of Race," *New York Times,* October 27, 2004.

8. Max Müller, as quoted in *Gerald Massey's Lectures* (Brooklyn, NY: A&B Books, 1998), 165-166.
9. *CNN,* November 8, 2001.

CHAPTER NINE

1. J. Ki-Zerbo, *General History of Africa,* 16.
2. *Ibid.,* 18.
3. Curtis Church, *The Golden Bough,* vi.
4. Terrence Deacon, 340.
5. Edward Whitmont, *The Symbolic Quest: Basic Concepts of Analytical Psychology* (Princeton, NJ: Princeton University Press, 1969), 20.
6. *Ibid.,* 136.
7. *Ibid.* 176.
8. Terrence Deacon, 417.
9. *Ibid.,* 340.
10. Gerald Massey, *Natural Genesis,* 12.
11. *Ibid.,* 13.
12. Curtis Church, *Ibid.,* 4.
13. Frazer, *The New Golden Bough,* 10.
14. *Ibid.,* 10.
15. *Ibid.,* 58.
16. *Ibid.,* 122.
17. John Fiske, *Myths and Mythmakers: Old Tales and Superstitions Interpreted by Comparative Mythology* (New York: Houghton, Mifflin & Co.,1901), 16.
18. *Ibid.,* 214.
19. Cheikh Anta Diop, *African Origins of Civilization: Myth or Reality,* 43.
20. *Ibid.,* 242.
21. Joyce Marcus and Kent V. Flannery, "The coevolution of ritual and society: New 14C dates from ancient Mexico," PNAS, Vol. 101, No. 52, p. 18257, 12/28/04 (Copyright 2004 National Academy of Sciences USA).
22. *Ibid.,* 18258.
23. *Ibid.,* 18259.
24. G. Mokhtar, Ed., "Origins of the Ancient Egyptians," *UNESCO General History of Africa Series,* Volume II (California: James Currey, Ltd., 1990), 20.
25. Diop, *Ibid.,* 149-150.
26. Diop, *Civilization or Barbarism,* 105.
27. Diop, *The African Origin Of Civilization: Myth Or Reality,* 150.
28. Max Müller, *Comparative Mythology,* 14.
29. William Adams, as quoted by St. Clark Drake, *Black Folk Here And There,* 217.

30. *Ibid.,* 217.
31. Martin Bernal, *Black Athen,* Vol. II, 54.
32. Dupuis, *Origins of all Religious Worship,* 12.
33. *Ibid.,* 25.
34. *Ibid.,* 314.
35. Diop, *Civilization or Barbarism,* 149.
36. M.M. Arnault, A. Jay, I. Norvins, "Memoir on the Life and Writings of Dupuis," in *The Origin of All Religious Worship,* by Charles Francois Dupuis (Ann Arbor: University of Michigan, 1872), 11
37. Dupuis, 300-301.
38. Dr. Theodore H. Gaster, *The New Golden Bough,* xix.
39. *Ibid.,* xix-xx.
40. *Ibid.,* 668.
41. J. Rendel Harris, *Origin and Meaning of Apple Cults,* The John Rylands Library (1918), 42.
42. Frank Browning, *Apples* (New York: 1998), 74.
43. Mark Rossenstein, *In Praise of Apples* (Ashville, NC: Lark Books, 1996), 23.
44. Cheikh Anta Diop, *African Origin of Civilization: Myth or Reality* (Westport, CT: Lawrence Hill & Co. 1974), 43.
45. Deacon, 404.
46. Spencer Wells, *The Journey of Man* (New York: Random House 2002), 1.
47. *Ibid.,* 1.
48. Charles S. Finch, III, M.D., *The Star of Deep Beginnings: The Genesis of African Science and Technology* (Decatur, GA: Khenti, Inc.,1998), xx.
49. Frazer, *Ibid.,* 584.
50. *Ibid.,* 585.
51. *Ibid.,* 362.
52. Diop, *Civilization or Barbarism,* 105.
53. *Ibid.,* 149.
54. Dupuis, 300.
55. Tim Burt and Tobias Buck, "Dominant Operators Win Symbolic Victory," *The Financial Times,* July 21, 2004.
56. Cheikh Anta Diop, *Great Afrikan Thinkers: Volume 1: Cheikh Anta Diop,* Ivan Van Sertima, Ed. (New Brunswick, NJ: Transaction Books, Rutgers University, 1986), 296.
57. Herbert Read, "Foreword," in *A Dictionary of Symbols,* by J.L. Cirlot (Mineola, NY: Dover Publications,, 2002), x.
58. *Ibid.,* 56.
59. *Ibid.,* 60.
60. David White, "Darfur is a Disturbing Symptom of a Wider Problem," *Financial Times,* June 12-13, 2004, 7.

61. Stephen, Kinzer, "A Clash of Symbols: Defining Holy Sites on Faith," *New York Times,* April 28, 2002.
62. Mahathir bin Mohamad, "We've Failed to Manage the World," *New Africa magazine,* March 2003, 66.
63. Dupuis, 300-301.
64. Diop, *Civilization or Barbarism,* 149.
65. Diop, *The African Origins of Civilization,* 242.
66. *Ibid.,* 242.
67. Massey, *Gerald Massey's Lectures,* 188.
68. Massey,143.

Chapter Ten

1. Max Müller, Lectures on the *Science of Language,* Second Series (London: Longman, Green, Longman, Roberts & Green, 1864), 117.
2. *Ibid.,* 105.
3. *Ibid.,* 358
4. Julinda Lewis-Ferguson, "Kwanzaa Festival," Richmond Free Press, December 31, 1998-January 2, 1999.
5. Marian Burros, *New York Times,* undated.
6. Müller, 397-398.
7. J. Rendel Harris, *The Origin and Meaning of Apple Cults.*
8. A.B. Cook, as noted in J. Rendel Harris' *The Origin and Meaning of Apple Cults.*
9. Celia W. Dugger, "Study Finds Small Developing Lands Hit Hardest by 'Brain Drain'," *New York Times,* October 25, 2005.
10. Yossi Sheffi, *The Resilient Enterprise: Overcoming Vulnerability for Competitive Advantage* (Cambridge, MA: The MIT Press, 2005), 35.
11. *Ibid.,* 35-40.
12. Mahathir bin Mohamad, 66.
13. Massey, *Natural Genesis,* Volume I, 11.
14. *Ibid.,* 12.
15. Michael M. Phillips, "Unanswered Prayers: In Swaziland, U.S. Preacher Sees His Dream Vanish," *The Wall Street Journal,* December 19, 2005.
16. Dupuis, *The Origin of All Religious Worship,* 319.
17. *Ibid.,* 303.
18. *Ibid.,* 300-301.
19. Deacon, 22.
20. *Ibid.,* 300.
21. Garber, 5.
22. Massey, *Ancient Egypt: Light of the World,* 15.
23. Herbert Read, as quoted in Cirlot, J.E., *Dictionary of Symbols,* x.

24. Deacon, *Ibid.*, 437.
25. Massey, *The Natural Genesis,* 14.
26. Dupuis, 301.
27. Massey, *Ancient Egypt,* 3.
28. Deacon, 77.
29. Dupuis, 320.
30. *Ibid.,* 321.
31. *Ibid.,* 323.
32. Yosef ben-Jochannan, *Black Man of the Nile and His Family* (Baltimore: Black Classic Press), 40.
33. Fred Jerome and Rodger Taylor, *Einstein on Race and Racism* (New Brunswick, NJ: Rutgers University Press, 2005), 142.
34. ben-Jochannan, 53.
35. Diop, *African Origin of Civilization,* 242.
36. Cirlot, 77.
37. Zizêk,155.
38. Deacon, 401.
39. Dupuis, 100.
40. *Ibid.,* 300-301.
41. *Ibid.,* 301.
42. Langer, ,57-59..
43. David Leonhardt, "Why Doctors So Often Get it Wrong," *New York Times,* February 21, 2006.
44. Alex Perry, "Could You Please Make Me a Shade Lighter?," TIME magazine, December 5, 2005, 49.
45. *Ibid.,* as stated by Cory Wallis.
46. Dupuis, 5.
47. *Ibid.,* 355.
48. *Ibid.,* 341.
49. *Ibid.,* 321.
50. Diop, *Civilization or Barbarism,* 213.
51. George G. M. James, *Stolen Legacy: Greek Philosophy is Stolen Egyptian Philosophy* (New York: Philosophical Library, 1954), 51.
52. Dupuis, 325.
53. John Thornhill and John Burton, "Mahathir Warns US on Iraq Attack," *The Financial Times,* September 17, 2002.
54. Mahathir bin Mohamad, 66.
55. Dupuis, 318.
56. Diop, *Civilization or Barbarism,* 149.
57. Sir James George Frazer, *Man, God and Immortality: Thoughts on Human Progress* (New York: The MacMillan Co., 1927), 4.
58. *Ibid.,* 319-320.
59. Jules Cashford and J.D.F. Jones, "Death is Outwitted by Gods Reborn in Spring," Weekend *Financial Times,* April 3, 1994, X.

60. John Postgate, "Religion: Are We Better Off Without It?" Weekend *Financial Times*, June 18-19, 1994, 11-1.
61. Ridley, *Symbolism Revisited*, 74-76.

CHAPTER ELEVEN

1. J. Ki-Zerbo, Ed., *General History of Africa – Volume I, Methodology and African Prehistory*, vii.
2. *Ibid.*, vii-viii.
3. *Ibid.*, 102.
4. *Ibid.*, 18.
5. J. Rendel Harris, 31.
6. *Ibid.*, 42.
7. Benjamin Foster, *Notes on The Symbolism of the Apple in Classical Antiquity*, J.W.H. Walden, 39.
8. Frank Browning, *Apples* (New York: North Point Press, 1998), 69.
9. John Fiske, *Myth and Myth-makers: Old Tales and Superstitions Interpreted by Comparative Mythology* (Cambridge, MA: The Riverside Press, 1901), 209.
10. Gerald Massey, *Gerald Massey's Lectures* (Brooklyn: A&B Books Publishers, 1998), 165-166.
11. Marimba Ani, *Yurugu: An African-Centered Critique of European Cultural Thought and Behavior* (Trenton, NJ: Africa World Press), 29.
12. Francis Cress Welsing, *The Isis Papers: The Keys to the Colors* (Chicago: Third World Press, 1991), 56.
13. *Ibid., Herodotus*, Book II, 140.
14. Ridley, *An African Answer*, 36.
15. Robert Graham , "President's Wife Brings U.S. Into UNESCO's Fold After 19-year Stand Off" (London: *Financial Times*, September 30, 2003).
16. Alan Riding, "UNESCO Adopts New Plan Against Cultural Invasion", *New York Times*, October 21, 2005.
17. *Ibid.*
18. Garber, 7.
19. Dennis Overbye, "Astronomers Find the Earliest Signs Yet of a Violent Baby Universe," *New York Times*, March 17, 2006.
20. Deacon, 404.
21. Deacon, 437.
22. DuPuis, 301.
23. Deborah Solomon, "The Downtowning of Uptown," *New York Times Magazine*, August 19, 2001, 44.
24. Massey, *Gerald Massey's Lectures*, 143.
25. Frazer, *The Golden Bough*, 584.
26. *Ibid.*, 585.

27. Kast, 11.
28. Patricia Leigh Brown, "In A World of Symbols, One Brings Confusion," *New York Times,* January 30, 1992.
29. *Colors 41 magazine,* December 2000.
30. Kast, 14.

Index